T0399408

A Studio Guide to Interior Design

A Studio Guide to Interior Design leads you through the creative process of developing an interior design proposal. From reading existing buildings, to presenting the final design, each stage is illustrated with analytical diagrams demonstrating clearly the workflow, processes and skills needed at each stage of the design process. Throughout the book there are key references to drawing, digital practice, author illustrated diagrams and design precedents.

The book shows how to effectively read existing architecture and interiors and sets out orthographic drawing principles, to be used as an integral part of conceptual design development. It also looks at the integration of technology within the design process. The book has a complementary focus towards hand drawing and digital practice and uses a case study driven, diagrammatic approach so students can readily apply programmatic concepts to their own project context.

Ideally suited to students at the beginning of their course, the book covers everything students need to get to grips with early on in their studies and features a wealth of pedagogical features.

Elys John is currently an associate lecturer and a visiting critic at the Welsh School of Architecture; previously he was the course leader and senior lecturer for BA [Hons] Interior Design courses at Bath Spa University and the University of South Wales. Prior to that, for over eight years he was a tutor on one of the first Interior Architecture programmes in the UK at the University of Wales Institute, Cardiff. In 2013 he published *CAD Fundamentals for Architects*; he has also had a number of papers published on architectural computer-aided design. While teaching he is also pursuing an Architecture PhD at the Welsh School of Architecture.

A Studio Guide to Interior Design

Elys John

LONDON AND NEW YORK

Designed cover image: David Connor Design and Kate Darby
Architects 2017
Photo credit: David Connor

First published 2024
by Routledge
4 Park Square, Milton Park, Abingdon, Oxon OX14 4RN

and by Routledge
605 Third Avenue, New York, NY 10158

Routledge is an imprint of the Taylor & Francis Group, an informa business

British Library Cataloguing-in-Publication Data
A catalogue record for this book is available from the British Library

Library of Congress Cataloging-in-Publication Data
Names: John, Elys, author.
Title: A studio guide to interior design / Elys John.
Description: Abingdon, Oxon; New York, NY: Routledge, 2024. |
Includes index. |
Identifiers: LCCN 2023009561 (print) | LCCN 2023009562 (ebook) |
ISBN 9780367637781 (hardback) | ISBN 9780367637798 (paperback) |
ISBN 9781003120650 (ebook)
Subjects: LCSH: Interior decoration—Design. |
Interior decoration—Computer-aided design.
Classification: LCC NK2114 .J64 2024 (print) |
LCC NK2114 (ebook) | DDC 747—dc23/eng/20230412
LC record available at https://lccn.loc.gov/2023009561
LC ebook record available at https://lccn.loc.gov/2023009562

ISBN: 9780367637781 (hbk)
ISBN: 9780367637798 (pbk)
ISBN: 9781003120650 (ebk)

DOI: 10.4324/9781003120650

Typeset in Minion Pro and Avenir
by codeMantra

Contents

INTRODUCTION

The project to write a studio guide for interior design students started some years ago. It's always struck me that interiors is a grey area, open to interpretation and various levels of subjective thought. There are quite a few good books on interiors in circulation today that cover the empirical and practical considerations of interior design [as an academic subject]. That said, it can be quite hard to unpick that information to be relevant to a design project, or to know at what stage the information being presented is of use or even relevant.

The context of today's interior design teaching is very different to interior design and interior architecture education of the past. When studying interior architecture in 1993 a copy of architecture, form, space and order by Francis D. K. Ching was issued as our key text, whose relevance, I readily admit, I didn't understand until I left university. That combined with an architectural process that was 'mystical' [you either knew it or didn't] has led me to clarify the process both here and within my teaching practice.

With the rise of the computer age we are also led by compelling digital resources. Visual resources such as Pinterest and Dezeen are an 'inspiration' to us all. CAD has also added a level of 'readymade' to today's interior design process, and programs such as SketchUp list a marketplace of objects that can be easily imported into a model to fill it up with interior elements. On the one hand, I've embraced CAD and visual resources, even writing a book *CAD Fundamentals for Architecture* in 2013. As a design tutor I've also found it can be a hindrance to the development of a project work because those quick found references [CAD or imagery] can often override and undermine the development of a project to a higher level. Those 'resources' can become superficial references not playing the full role you would expect from the analysis gained from a precedent study.

A *Studio Guide for Interior Design* leads you through the creative process of developing a design proposal. From reading existing buildings to presenting the final design, each stage is covered through analytical diagrams clearly demonstrating the workflow, processes and skills needed at each stage of the design process. Throughout the book there are key references to drawing, digital practice, illustrated diagrams and design precedents.

The structure of the book follows a set path in terms of its approach to a hierarchical design process. Read the context space, evaluate any spatial or structural interventions, defining a clear series of concepts to work with, testing them out through plan and section and developing the level of detail to make it work! The intention is that you touch base with each chapter in a sequential manner. Hopefully, some of the language used within the book will also help you gain a better understanding of the terminology that is used within the academic and professional environment.

CHAPTER OVERVIEW

Initially in the book key skills are defined to make informed contextual readings of existing architecture and explain the methods required to record that information accurately. The 'reading' of the existing building and site is the starting point of any interior design project. It is at these

DOI: 10.4324/9781003120650-1

initial stages the first conceptual design responses may be formed – today at a conceptual level with sustainability in mind, decisions may well be made to leave things as they are rather than change, modify or renew. Something we are seeing increasingly as a forward-looking strategy.

Early on in the design process it is important to form a series of key conceptual moves. These key moves can range from external to internal spatial considerations and are often focused on interventions to 'existing' architecture. I've based these around three facets of 2D conceptual design: 2D drawing, diagramming ideas and developing a set of key moves to work with. There is a very valid argument that 3D and 2D are symbiotic in terms of conceptual development [which is picked up in Chapter 3]; that said, at the very initial stages 2D drawing principles such as point, line and shape can be a very effective way to apply spatial concepts diagrammatically, especially at the formative stages of an interior designer's education. Diagrams are used to illustrate design thinking; they are sufficiently abstract to communicate the IDEAS behind a project proposal without getting involved in the problems of applying them. What is important to retain is the legibility of the initial concepts throughout the project development and not to make shapes or patterns that have no conceptual base.

The 3D environment is the natural home of the interior designer. 3D spatial design defines the profession past the perception of surface treatments and the dressing of spaces associated with interior decoration. Today 3D drawing has become more accessible and easier for the draughtsperson. CAD programs such as SketchUp actively encourage the designer to go straight in with 3D drawing, which has been problematic for me on a series of levels, as quite often the conceptual base provided by clear diagrammatic principles is bypassed and replaced by a 3D warehouse or 'blocks.' The 3D chapter starts with the premise that drawing in 3D and modelling by hand is more appropriate at the initial stages of a design, whereas using 3D CAD may be more appropriate when a design concept has been realised. Within the 3D chapter the process of exploring design is broken down to be sequential/logical, with the appropriate scales set to match the design process along with introducing an understanding of when to move into detail development.

I'm very aware there is a conflict of interest in the above, whilst a steady and sequential approach to interior design is essential to an effective workflow, on the other hand many other factors may come to play within the formation of a 'creative' design. This additional layering of conceptual principles is so important to develop and may come from other creative disciplines or through technological development. For quite some time the idea of movement and transformation has played an important part in space efficiency or immersive environments. When developing the functionality of space pragmatics can often take over such as a table being a table or a wall being a wall [static objects in space]. It is through the transformation chapter that the discussion is expanded into the possibilities of using flexible design strategies to enhance our perceptions of space, such as a wall that can move and transform a space from open to enclosed, or 'thickened up' to provide extra layers of functionality. These are often basic interior elements that if approached differently in conceptualisation can add extra layers of design inventiveness.

Regardless of how small or big the space is that you are dealing with, materials are integral to every aspect of interior practice. As a designer entering well into the 21st century there are serious issues that arise from the environmental impact of materials used in interiors and architecture. From short-lived interiors to landfill, to the use of plastics and vinyl for cost and convenience, interior design is a major contributor to unsustainable practice.

The material chapter introduces traditional materials, contemporary finishes and surface treatments; it is a comprehensive list that covers all aspects of material use from construction to applied finishes, which is important for the interior designer to know so that they can discuss them on an informed level with construction professionals. While facing the climate and global cost crisis the selection of honest materials within interior design practice has never been a more important specification. The materials chapter has an unapologetic focus on honest materials and away from the material stereotypes such as wallpaper and fabrics, encouraging the designer to play an active role in material sustainability.

Finally, the successful communication of a design proposal is one of the most important skills a designer needs to develop. You can have the strongest conceptual base but if you cannot communicate it visually using the correct mediums or the correct drawing conventions soon the academic or professional focus moves towards the illegibility of the project proposal. The output and CAD chapters define the key principles that should be retained whilst preparing your project work for presentation.

For us orthographic drawings are the key content, the testing out of spatial ideas, the working out of them before they are built to ensure that the contractors or the client can understand how it will work and how much it will inevitably cost.

At its base *A Studio Guide for Interior Design* introduces the understanding to effectively read existing architecture. It sets out orthographic drawing principles, to be an integral part of conceptual design development. It indicates the next stages of design development and final communication. The book has a complementary focus towards hand drawing and digital practice; it also has a diagrammatic approach [with case studies] so you can readily apply programmatic concepts to your own project context. Overall it's a studio guide for interior design to be consulted at key stages of your formative design studies, a primer so you get a better insight into the design process and the environmental issues of interior design practice.

Interiors has always been a subjective subject [as with architecture] but even so a clear definition of the design process along with a definitive definition of hierarchy will hopefully help students of interior design develop an effective linear workflow from the outset rather than be left to the mercy of personal tastes and opinions!

CONTEXT AND SITE

- Introduction
- Reading a Building
- Documenting Interior and Exterior Space
- Global Considerations, Sun, Climate
- Site Research
- Recording and Documenting: Onsite the Building
- Surveying and Understanding Space Digitally
- Case Study: Repurposing

INTRODUCTION

Chapter 1 introduces an understanding of how to read and record a building [including its site context]. The chapter is focused on the importance of understanding significant attributes of an existing architectural space. Highlighted are the methods to record the information diagrammatically with a sketch book and digitally. To gain a wider understanding of building analysis the chapter looks at global climatic variations and digital resources available to the interior designer.

An interior designer has a complex contextual tool set to engage with, which enriches the practice of interior design by understanding the context of a site and existing architecture the interior designer has the potential to remodel, repurpose, refurbish and intervene at an intellectual level.

Figure 1.1 The stripped back interior of the Palais de Tokyo, Anne Lacaton and Jean-Philippe Vassal, 2012. An example of 'stripping back' of the interior rather than cladding/hiding the structure and services

DOI: 10.4324/9781003120650-2

Context

Interior design shares many attributes with architectural practice; the reading of site and context is one of them and the starting point of a design proposal. Context can be described as many variable factors as possible that engage with a site. In interior design terms, the contextual restraints or potentials can range from the surrounding landscape to the interior enclosure. A responsive design proposal will consider site and contextual readings to help inform the design concept. The overall objective is to get a sense of place and space.

An interior designer will inevitably start with an interior space that can range from a singular space to a series of spaces that form a building. Within this 'existing' context there is the added layer of complexity that sets a given boundary to design concepts.

Reading of the existing space is the starting point of any interior design project. It is at these initial stages that the first conceptual design responses may be formed – at a conceptual level decision may be made to leave things as they are rather than change, modify or renew. Potentials in narrative can be developed from historical readings, an event, a timeline, a tale; they can all add to the authenticity of a project proposal.

When the boundaries are broken down between the interior and exterior context some exciting spatial moves can be realised.

Figure 1.2 Bristol Old Vic, Haworth Tompkins Architects, 2018. Photo Credit: Philip Vile

> *The foyer is conceived as an informal extension of the street, as much a covered public square as a discrete building. The space is framed and covered by structural timber and glass to bring daylight deep into the room. The centrepiece of the space is the much-altered façade of the Georgian auditorium, visible from the street for the first time, illuminated by a large light well and punctured by new openings to overwrite the visible evidence of historic alterations.*
>
> (Haworth Tompkins Architects)

Existing and New Build

An interior designer is likely to encounter two types of interior built environments, one existing and the other a new built interior. The latter allows the designer to be involved in the spatial and architectural development of the building. In mainstream architecture it is more likely to be the development of interior furniture and finishes.

Within existing architecture there is a rich heritage that spans millennia; in this context the interior designer has exciting possibilities in the altering and intervention of the existing. Fred Scott's 'On altering architecture 2007' discusses in detail the contextual issues that confront the designer in altering existing architecture. From restoration to interior intervention the interior designer has a responsibility to find a balance in the existing building and its future use.

Sustainability and Reuse

Considering sustainability concerns, global emissions [concrete production in particular] and the re-use of existing architecture is a paramount concern for us all. It is within this context that the role of the interior designer, architect and interior architect in developing a sustainable built environment becomes of utmost importance. Yes, we can use 'eco' materials and develop buildings with exceptional U values, but this only goes partway to responding to the environmental impact of the built environment. The real creativity in the built environment comes in how we develop strategies for the repurposing of existing spaces and find new uses for old buildings rather than demolishing and rebuilding.

Figure 1.3 Brynmawr rubber factory. Photo Credit: Elain Harwood. Landschaftspark Duisburg. Photo Credit: Thomas Burns

Two important industrial sites with architectural and interior significance that met vastly different fates: Brynmawr rubber factory was demolished in 2001 despite being a listed structure and impressive example of mid-century concrete construction. It has now been replaced with new housing and retail.

Landschaftspark Duisburg is an industrial site that produced pig iron between 1901 and 1985, in concept a living industrial monument. Designed in 1991 by Latz + Partner, to preserve and work with the industrial past, creating a city oasis.

READING A BUILDING

Existing Building

Site Boundary Is the area of surrounding land that belongs to the building plot. In some cases, there may be no or an extremely limited amount of site, such as a high-density high rise. At the other end of the scale, it could be secluded within acres of its own land.

A factory built in 1976–1977 to a design by Nicholas Grimshaw of Farrell & Grimshaw Architects, for the American furniture company Herman Miller Inc. 2D site plan, 1976, using a bold colour palette to diagrammatically explain the site: a more recent Revit [computer-generated] 3D site plan, 2019, showing the extents of the site, the interior plus key contextual references such as the river and bridge.

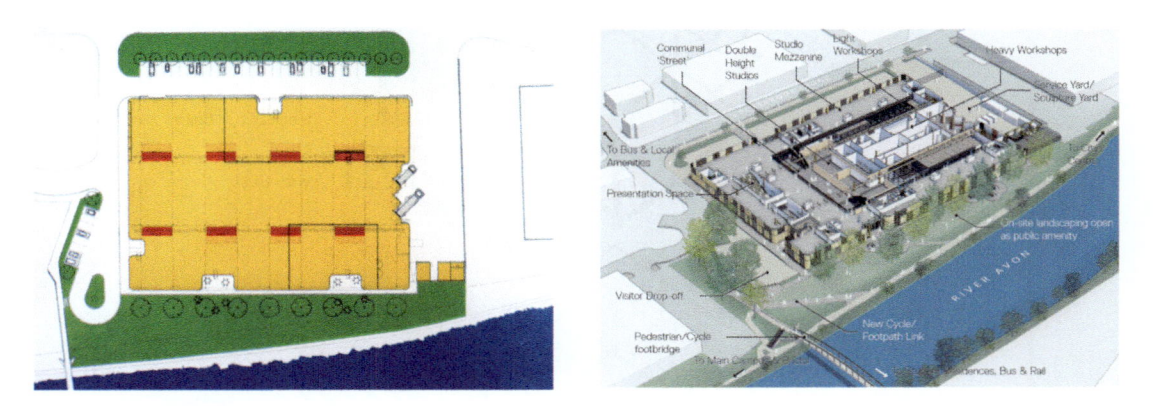

Figure 1.4 1970s site plan and a recent Revit site model: Courtesy of Grimshaw Global: Herman Miller Factory

Building Style – It can be categorised by many factors and may require some further research to define correctly. The age and the period of the building may be a starting point, for example, Georgian, early 20th century, or it could be related to a movement such as hi-tech or brutalist. In all cases – even if dealing with a mundane everyday office space – try and pin down the architectural style as it can provide the starting point/inspiration for a design concept.

Figure 1.5 Theis + Khan Architects. Bat & Ball Station restoration and refurbishment project, 2019. Photo Credit: Nick Kane

A careful judgment was made to balance a sense of historic enhancement with contemporary design, so lighting, radiators and sanitary fittings are carefully chosen to complement the original 'Victorian' style of the station.

(Theis and Khan Architects)

Building Construction – This is often influenced by the type but can often be categorised into a series of well-defined construction types. Another variable factor is that your building may be made up of more than one construction type; buildings with additions often have a change in construction methods and materials.

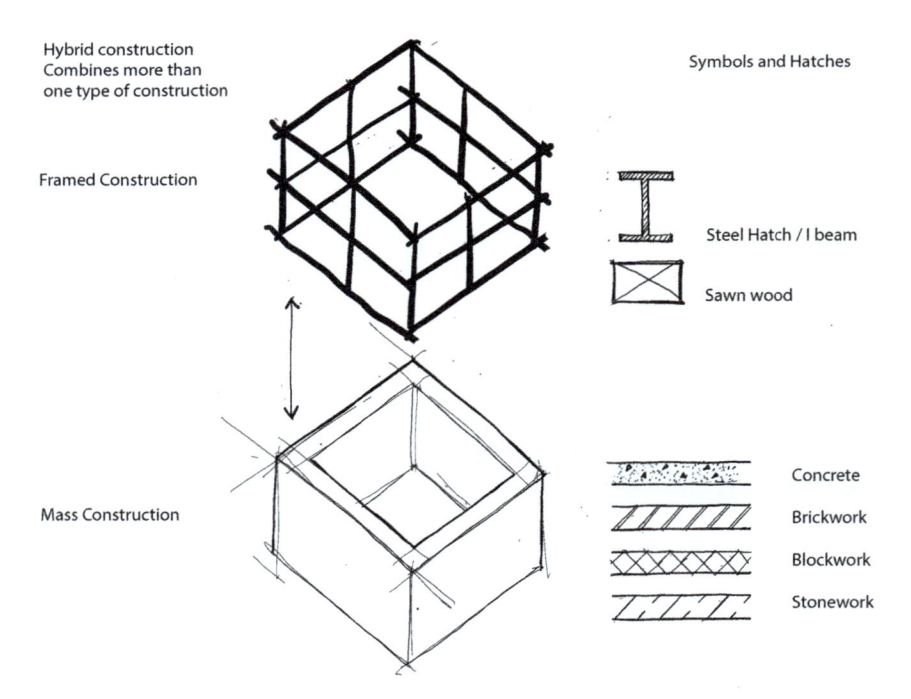

Figure 1.6 Types of material used commonly in construction. With the hatch patterns that normally represent the material in plan and section

Hybrid construction
Combines more than one type
    of construction
Framed construction
Mass construction
Symbols and hatches

Steel hatch/I beam
Sawn wood
Concrete
Brickwork
Blockwork
Stonework

The building envelope can comprise different constructions and it is useful to get a good understanding of this at the beginning so any new modifications can work with the existing construction.

Construction Types

Masonry – Brick, block and stone, often a load-bearing material; it is also used as a cladding.

Timber – Timber frame construction [one of the oldest types of construction] is also used as a cladding. In typical domestic dwellings the pitched roof spaces are constructed in timber whereas the building enclosure is a masonry construction.

Steel – Steel is one of the most used construction materials today. As a structural material it is used in a framed construction. It is also used in multiple applications within exterior cladding and in interior construction such as wall partitions.

Reinforced Concrete – Concrete is made up of aggregate [commonly stone chippings], cement and water. The reinforcement is normally steel bars set in the concrete.

Glass – Glass is found as a structural material in recent modern architecture and can be spectacular in both appearance and performance. Structural glass is made up of laminated glass; the more the laminations the stronger the glass.

Hybrid Construction – It could be that the building is a hybrid construction [particularly if it has had additions]. For example, a building may have a masonry or concrete ground floor then a second floor that is of timber or steel construction. The term hybrid construction refers to the combination of two or more types of construction in a singular building.

DOCUMENTING INTERIOR AND EXTERIOR SPACE

The following is a list of common building components: both exterior and interior. They highlight the areas of a structure that may be of significance or of interest when visiting a building and interior space. In a listed property many of the elements may be listed for preservation.

Figure 1.7 Library Delft University of Technology, Delft, the Netherlands. Mecanoo Architects, 1995. Photo Credit: Mecanoo/Bristol Old Vic façade, Haworth Tompkins, 2018. Photo Credit: Philip Vile

Using a simple geometric composition Mecanoo's Delft Library carves out a dramatic angled entrance sequence into the monumental mass of the main building. The building path/approach is often used as a symbolic or ceremonial approach to a building.

Bristol Old Vic, Haworth Tompkins, 2018. The classical Georgian façade and glass curtain wall façade work together to clearly define an outside-inside, old and new relationship.

Exterior Building Elements

The Façade – The façade is the outward face of a building. It can be one principal elevation or made up of multiple elevations. It is typically where the entrance is made into the building. A building façade can range from highly embellished with ornamentation to minimal glass curtain walling.

Juxtaposition – In contemporary architecture and design you often see the simplicity of glass juxtaposed against more elaborate architectural detailing.

The Roof – It is an exterior element that can play a significant role in the visual impact of a building or be minimised to insignificance by hiding behind a parapet wall or flat construction. Some of the most common roofs we come across are gable roofs, hipped roofs and valleyed roofs.

> *Often in period properties the roof may be projected to create a verge. Some roofs contain a continuous roof light, a dormer window or a lantern roof light.*

Openings – Within a building's elevation [or façade] there are openings; they can be a window or door providing light and access to the building. Further openings may have been made to provide more complex interior/exterior relationships.

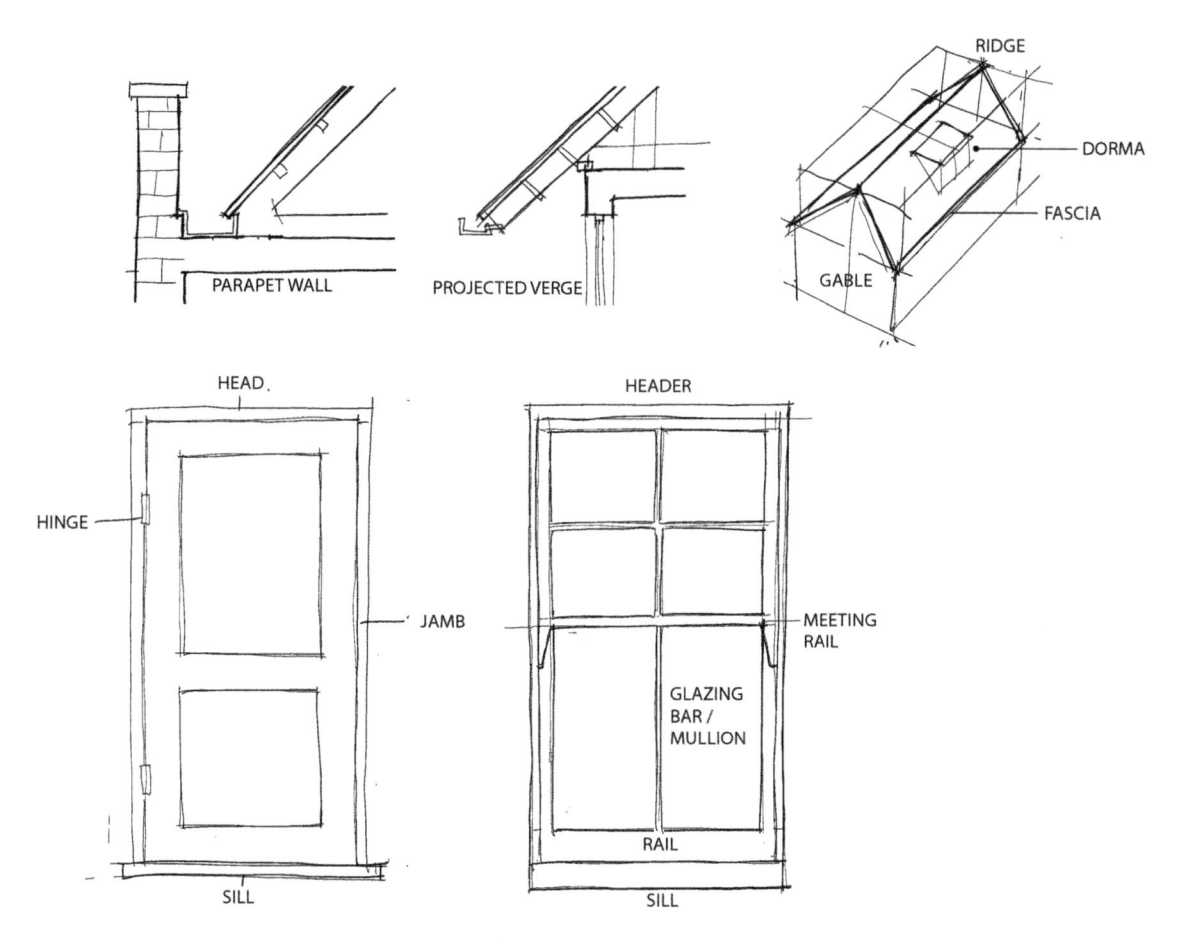

Figure 1.8 Two different approaches to roof detailing – parapet wall, projected verge or eaves /basic common exterior roof components. Basic door and window terminology/details

> *The detailing of windows and door openings is rarely the same. Most listed building elements can be dated through the architectural detailing of the openings.*

Porch – A porch is often present in domestic period properties; the porch provides some protection from the elements. In modern architecture this is often incorporated inside the building shell to provide an entrance lobby or foyer.

Interior Building Elements

Entrance – It marks the entrance of a building from outside to inside, normally through a doorway. It is often celebrated as a design opportunity, embellished with ornamentation or decoration.

Threshold – It marks the transition of one interior space to another. The entrance normally defines the first threshold.

Modern architecture and interior architecture play with the notion of threshold by diminishing its physicality, to create spaces without thresholds that are interlinked spatially. The Barcelona Pavilion is one example of inside and outside spaces being spatially linked rather than there being physical thresholds.

Figure 1.9 A traditional Victorian entrance/threshold. The Barcelona Pavilion where the transition between the inside and the outside has been broken down, Mie's van der Rohe, 1930

Hallway/Lobby – This is normally the first space you enter within a building. In classical interiors this is often amplified in scale to give a sense of grandeur. In modern architecture it can be subverted to add a level of tension/compression before entering a main volume.

Circulation/Route – Circulation of the interior is a major consideration of interior design practice. The internal path space relationships are often the primary design consideration in a building's interior. Movement around a building can be subterranean, level or elevated. This configuration is often organised to optimise the spatial experience of the building's form and spaces. Circulation may pass through, be adjacent to or terminate in an interior space.

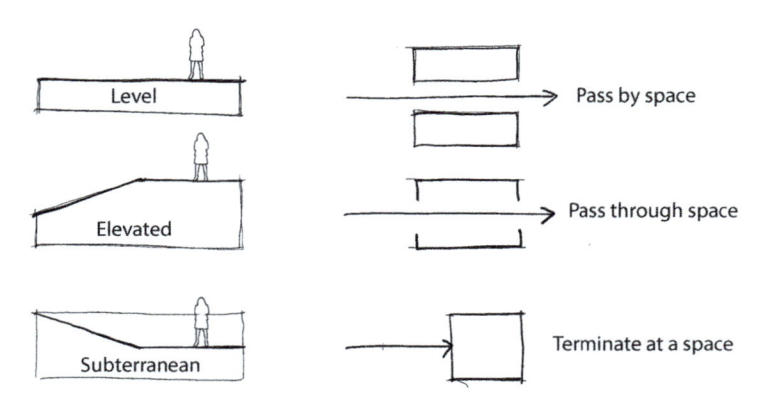

Figure 1.10 Left: definitions of different levels within a spatial context: level, elevated, subterranean. Right: different options to move through space: pass by, pass through, terminate at a space

In an existing building the original circulation may have been altered, things may not work as well as they should spatially, and this is normally through inappropriate design modifications in the circulation and route. It is worth diagramming out a building's existing circulation to understand it and see if it can be improved.

Stairs – Stairs, ramps and lifts allow us to move between spaces vertically, from one floor plane to another. They are often celebrated as an interior design feature ranging from highly ornamental to minimal. Interior stairs in older properties are often a listed element.

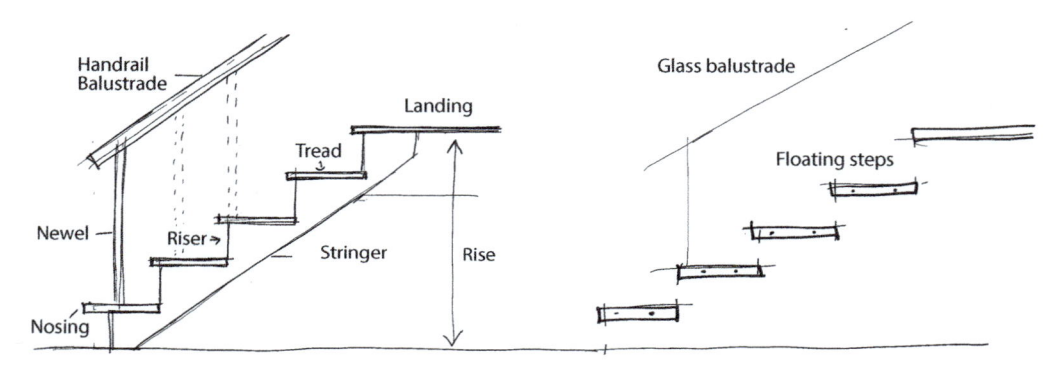

Figure 1.11 Traditional and contemporary approaches to stair design

In contemporary design a 'traditional' staircase is often substituted for a floating step design which minimises the stair to just treads with no stringer or glass balustrades. This adds to the weightlessness of the element.

Figure 1.12 House in Takatsuki, Tato Architects, Yo Shimada, 2018. Photo Credit: Shinkenchiku Sha

Changes in floor level defining different spaces: the spaces between different floor levels are left open to create a floating effect, allowing the floors to be used as desks and shelves where objects can be stored.

Note: any significant details of stair elements on a site visit along with the basic dimensions of the risers and treads.

Interior Envelope – The interior envelope is an enclosure within a building envelope. It is a defined space made up of a floor, wall/s and a ceiling plane. In older properties the elements are often celebrated with ornamentation such as a ceiling rose, cornice, architrave, dado rail and skirting. In modern architecture the level of interior enclosure is often reduced dramatically to produce open plan spaces that rely on spatial rather than physical interventions.

> *Note: primary elements and any significant features within an existing space such as a chimney stack or built-in furniture. Even in a listed interior there may be the opportunity to explore the level of enclosure of an existing space which can provide a dynamic spatial interior intervention.*

GLOBAL CONSIDERATIONS, SUN, CLIMATE

Global Considerations

Location, orientation and climate are fundamental starting points of architectural design. In newly built sites, with ample land availability, the building location and orientation are normally set to provide maximum thermal performance and climate control.

Within existing old buildings, the performance of the building may be extremely poor and site constraints such as terrace housing might need to be fixed.

When recording a building and interior it is especially important to be aware of the building's existing orientation:

The facing direction of openings and the type of openings
The buildings relationship with its climate
Existing climate controls [if any]
Any potentials for natural energy adaptations [such as solar]

Northern Hemisphere

In the Northern Hemisphere a building is:

Typically orientated towards the south to maximise thermal comfort.
Southwest to southeast is the preferable direction for a principal façade.

Southern Hemisphere

The problem of cooling is an issue in the Southern Hemisphere.

Building location and orientation are typically orientated towards the north to maximise thermal comfort.

The strategy of cooling involves:

Good airflow/cross ventilation
Smaller window openings
Overhanging roof to provide shade and monsoon protection
Low mass buildings to allow dissipation of excess heat

Within the Bawa town house a series of buildings have been stitched together with indoor outdoor spaces that break down the traditional threshold of indoor and outdoor space – a practice that is more common in a Southern Hemisphere building due to the mild climate. Light green = indoor outdoor space/white internal space.

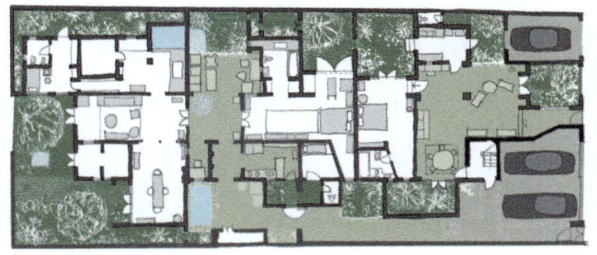

Figure 1.13 Geoffrey Bawa Town House, 1960–1969

Southern Hemisphere climate response:

Deep verandas, overhanging roof, interior courtyards, minimal glass; a blurred relationship between inside and outside environments

Ventilation

Naturally, ventilated spaces have been a part of western architecture since before Georgian times. They provide an effective climatic strategy [control of internal climate and ventilation] in the Northern Hemisphere. Today, in larger new builds, mechanical ventilation is usually integrated into the structure as these often have closed façade systems such as curtain walling or glass façades.

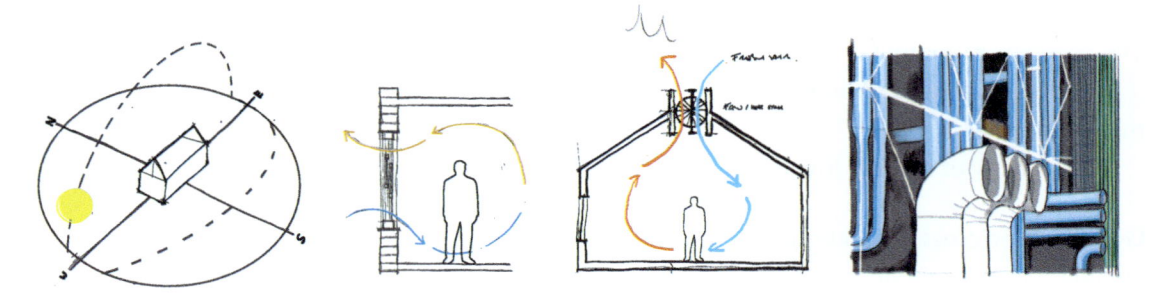

Figure 1.14 Sun path diagram; natural and mechanical ventilation ducts

Sash windows aid natural ventilation; as window design has moved into single casement designs the ability to have this type of air circulation has reduced.

In modern curtain wall buildings [where the windows don't open] mechanical ventilation with fans imports fresh air and exhales warm air.

Centre Pompidou, Rogers Stirk Harbour + Partners (RSHP) 1977. Mechanical services are visible on the exterior of the building and used as an architectural expression of the building's façade.

SITE RESEARCH

A site survey is the inspection of an area either indoors or outdoors to gather information/data. In design it forms part of an appraisal of the existing space along with the collection or verification of key measurements that are transferred into a technical drawing.

Before a site visit there is a lot of preparation that can be collated to understand the site conditions in more detail, leading to an informed visit.

Ordnance Survey Maps

Sourcing an ordnance survey (OS) site plan can give you an excellent overview of a building's surroundings.

Make a plan of areas to investigate.

Mark up the different building types that surround the site such as housing, shops and industrial units.

Mark up any other areas of interest such as landscape elements, trees, the river, bridge, boats....and anything YOU think is identifiable with the site.

Figure 1.15 Digi Roam example. Google street view, Reichstag, Berlin, Norman Foster partners, 1999

As a student in an academic institution you will probably have access to DIGI Roam, which is free to use for students; it not only has digital access to OS maps but historical data and digital CAD/GIS maps. The historical data can be especially useful when you are researching an old building.

Google Maps

Google Maps is the most accessible internet site in the world. There is detailed information on the site surroundings such as the types of businesses, landscape elements, rivers and so on; all are set at an excellent resolution and available as a hybrid map. The real potential of early site research in Google Maps is the street view where you can take a remarkably close look at public site locations.

Existing Building Research

Most buildings will have a past and would have been subject to changes. New built structures will have a record in terms of site plans, plans and sections. It is a good practice to gather as much information on the existing building as is possible before carrying out any site survey. You may even find that you can source the dimensional information from a previous survey. If you are lucky enough to come across a full set of plans, sections and elevations it would always be beneficial to check some key measurements on site for accuracy.

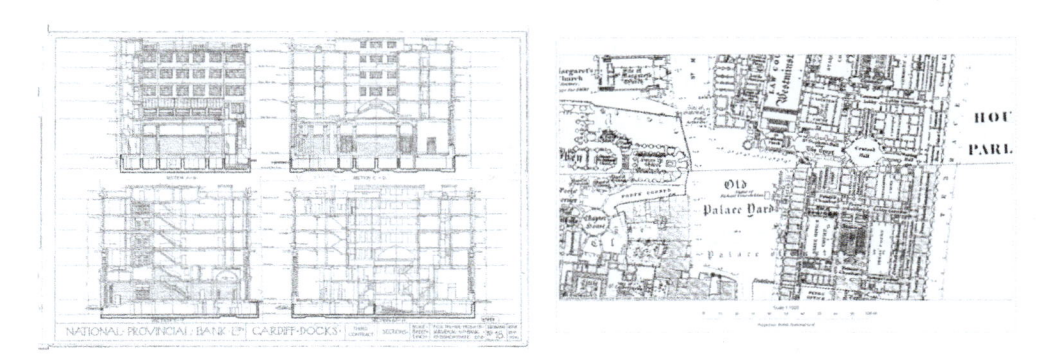

Figure 1.16 A set of hand-drawn sections found with an online search. A local archive map

> *In the case of an old building there is a good chance that the drawings were by hand, which is not as accurate as CAD drawings. They often give you an additional level of drawing detail that you can include in your final presentation to emphasise the age of the building you are working with – such as window details and original interior elements.*

Local Archives

A local archive is a particularly good place to start gathering additional information on a building. They will often have original plans along with any other relevant information related to the structure. Increasingly, this information is being transferred to a digital resource and is keyword searchable.

A local archive will possibly give you not only the building history but also any newspaper and local history associations. Some of the information that may be available are maps, plans, images, newspapers, directories and books. As some of this may not be digital [much is not] you will need to visit the archives, which will often involve pre-booking.

> *Information from a building's history is often appropriated as a starting point within the conceptual design process. Designers will use imagery from the building's past or a story from the past to add a sense of nostalgia to the repurposing of an old building.*

Planning Portal

Since the 1990s most planning applications have been digitised [originally held as drawings at the planning office]. Whether the planning system is digital or a drawing archive, most modifications to buildings, street signage and repurposing require some degree of planning permission. As most planning procedures are open to public scrutiny, it is normally possible to access the information.

> *A planning application normally carries a set of plans to confirm the 'alteration,' further information such as site plans. Sections and elevations can also be readily available. In the case of listed [old buildings], there is often extensive information such as listing documents, details of listed elements and historical statements.*

A General Internet Search

Typing in the address, postcode or zip code for a building can bring up some interesting information! In the news section, you will get information on past and future developments along with any notable events that have happened or are due to happen.

RECORDING AND DOCUMENTING: ONSITE THE BUILDING

One of the first premises that should be made when going on a site visit is that it will be the only visit, so it is important to gather as much information as possible on that visit. If you do not have a site plan, plan or section of the space you are recording then you will need to gather that information. Even with a satisfactory level of information it is worth double-checking dimensions on site to ensure the accuracy of the drawings.

> *Equipment checklist:*
>
> *sketch book or and graph paper and clipboard*
> *clutch pencil/technical pens/rubber*
> *5 m tape measure/surveying tape [for larger interiors]*
> *mobile phone = camera and calculator*
> *optional – laser measure*

External Recording and Documentation

Sketch – Draw a series of quick sketches using analytical sketching techniques to work things out.
   Use simple perspective when drawing 'Views.'
   Use PLAN diagrams to describe the site.
   Measure – Use a surveyor's tape or laser measure [work in pairs if you can].
   A surveyor's tape can cover greater distances when measuring up large spaces/buildings

| Axo | Perspective | Site Plan | Sketch plan and section |

Figure 1.17 A sketch axo, perspective and site plan drawn on site. A traditional building sketch plan indicating doorways, windows, stairs, chimneys and internal/external walls

| Tape | Overview | Zoom In | Sketch dims |

Figure 1.18 Different types of tape measures. Photos taken on site and a sketch of dimensions taken on site

Basic measurements can be gathered using rule of thumb measurements such as a standard brick size, window openings or a modular façade element. You can then multiply the object to give an estimate of size.

If an OS plan has been sourced, then that will be to scale and can be set to about 1:100 [accurate to about 20cm but that varies to 1mm].

Photograph – Key elements of structures and landscape

Record as much targeted information as possible.

Take an overview of any buildings or elements, then focus on the details.

> *Use a 5m tape for details and a 50m surveyor tape to get the overall dimensions. Take photographs at different scales, a general overview: zoomed in shot. Make a sketch of dimensions on site.*

Interior Recording and Documentation

Sketch – Draw the main elements in the space such as windows, doors, flooring and celling details. Try and get an idea about the relationship of spaces and the material make-up of any floors, walls and ceilings. As a starting point draw up a sketch plan, not to scale and add key dimensions to it.

Draw in structural elements and try to work out how they line up.

Indicate all door and window openings.

> *When measuring between columns, measure from the centre rather than from edge to edge. Keep an eye out and include elements of interior significance.*

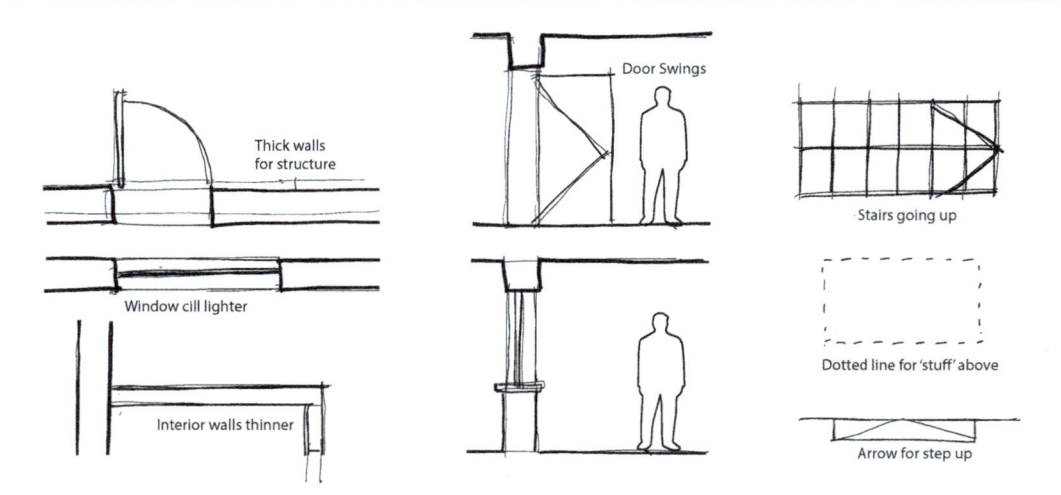

Figure 1.19 A series of interior technical drawing symbols that should be used [drawn up] whilst onsite preparing a draft plan and section

Door

Window

Exterior/interior wall

Door and window in section

Stairs up in plan

Overhead element dotted in

Step up

Measure – If there is an apparent grid such as a steel structure, ceiling grid [suspended ceiling] or floor grid, draw it in as it will help you plot out elements in the space – they are more often modular elements. Ceiling and floor tiles come in standard sizes, 600 mm × 600 mm being most common for ceiling tiles.

When trying to understand bigger buildings, taking key measurements between columns will help you identify the structural layout – there is likely to be a structural sense [an even distance] to their placement; an apparent grid helps you gauge the size of the space and plot out elements. In larger buildings the structural rhythm of the building is a good point to start.

A plan can often be sourced for an existing space or building. A section is normally much harder to come by so ensure you do take enough vertical measurements as you can with a section drawing in mind.

A lot can be learnt from a knock! A hollow sound may indicate a partition wall and a solid knock: load bearing. Remember: these are initial assessments and in all cases any alterations would be undertaken with the advice of a structural engineer.

We often become fixated on the bigger elements when surveying a space. Remember to take plenty of photographs and measurements of smaller details such as window mullions or door architraves.

Measuring is traditionally done by using tapes and measuring rods for height. Today it is more likely that a laser measure is used. Site visit aside, it is always handy to always have a 5m builders' tape with you.

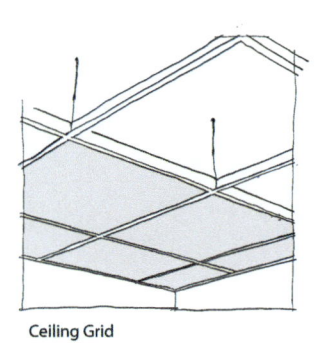

Ceiling Grid

Structural grid of a building

Figure 1.20 Ceiling tile image: Locksbrook building structure frame example. Photo Credit: Grimshaw Global

Basic Measure Principles

Defining control lines/main elements/work on the biggest area first.

Look for structural/interior rhythm/grid.

Measure columns from centres.

Triangulation measurements will help control the plans of small or irregular building shapes.

Photograph key interior spaces. Record as much targeted information as possible. Take an overview of the interior envelope, then focus on the detail. It might be useful to hold a tape measure against the area to be photographed.

Historic Building Checklist

When surveying an old or listed building it is important to take note of significant attributes and listed features. When visiting a historic or listed building pay particular attention and document exterior and interior fabric.

Look For – Evidence of phasing (e.g., masonry joints) development between Architectural styles

Plan elements

Decorative schemes

Fixtures and fittings or other details which help to date the building or its various stages of evolution

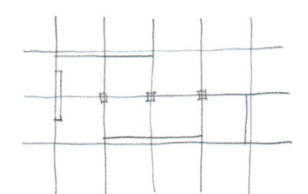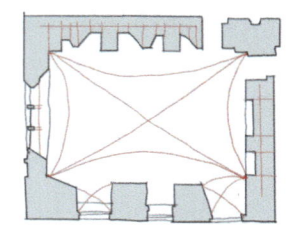

Figure 1.21 Marking out the columns on a grid plan/triangulation/tape measure used to read size

Figure 1.22 Interior of the Museo Fortuny exposing the many layers of change within the building whilst introducing new contemporary interior elements. The original Locksbrook factory floor from the 1970s which has been kept as part of the recent remodelling of the interior

Photograph – The building in its wider landscape

The elevations of the building along with any corner details that are important such as a Column detail

Views of any principal rooms

Any external or internal detail that is relevant to the building's design

Any signage or graffiti that is of historical interest

SURVEYING AND UNDERSTANDING SPACE DIGITALLY

Increasingly, digital technology is becoming integrated into the drawing process. One of the advantages of using a tablet/iPad to draw in your sketch measurements is that they can, in some cases, be in vector format, which is useful for integration into the mainstream CAD package.

Drawing Apps

Autodesk Sketchbook

Morpholio Trace

Adobe Fresco [screen shot]

Pro create

For example, a line that is sketched in can be easily modified to the actual dimension and blocks of stencils can be inserted to indicate the main interior elements, such as door swings or window openings.

Drawing Web Apps – With the introduction of CAD web apps for mainstream CAD software such as AutoCAD, the need to have a dedicated workstation to draw up CAD plans diminished. Access to the internet allows you to directly input dimensions into a web browser.

> *Web apps are allowing you to use CAD software regardless of operating system, system hardware or device type.*

Surveying Apps – Room scan – app-based survey has been a bit of a hit and miss in the past. With the introduction of laser technology to the latest devices, things will improve radically. If you are lucky enough to own a newer device, then it really does change the capabilities and the potentials of survey apps. With the accuracy of a laser and CAD apps, fully accurate floor plans can be generated in seconds.

GIS CAD

> *A geographic information system (GIS) is a framework for gathering, managing and analysing data. Rooted in the science of geography, GIS integrates many types of data. It analyses spatial location and organises layers of information into visualisations using maps and 3D scenes – source.*

While rooted in geography, GIS, and GPS [global positioning system] are becoming increasingly accessible to mainstream surveying and integrated into our daily lives. In principle a very accurate location point is taken and entered into 3D CAD data [allowing heights to be accurately recorded].

Much of this information can be accessed using the DIGIMAP portal.

We are not far off the time when we will be able to enter a room and a mobile phone will be able to record spatial information accurately and automatically as we move through spaces using both LIDAR and a GPS data 3D room scanner.

Laser Measuring

Of all the surveying equipment you encounter the laser measure is the most likely that you will encounter as an interior designer.

Once the measuring tool has been switched on, the rear edge of the measuring tool will be selected. (A) You can change this to the front edge of the laser measure if it is more appropriate. (B) In continuous measurement mode (C) the measuring tool can be moved relative to the target. For example, move a desired distance away from a wall while reading off the current distance at all times.

Pressing the measuring button will switch the laser on [not take the initial measurement].

Use the laser beam to locate the area to measure from (e.g., wall).

Pressing the measuring button again will take the measurement.

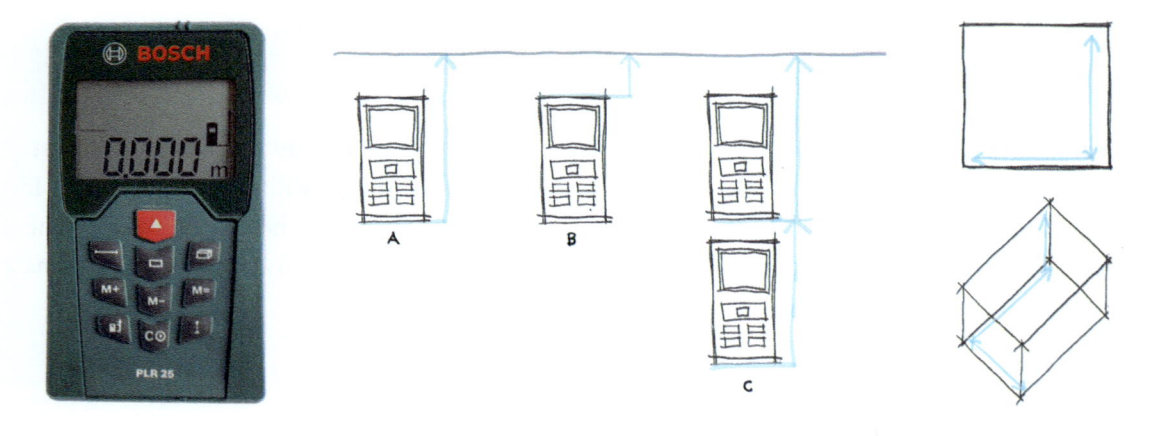

Figure 1.23 A standard laser measure: three different ways of measuring with a laser measure – (A and B) laser position, (C) adding sequential measurements. Different types of area measurement: 2D plan measurement/3D volume measurement

Area Measurement – A basic area measurement will involve width and length [in more sophisticated measures you can add more than two for irregular rooms]. Select the area measurement function on the laser measure, and the width and length one after the other. The laser beam remains switched on between the two measurements.

Volume Measurement – Select the volume measurement function. Then measure the width, length and height one after the other as with a length measurement. The laser beam remains switched on between the three measurements.

> *If you are on a gradient/slope it might be useful to use a level to position the laser horizontal to get an accurate distance.*
>
> *If the area you are aiming at is busy with interior objects or details it might be useful to set up a target; an A4 piece of paper can help define a target as can a sketchbook.*
>
> *Pro Laser measures often have apps that work with the laser measure to create a floor plan as you take the measurements – using Bluetooth GLM 100 C Professional and GLM floor plan app.*

CASE STUDY – REPURPOSING

LocHal Library – Tilburg 2019

Project Partners: Braaksma & Roos Architecten, Civic Architects (Project Architects)
   Mecanoo Architecten [Library Interior], Inside Outside, Petra Blaisse

---

The LocHal is a good example of a repurposing project that takes many elements of contextual and historical readings to develop a sophisticated intervention into the existing structure.

The design strategy celebrates its site position at the centre of a new city development, the historic structure, and the patina of industrial use. The structure is complemented by new insertions such as the landscape stairs, architectural curtains and a winter garden with a view over the city.

Unusually the project is attributed to four practices, each bringing their own individuality to this project; the project was overseen by Civic Architects.

Reading of the Context

The LocHal was an industrial workshop where wagons and locomotives were developed and repaired from 1932 until its closure in 2009 – the building is located next to the central station, an area that is being developed as a new city area.

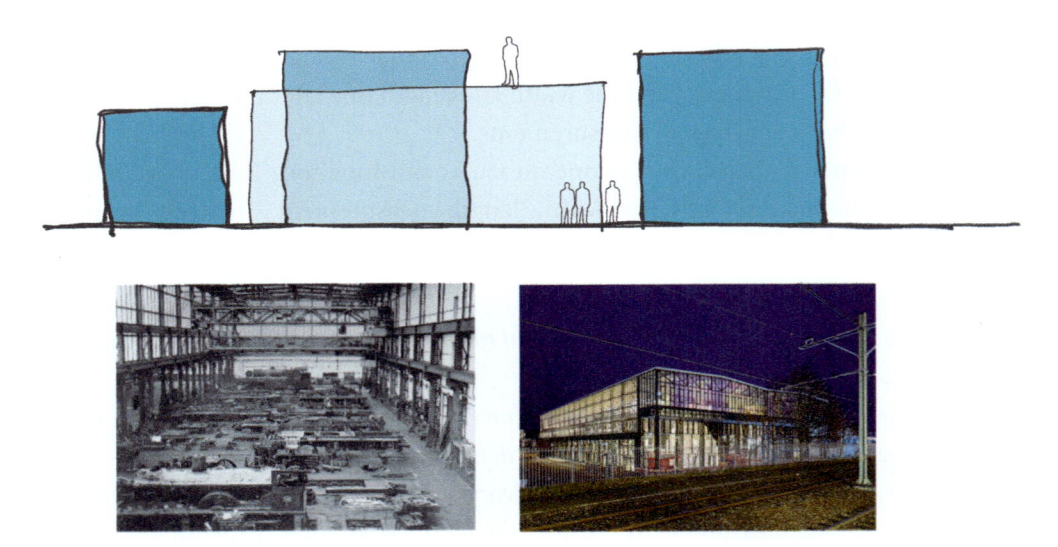

Figure 1.24 Three core conceptual diagrams. A glass and steel cathedral space for the city. A covered square where crowds can gather, more than a building/balcony city views. Original bustling workshop, courtesy of Civic Architects/new building façade. Photo Credit: Arjen Veldt

Civic Concepts

The building is further enhanced by connecting it with the city through civic functions – library, co-working spaces, conference rooms, arts education spaces and a large city hall for international events ('LocHal Library: from former locomotive hangar to a social…')

A mixed-use facility enhances the functional sustainability of the building. A program of many layered activities ensures that the 'new' library has a functionality that goes beyond a traditional library resource.

> *An effective program of use is often as important as the design itself in terms of the [use] sustainability of a building.*

Reading of the Space

The building had always been part of the city with its heavy construction; the structure becomes lighter towards the top providing a fantastic spatial experience.

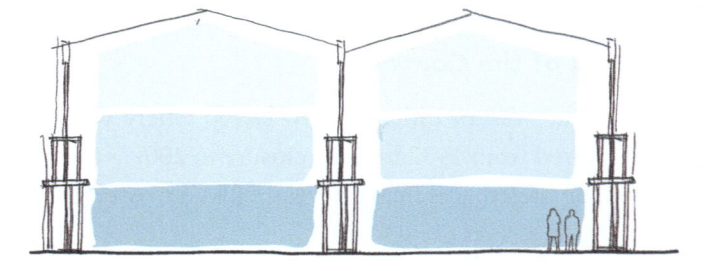

Figure 1.25 Stripped out and restored interior before insertions. Photo Credit: Braaksma Roos

Figure 1.26 Rolling stock table/library area integrated into the existing columns. Photo Credit: Ossip van Duivenbode

The original height and volume are preserved in the space to retain the spatial grandeur of the structure. The original structure is preserved in its original state to juxtapose against the new materials introduced.

Historical Reading/Design Concepts

Retaining the Industrial Past – The project retains the crane, crane tracks, the rails and the imposing steel construction with their original old layers of paint. This structure is embraced with furniture elements for reading and study.

The existing rolling stock and industrial structure have been appropriated to accommodate the library functions and to provide a dramatic integration of the old and new.

> *Old tracks remain visible in the concrete floor and are used to move three large wheeled 'train' tables. A single table can become the extension of the bar or, when combined with another table, forms a stage with the stairs as a tribune. They can also be moved outside to form a stage for outdoor events.*
>
> (Mecanoo Architects)

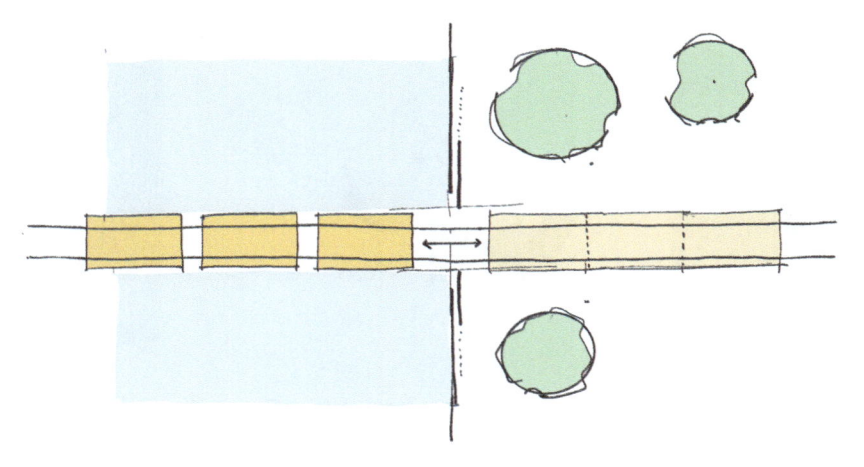

Figure 1.27 Moving train table diagram, expressing the inside-outside relationship of the rolling stock tables

Spatial Concepts

INTERIOR ARCHITECTURAL ELEMENTS – A large major open landscape staircase has been inserted into the hall. Taking you up two levels to the full height of the building the insertion provides a vast expanse of staging and informal seating. A series of curtains in the space give privacy and allow the whole space to open up when they are drawn back.

> *Movable textile walls – accentuate the scale of the building, define different spaces, and improve the acoustics. They soften the industrial hall and divide the space into larger or smaller activity areas. The transparency of the curtains allows you to read the space as whole.*
>
> (Inside Outside Design Studio)

Figure 1.28 Landscape stair element. Photo Credit: Ossip van Duivenbode /landscape stair element setting up the main space

 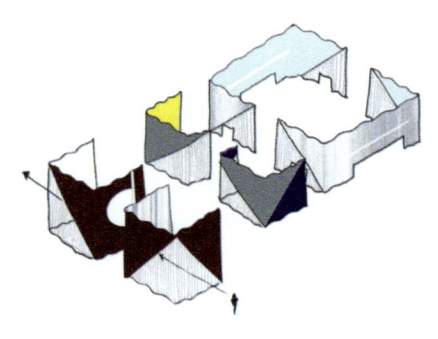 

Figure 1.29 Architectural curtains define space. Diagram courtesy of Inside Outside, Petra Blaisse. Photo Credit: Peter Tijhuis

◆ Locomotive hall

The hull of Nedtrain's historic Locomotive Hall forms the basis for the architecture. All traces of use have been retained. They set the key-note for the new architecture.

- Braaksma & Roos Architectenbureau

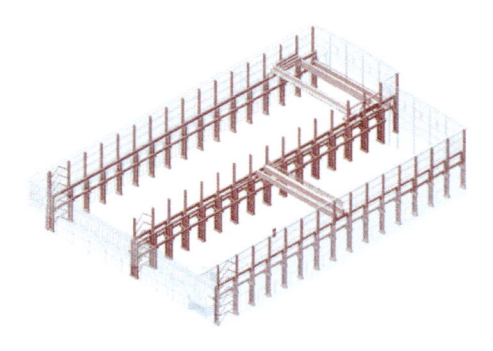

◆ Interwoven architecture

The solid architecture coincides with the hall and makes the LocHal an impressive public place: An open knowledge workshop with various labs and space for events.

- Civic A rchitects
- Braaksma & Roos Architectenbureau
- Inside Outside / Petra Blaisse

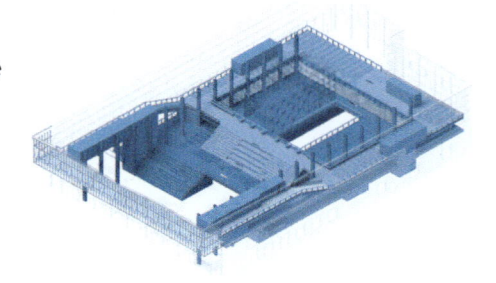

◆ Movable textiles

Six massive movable screens make it possible to divide the hall and stairwell into different zones for lectures, events and exhibitions.

- Inside Outside / Petra Blaisse
- TextielLab

◆ Colorful life

Many different activities and target groups are located side by side in the hall, with different design themes: An interior that is full of diversity.

- Meca noo
- Academy of architecture Tilburg

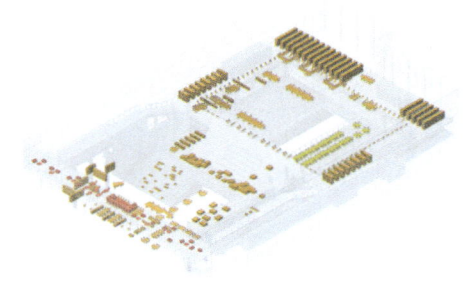

Figure 1.30 A diagram expressing the four main interior architectural conceptual layers of the scheme. Courtesy of Civic Architects

CHAPTER 2

2D

INTRODUCTION

Chapter 2 covers 3 facets that make up the 2D conceptual design process: 2D drawing, diagramming ideas and developing a set of key moves to work with.

The creation of point, line and shape are explored along with sketch analytical drawing techniques to emphasise the relationship of 2D drawing to conceptual design development. The 2D drafting environment maps closely to a 2D CAD drawing environment. The overriding conceptual design emphasis in this chapter is to develop a good understanding of 2D drawing conventions and to transcend them into a series of key moves early on in your design process.

Concept development is introduced as a starting point to the design process [and expanded on in Chapter 3], with an emphasis in this chapter given to developing a scheme proposal in 2D through plan and section development.

2D Overview

For a design process it is important that a series of key conceptual moves be formed at the initial stages of a design project. These key moves can range from external to internal spatial considerations and are often focused on interventions to 'existing' architecture. When applied in context [see Chapter 1] they can readily be adopted to become one or more key concepts in the development of your own scheme proposals. Diagrams are used to illustrate design thinking; they are sufficiently abstract to communicate the IDEAS behind a project proposal without getting involved in the problems of applying them – this is the main advantage of diagrammatic thinking.

The process of design for an interior designer is as follows:

Read the context space
Evaluate any spatial or structural interventions [big or small]
Define a clear series of concepts to work with [and stick to them]

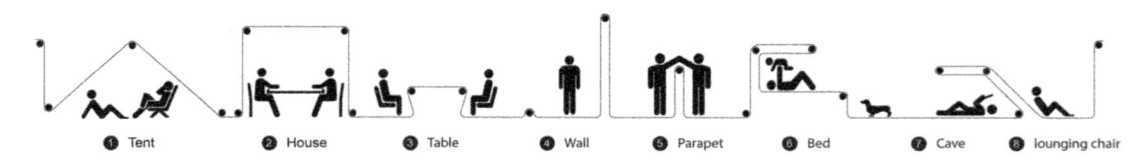

Figure 2.1 The diagrammatic principles for paper roll space creation – Happier Café, Taiwan. Courtesy of JC Architecture, 2016

DOI: 10.4324/9781003120650-3

Test them out through plan and section [draw it out]
Develop the level of detail [make it work]

2D DRAFTING ENVIRONMENTS

As discussed in the previous chapter, understanding existing space is fundamental to the role of an interior designer. 'Measuring up' records an existing building or space, and collates measurements, dimensions and notes of any significant features. After all the information is gathered an accurate measured drawing is needed. In these preliminary stages, it is embedded in the process of drawing up a basic plan and section. As a starting point a good plan and section drawn by 'hand' will go a long way to further your understanding of a surveyed space and of the principles of 2D drafting.

Hand drawing is the default go-to method of orthographic drawing that every interior designer should master. At some point in your development as a designer you should draft up using a drawing board as it helps you understand 2D drafting as a hands-on process; it also helps you understand and develop your orthographic skills without the additional burden of trying to master a CAD software interface. As you gain confidence and understanding then CAD will be your chosen method.

The Drawing Board

There is a sense of formality in using a drawing board. It is the place where you draw up your initial building plan to a chosen scale. It is the start of the 'testing' of your design ideas which would have been generated through diagrammatic explorations in 2D and 3D.

Setting a Scale to Work with

When drafting by hand the drawing board and paper size define the applicable units [it is also a CAD principle utilised by Vectorworks]. Set the scale of the drawing in accordance to your building size, paper size and drawing board.

By getting a good understanding of the appropriate scale you can work out the correct scale for your drawing prior to drawing it out. For example, a building that is 6 m × 6 m will comfortably fit on an A2 piece of paper drawn at a scale of 1:20.

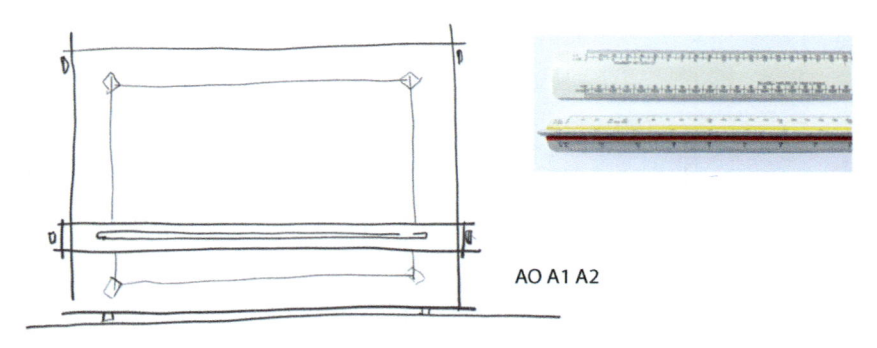

AO A1 A2

Figure 2.2 Available sizes for drawing boards A0, A1, A2/two types of scale rule, flat/triangular

> *Architectural scales are set to 1:200, 1:100, 1:50 and 1:20.*
> *The bigger the scale the more detail is needed in your drawing.*

Understanding Scale

A drawing at a scale of 1:20 means that the object being drawn is 20 times smaller than in real life scale 1:1. It will be the same size drawing regardless of the paper size.

Always read the end of the scale rule to see what units are being used.

While scale is not necessarily appropriate at the initial stages of concept design you might want to format an existing plan, section and elevation into a diagrammatic scale to use as an underlay, typically 1:500, 1:200 or 1:100.

> *A drawing board is a mechanical bit of kit that is prone to small failures:*
> *Check if the sliding rule is attached firmly and moves smoothly or everything will end up wonky.*
> *Make sure that you firmly attach any paper or trace to the board with masking tape – [no Sellotape] or the paper will move around, and everything will end up wonky.*
> *Check that the slide rule can clearly travel over the paper before you start drawing to avoid ripping the paper.*

Drawing Up

Start in the right-hand corner and work towards your left rather than starting in the middle. It is important to pick the correct point to start your drawing as you might well run out of paper and not fit your drawing on [when in draft you can add extra paper]. A good way to start is to measure out the limits of the building.

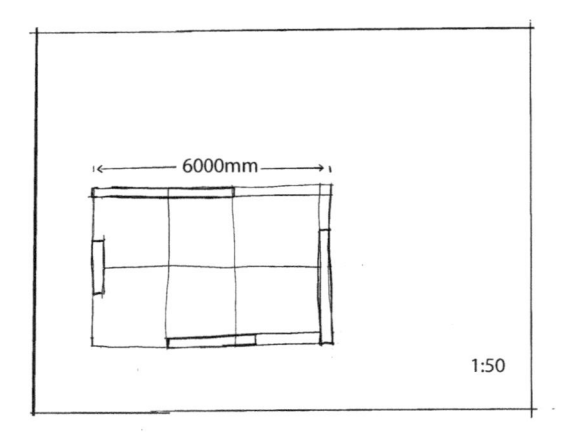
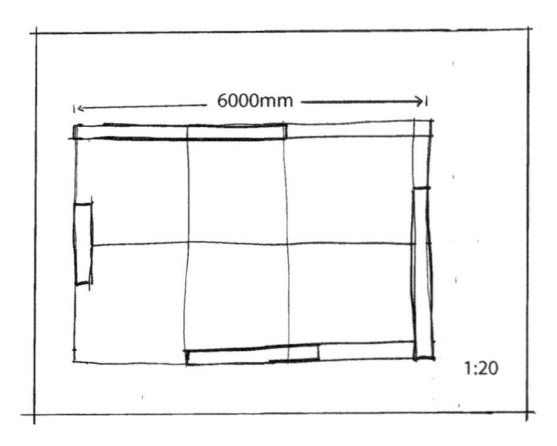

Figure 2.3 A4/A3 paper scale size diagram

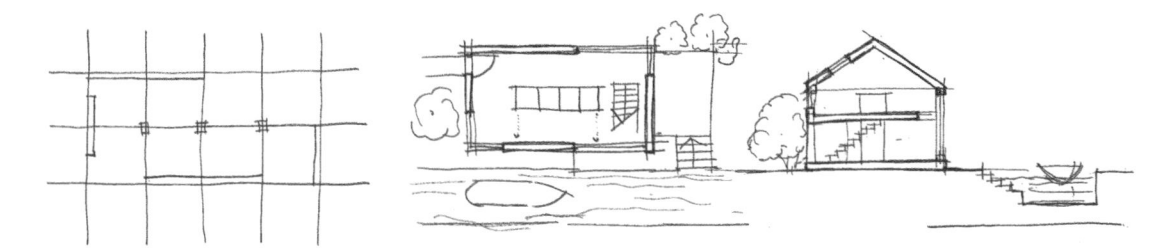

Figure 2.4 Start by defining the control lines/a sketch plan and section drawing

Define the structural walls and columns. If a grid is present in the building [even a ceiling grid] draw out that grid in singular lines as it will help you locate elements and draw more quickly/accurately.

When you have set up the primary elements, draw thickness to walls, add openings, then follow by adding window details, door swings, stair details and furniture.

> *As explained in Chapter 1, a column should be measured from its centre; thus, the crossing point of the single line becomes the centre of the column.*
>
> *A good 'drawing' practice task is to take an existing drawn plan and 'scale it off', take it from scale 1:100 and draw it up at 1:50 [Detail Magazine has lots of plans to a given scale].*

Plan and Sections

A plan and section are 2D drawings; they are always 2D [apart from a sectional perspective]. It is an 'orthographic' drawing; everything is drawn parallel and there is no 3D perspective.

A Plan is typically cut at 1m [window sill height] defining a cut taken horizontally through the structure. It helps you organise your internal arrangement, specify wall thicknesses, indicate door and window openings.

A Section is a vertical cut taken through the structure; it helps you develop height and spatial relationships, floor and roof thicknesses. It should be taken through the point of most information such as window openings, voids, landscape furniture elements.

POINT-LINE-PLANE-SHAPE

The 2D creation section introduces 2D geometric principles, starting with point and then proceeding to shape creation. While these are simple geometric representations, these elements also have a role in the conceptual design process and can in many cases be the representation of a series of significant key moves.

We start with the basic definitions and then look at the transformative potentials, such as applied attributes and transformations [move, multiply, scale, mirror, etc.]. To accompany the section there are references to CAD software so you can associate with the terminology [also covered in Chapter 7]. These 2D principles are 'one' [+3D] of the foundations to effective conceptual design development.

Point

A point is a position in space. It has no attributes until you start to view it in a context such as a screen or picture plane. In this environment it will act as a visual focus/area within a given field. A point also acts as a marker within a shape, e.g., endpoint.

Applied Attributes

A point carrying attributes can take on many complex roles in the conceptual design process. It might be offset to create a circular enclosure, be the central point of a shape or carry thickness to express solidity. As an organising principle it particularly comes alive within a point cloud organisation.

Design Principles

Points play an important conceptual role in the design process:

Setting up a design grid
Acting as a node in complex shapes
Defining a central point in a spatial organisation
Clustering to form particle clouds

Line

A line is an extended point or a drawn distance between two endpoints. Conceptually it has length defined by two points but no initial thickness or depth unless attributes have been set to do so. When a combination of lines are drawn they can describe a shape which can be open or closed [shape]. By applying a degree of thickness, a line can be used to define depth or a cut in an architectural plan and section.

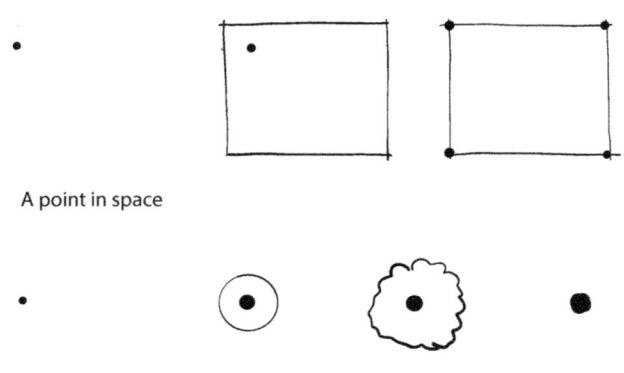

A point in space

A Point with attibutes

Figure 2.5 Point diagrams point in an open space, in a visual field and as a marker within a shape/a point with no attributes and with attributes. A point with no attributes and with attributes/put text on diagrams

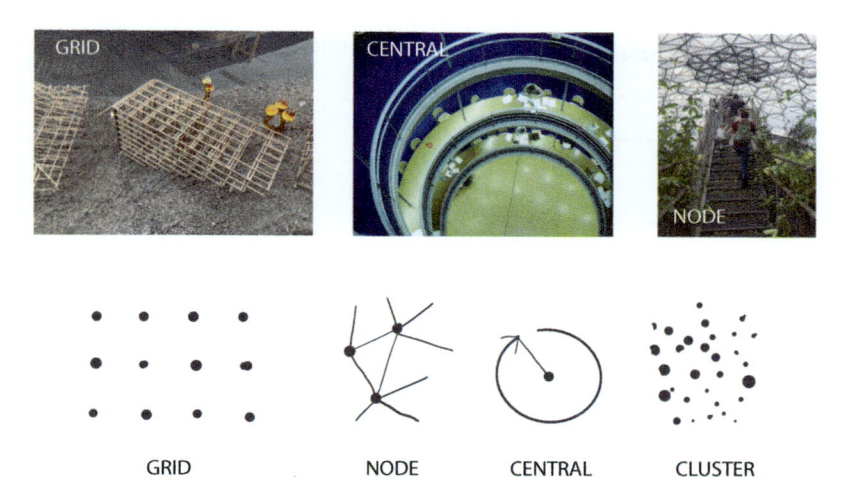

Figure 2.6 A gridded structure: There Are Walls that Want to Prawl. Venice Architecture biennale, 2020. Central 'cone' organisation Library Delft University of Technology, Mecanoo Architects, 1998. A hexagonal and pentagonal geodesic [node] structure. Eden project, Grimshaw Global 2000 diagram: diagrammatic expressions of the point grid, node, central, cluster

> *A dotted line can indicate something above or something hidden of importance to the design scheme.*
>
> *In orthographic drawing line attributes can indicate other design elements such as boundaries, materials, insulation, thresholds and pathways.*

While the simplest of geometric representations, the line has a great potential for complexity to develop intricate 2D shapes.

Design Principles

The line is used to express many key conceptual moves such as a path, a linear space organisation or an entrance approach. The placement of the linear route is often a major design feature in a contemporary interior design intervention. Other 'typical' conceptual moves may be:

To split a plan organisation with the placement of a line to create a dynamic spatial arrangement. To insert a linear wall element to divide space.

Enclosure – lines used to define an open enclosure, indicating four planes
Linear – organisation of adjacent spaces along a linear path
Radial – organisation indicating elements arranged in a polar arrangement and centralised
Path – configuration that is defining a specific route
Axis – defined at an angle to add spatial tension to a plan
Symmetry – line path used to intersect a space or mirror a shape
Asymmetry – line path used to reinforce asymmetrical arrangement
Datum – line acting as an anchor for a collection

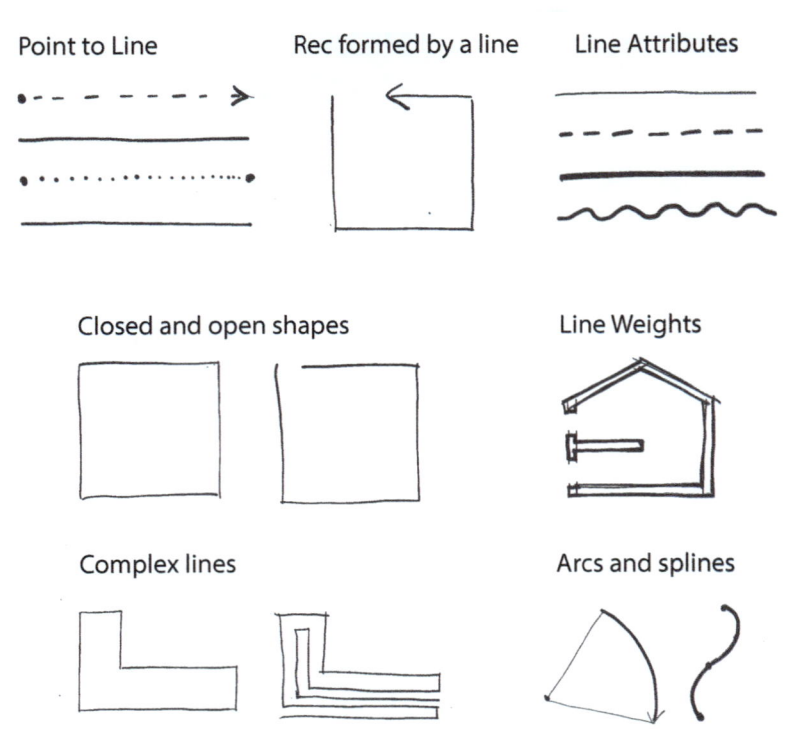

Figure 2.7 Line diagrams, line principles, point to line, rectangle formed by line, attributes assigned to a line, open closed shapes, attributes used to thicken a line in a section cut; starting with a simple outline the shape can be broken down to become more intricate. The arc and spline are a type of line that aligns to a specific point

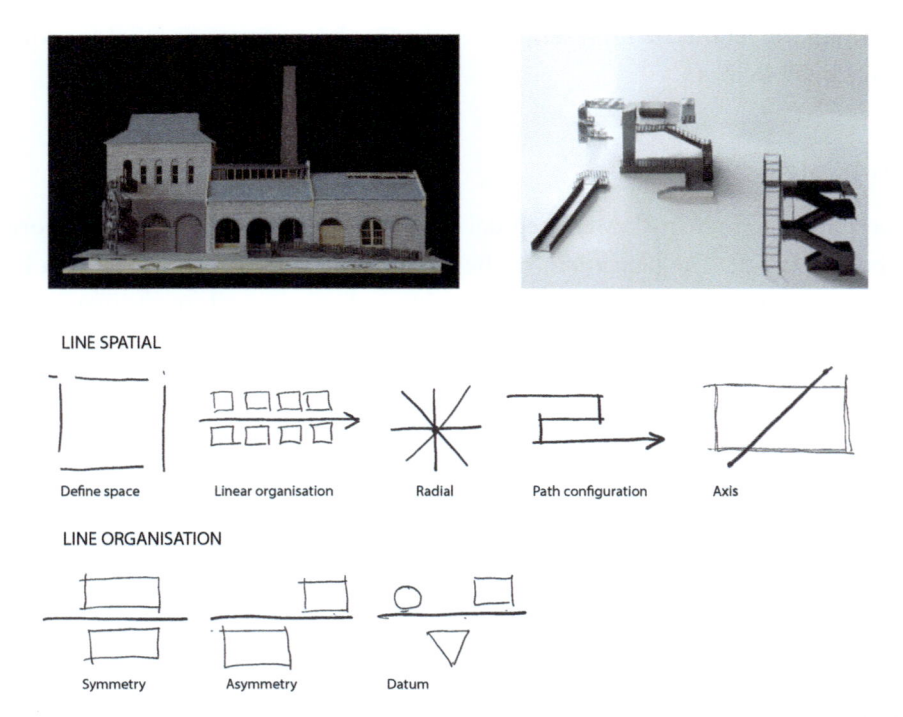

Figure 2.8 Walthamstow Wetlands project, WWM Architects, 2017. Line 'path' configurations inserted into an existing historic structure. Photo Credit: David Grandorge. Common path and spatial 'line' organising principles in diagrammatic form

Drawing Board Tips

When drawing a line, you will need to draw the line to scale, draw a continuous line [it's best to use a sharp pencil towards the H side of the HB] and then mark the two points, the beginning and end using a scale rule.

The drawing board has a parallel motion, and you should have a set square. It is important that all lines are drawn against the actual parallel motion ruler and not freehand with a ruler.

> *Draw horizontal lines with the parallel motion [not off a ruler].*
>
> *Any vertically straight or angled lines should be drawn against the set square or adjustable set square.*
>
> *When drawing an arc, you will use a compass; if the field of the arc is too big it is useful to plot out a series of points to follow or use a beam compass.*

Plane/Shape

A plane is a 2D object that has width and length; it does not carry any thickness. Conceptually it can be thought of as an extruded line [similar to the CAD process of extruding a line into a plane].

Shapes

Primary shapes are the building blocks of complex spatial compositions. When shapes are combined, they help define a series of spaces and the links between those spaces.

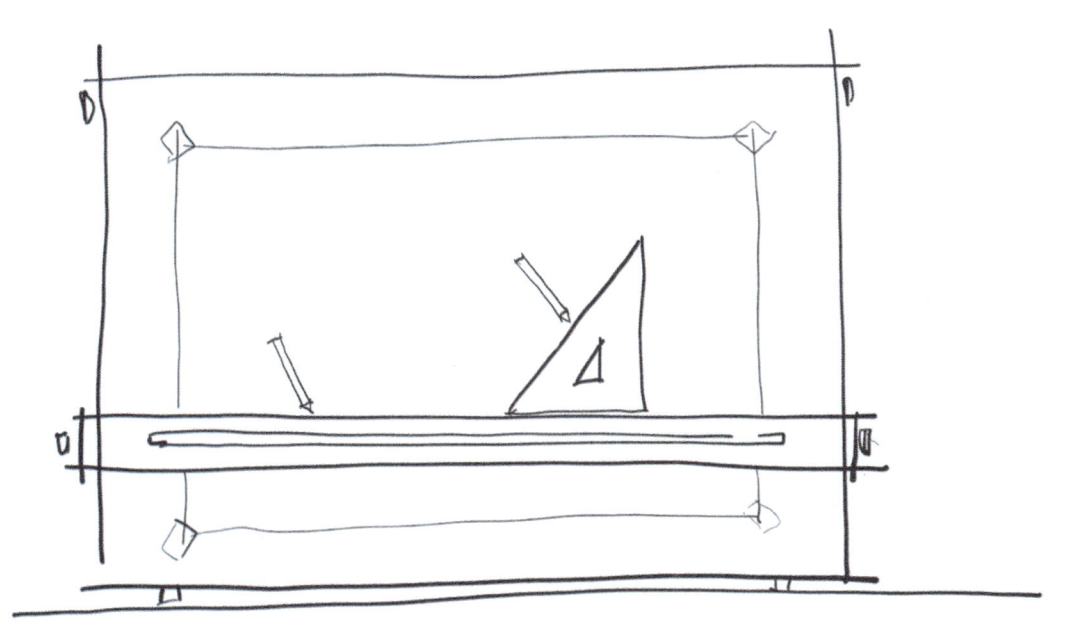

Figure 2.9 Use the drawing board aids, the parallel motion and set square

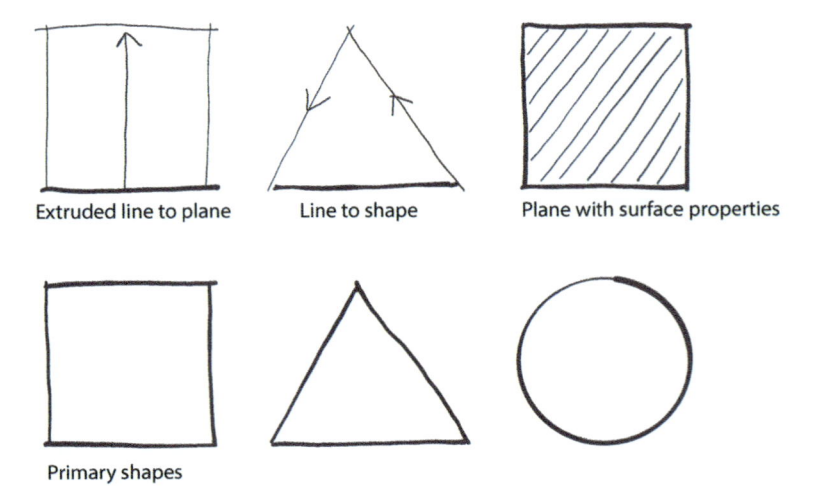

Extruded line to plane | Line to shape | Plane with surface properties

Primary shapes

Figure 2.10 The construction of different types of shapes using the line to create primary shapes. Square triangle, circle and properties assigned to a surface

> *There is little need to draw out more complex shapes in the first instance – a series of rectilinear shapes are always the best starting point for the designer in terms of both drawing up and spatial planning even if the end result is curved or organic in shape.*

Design Principles

In interior design the basic surface – 'the plane' – is an important interior element. Planes are used to define the enclosure of the internal envelope; ceilings, walls and floors are the primary planar elements within the formation of an interior space.

> *In contemporary design the degree of enclosure and the composition of the overhead, wall and ground plane, such as in the work of Mie's Van der Rhoe [Barcelona Pavilion], have helped to break down the traditional spatial solidity experienced in a typical 'room' enclosure.*

Applied Attributes

Shapes can carry the attribute properties of 'surface': a surface pattern, colour or reflection – these are attributes that can be linked to materials specified in the interior proposal and often used in CAD to represent material qualities.

Shape Composition

Shapes can be combined to set up complex spatial compositions; interlocking spaces, regular and irregular shapes can be combined to form dynamic spatial relationships. Within the interior space a curved or organic form juxtaposes well against a formal backdrop [such as a cube].

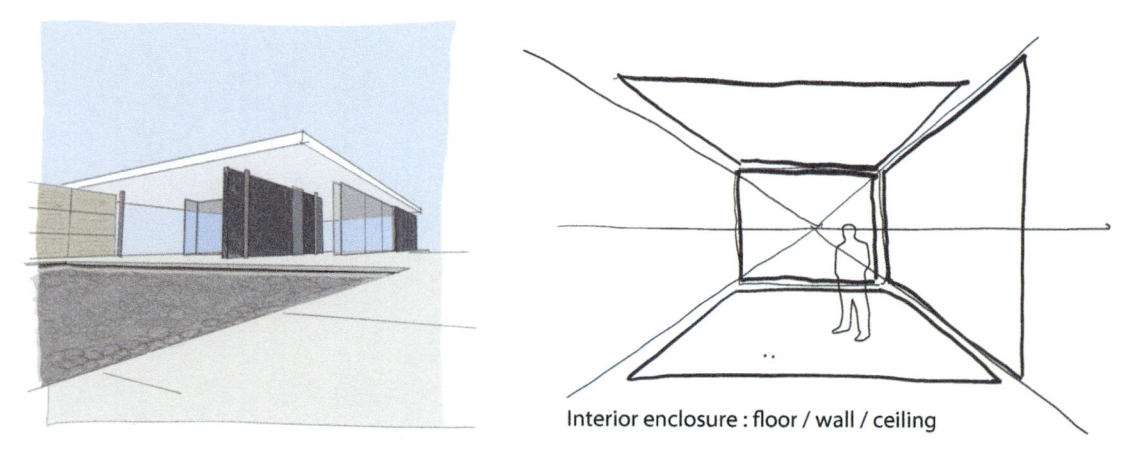

Interior enclosure : floor / wall / ceiling

Figure 2.11 Mie's Van der Rohe [Barcelona Pavilion] planar elements used to define space/plane elements that make up an interior enclosure

Formal Transformations

Transformations are a measured move, duplication or scale in the *XYZ* direction.

They can be applied to a single or multiple shapes in one or multiple transformations [more than one move such as copy and rotate].

> *The overlap and the gaps of a shape composition provide opportunities for defining multiple levels of spatial thinking such as enclosures, circulation routes, [interlinked] structural integrity.*

Intersections

Formal intersections can be additive or subtractive [and combined with transformations]. Spatial complexity can be developed when subtracting from or combining a formal shape. The 'in between' or the add-on spaces created can be representative of a void space, threshold or spatial transition [amongst many others!].

In contemporary design you often see the subtraction of the solid offering an additional function such as to provide seating, define another space or provide inside-outside relationships.

Shapes can be significant or insignificant to the actual physical form. Composition and transitions can create complex spatial and structural configurations.

> *Square, rectangle, triangle and circle are sufficient in detail in the initial stages.*
>
> *It is always easier to develop a primary form first such as a square and then break it down into other irregular shapes as it gives a field to work in and helps you locate the points.*
>
> *Think of shapes as a series of spatial envelopes – avoid 'graphically shape making.'*

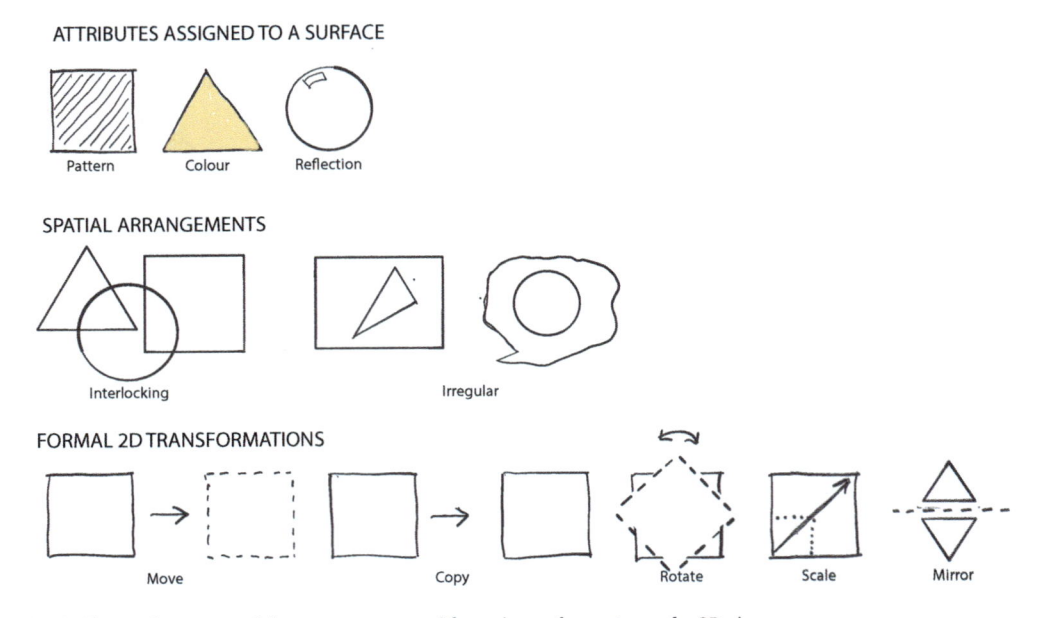

ATTRIBUTES ASSIGNED TO A SURFACE

Pattern   Colour   Reflection

SPATIAL ARRANGEMENTS

Interlocking   Irregular

FORMAL 2D TRANSFORMATIONS

Move   Copy   Rotate   Scale   Mirror

Figure 2.12 The attributes, spatial arrangements and formal transformations of a 2D shape

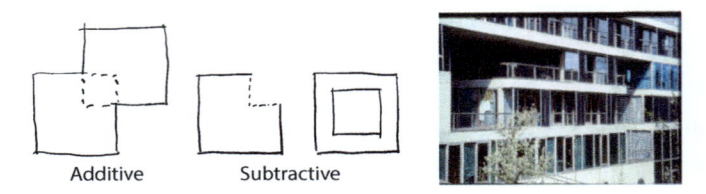

Additive   Subtractive

Figure 2.13 Diagram: add to and subtracting from a primary shape. Subtractive façade of the Villa VPRO, MVRDV Architects, 1997

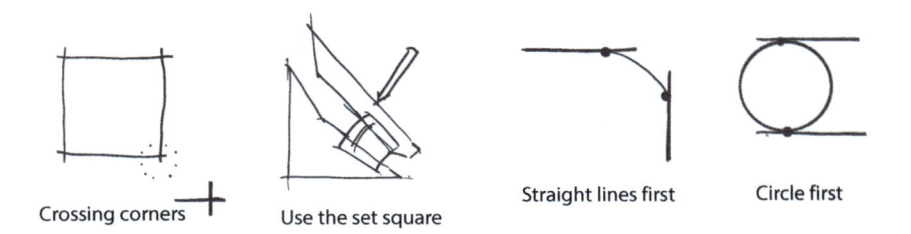

Crossing corners   Use the set square   Straight lines first   Circle first

Figure 2.14 Tips for drawing accurate-'looking' straight lines on the drawing board/tips for drawing curved lines on a drawing board

Drawing Board Tips

When constructing rectangular shapes, ensure that you use the parallel motion and the set square.

Develop a habit of leaving a tick/cross at the corners; it can visually make a square look 'squarer.'

You can use a circle template, compass, beam compass or French curves to draw circles and arcs.

If you are drawing with a compass it helps to set the drawing board flat so there is less chance of it slipping,

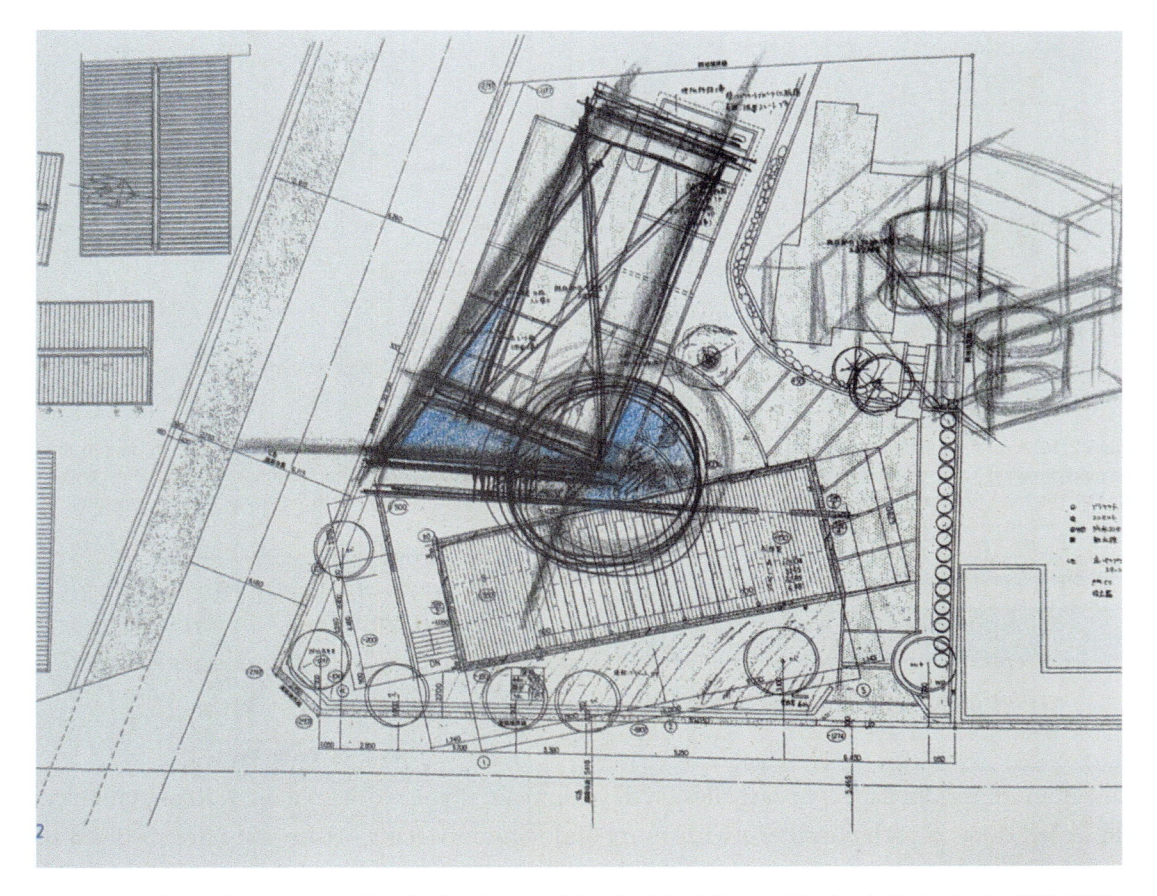

Figure 2.15 Tadao Ando Associates: Church of the Light and Sunday School Composition Study: Tadao Ando, 1997–1999

To make a good connection between curved and linear objects draw the straight lines before the arc and draw the straight lines after you have drawn a circle.

Use a set square or adjustable set square to construct angular shapes such as a triangle.

2D CONCEPTUAL DEVELOPMENT

Effective design development is embedded in developing a set of key moves to work with. They help guide a series of effective spatial, structural and organisational rules to work with. Without establishing a clear set of key moves a project is open to multiple interpretations and reiterations; it is open to be pushed around without any clear direction.

If you have established a clear set of key moves at the conceptual stage it is akin to forming a design contract with your client [or your tutor for that matter]. Your key moves should be sufficiently strong that you can recognise them clearly from the initial diagram to the finalised project drawings; they should also be fluid enough to be manipulated and developed further in conceptual complexity.

This section covers the process of conceptual development from methods of drawing out ideas to a series of established conceptual diagrams that can be adopted in your own project work.

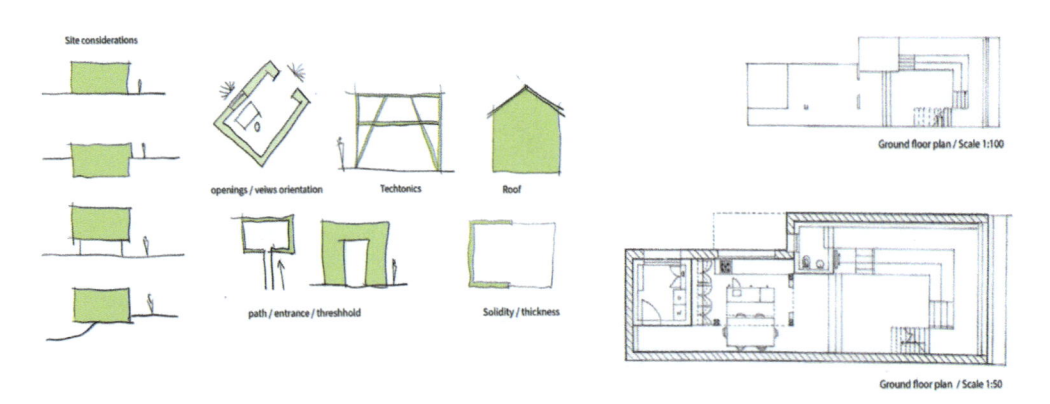

Figure 2.16 A series of simple 2D conceptual diagrams that can make up a strategy for design development. A student example of a plan drawn at 1:100 to explore the arrangement without the costly time of drawing in doors and furniture elements. Once resolved the level of detail can be developed at a scale of 1:50 as seen in the second drawing. Courtesy of Abigail Newton

> *It is ok to use 'just' 2D drawings to express conceptual ideas. It's often a better method of communication than a badly constructed 3D view. To start out you might want to focus on conceptual concepts derived from context information and apply them as a series of spatial, circulation and structural concepts.*

Scale is an important aspect of early design development; if you work on a big 1:20 plan then you will be led down a path considering furniture and window details before you have resolved the 'key moves' such as circulation, structure and approach. By bypassing the 'key moves' you will be continually backtracking to resolve fundamental problems.

Diagramming Principles

Your diagram/analytical drawings should try to explain key concept moves using singular lines; it is often the simplification of a complex design idea or set of ideas into a parti diagram [to make a decision in French]. The decision/drawing you construct should be clear so that it can be read clearly from concept to final proposal but also adaptable and easily modified if the design process demands it.

Consciously or unconsciously all design schemes contain three to five main moves within the final design proposal:

> *It is good practice to get main moves fixed at the conceptual stages, fixed so there is a consistent clarity to the future development of your scheme.*
>
> *Exterior context becomes particularly relevant if you are intending to develop a new entrance, make a new opening or add to the existing building any new architecture.*
>
> *Start by trying to compose the spatial and circulation system.*
>
> *Layer with organisational concepts not random shapes.*

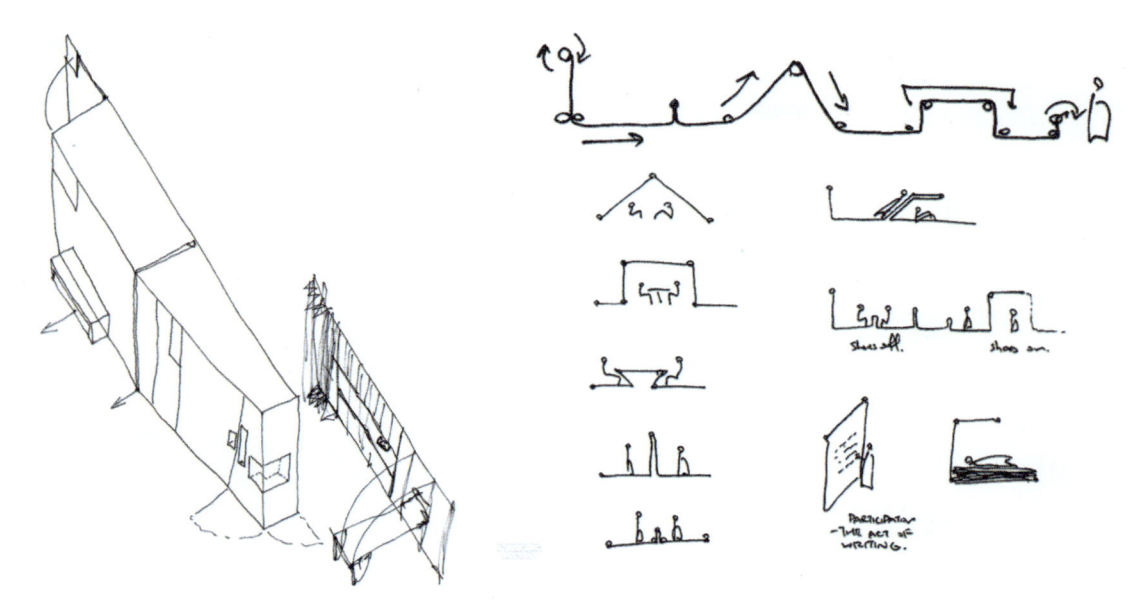

Figure 2.17 Peter Ebner Apartment K/a series of design moves sketched out in 3D not to scale, not tested out in plan and section but an explanation of all the moving parts of the scheme. JC Architecture; Happier Café, Taiwan/ diagrammatic principles of 'habitation' for Happier Café – expressing the spatial and functional principles to the paper roll interior

Diagram Development

In the preliminary stages of design development, you can use a diagram plan, section or model at a small scale 1:200 or 1:500 to quickly work through ideas. Do not make 'shapes' that look pretty as they will hinder the functionality; use 2D geometric principles to define and develop layers of spatial design thinking.

> *The orthographic plan and the section are the typical 2D formats used to express a conceptual diagram [along with sketch models].*
> *The plan to give the context, constraints, organisation, layout and openings.*
> *The section used to show height and reinforce spatial relationships.*

Sketch Pad Development

It is advisable to develop some small plans and section studies 'not to scale' in your sketchbook.

Draw out your key moves in the sketch book with a hint of the building context.

Use multiple trace overlays to develop your design concepts.

Draw in plan and section; leave out details that are not important at this stage, such as door swings or window details.

Go straight in with a pen, black ink and don't try and correct the line [optional].

For clarity and orthographic conventions start defining conceptual ideas with a singular line.

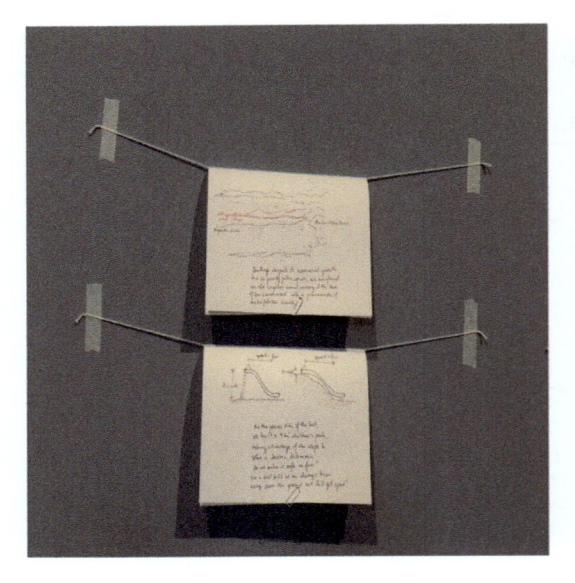
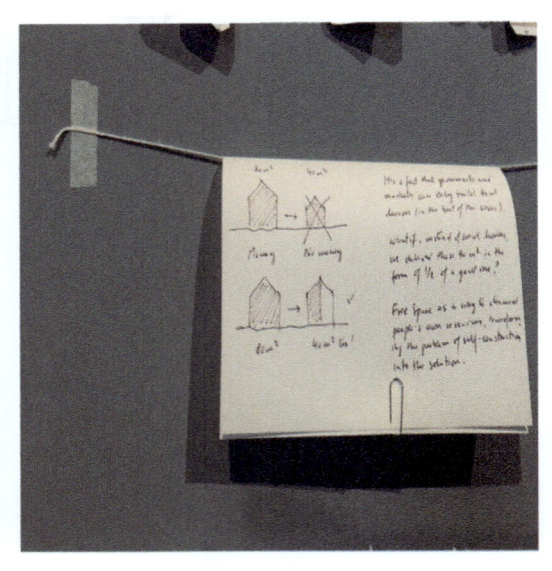

Figure 2.18 Parti diagrams used to explain the design thought process, Venice biennale, 2018. Elemental architecture

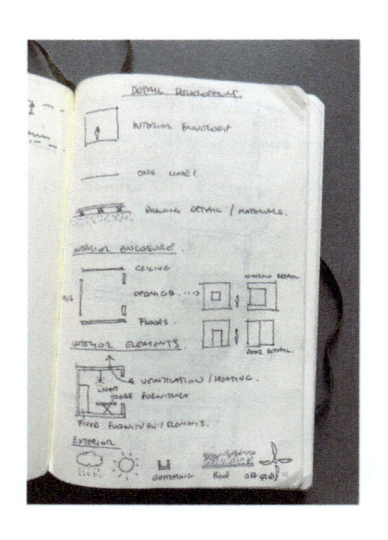
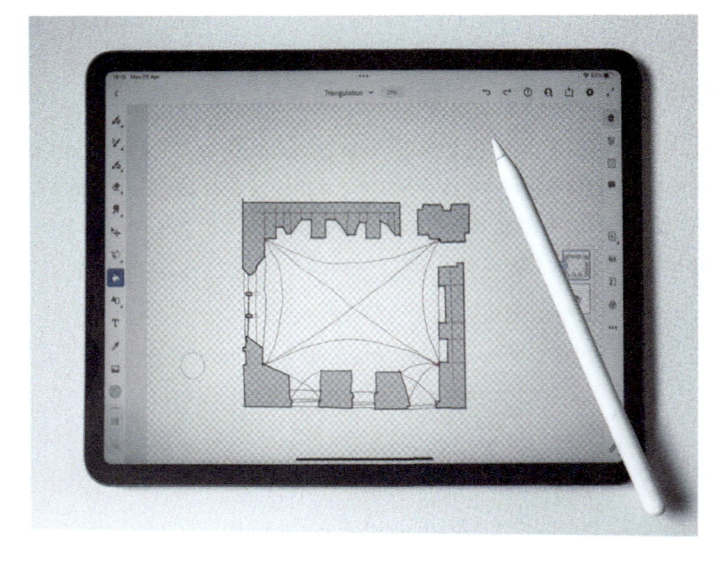

Figure 2.19 A sketch book example of key move diagrams. A tablet with sketching software, ideal for developing diagrams two-dimensionally

Use your hand and eye coordination to maintain lines that are parallel and don't worry if they don't meet up exactly.

Tablet Development

The iPad/tablet is becoming an increasingly useful tool in the world of drawing, especially with the latest addition of a pen. It encourages a singular line approach and is complemented by a

2D orthographic environment. If you are struggling with pen and paper this might well be the go-to interface to develop your drawings.

DIAGRAM EXAMPLES

 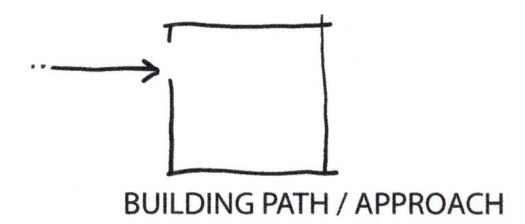

BUILDING PATH / APPROACH

Entrance path to the Hepworth Museum, David Chipperfield Architects 2011

EXISTING OPENINGS

Utilising existing openings Bristol Old Vic. Haworth Tompkins Architects 2018. Photo credit: Philip Vile

 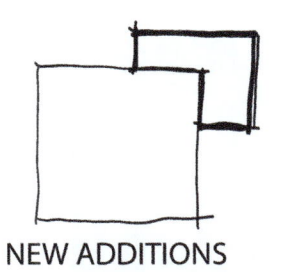

NEW ADDITIONS

The addition of a new architecture to the existing building: The Greifensee Cultural Centre, Jonathan Tuckey

 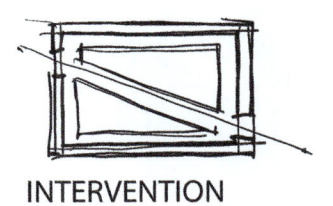

INTERVENTION

Intervention 'splitting of existing building' Gordon Matta Clarke, Splitting.

Figure 2.20 Diagrammatic examples of building path, existing openings, new additions and interventions

SUNLIGHT / OPENING

Daylight, Skyscape, Naoshima, Japan. James Turrell 2004.

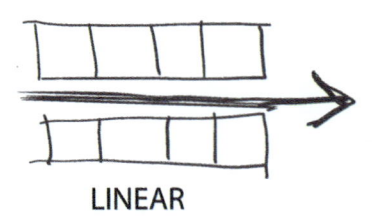

LINEAR

Defined linear route with fluorescent lighting The White cube, Casper Mueller Kneer Architects 2011.

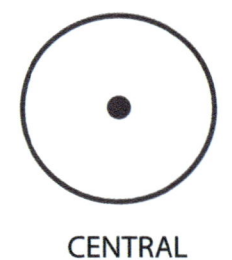

CENTRAL

Central double helix circulation of the Reichstag. Photo credit: Nigel Young Foster + Partners Reichstag Berlin1999.

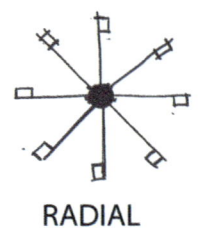

RADIAL

Radial stairs The Newport Gallery Caruso St John 2018.

Figure 2.21 Diagrammatic examples of openings, linear arrangements, central and radial organisations

CLUSTER

Clustered together spaces: Aldo van Eyck's Municipal Orphanage 1960.

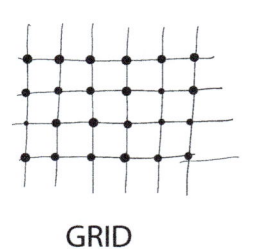

GRID

Grid organisation setting up retail space and display strategy. Camper Shop, Kengo Kuma 2015. Photo Credit: Zeno Zotti

CIRCULATION / ENCLOSURE / ROUTE

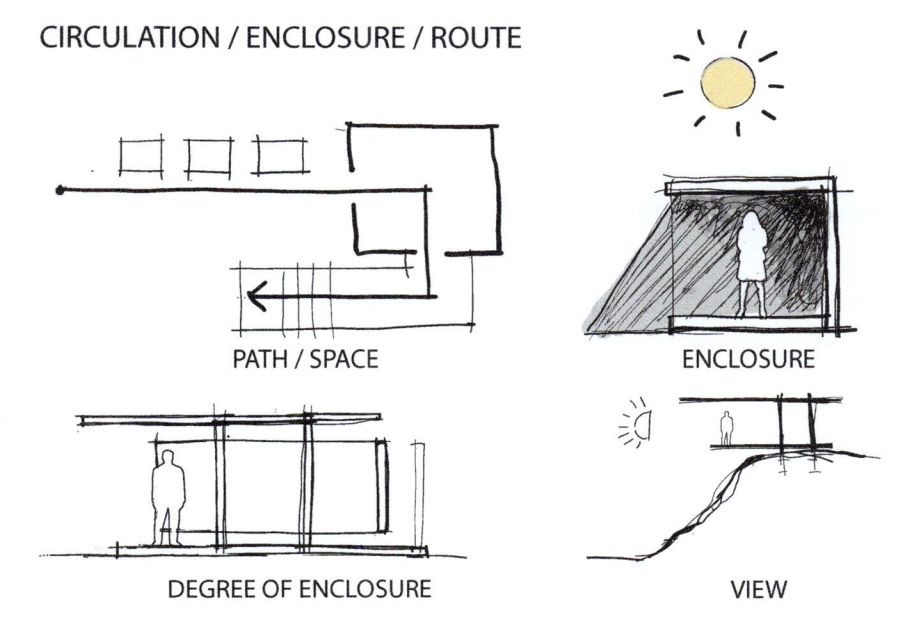

PATH / SPACE

ENCLOSURE

DEGREE OF ENCLOSURE

VIEW

Figure 2.22 Diagrammatic examples of cluster and grid organisations. Circulation, enclosure and route diagrams

---

CASE STUDY – ORGANISING PRINCIPLES

The Camper Shop – Milan, Kengo Kuma Associates, 2014

Design Team: Javier Villar Ruiz/Jaime Fernandez Calvache

The Camper shoe shop by Kengo Kuma Associates employs an organisational principle early on in the design process 'the grid.' In this interior-focused project, the grid organisation provides a structural system, an adaptive display strategy, and also carries the necessary services required in a shop interior such as lighting and electrics.

Context

The shop is located on Via Monte Napoleone, Milan, Italy. It is a historic area considered by many to be the most exclusive shopping area in Milan and home to all the top names in fashion and design concept stores. A walk around this area is an eye-catching immersive experience with different brands pitching new retail design concepts against each other to attract the consumer.

> *A shop enclosure is something that is often tackled by interior designers. One of the common contextual restraints of a shop interior is the lack of windows and light within the enclosure – more often than not the street-facing window will be the only source of natural light, meaning the interior will rely entirely on artificial lighting even during daylight hours.*

The shop window display is often the focus of any shop design; the project by Kengo Kuma embraces a holistic approach for the shop interior and shop window: it facilitates a seamless integration between internal and external display.

Key Concepts

The project combines a series of simple key concepts and rule sets to create a rich interior environment.

  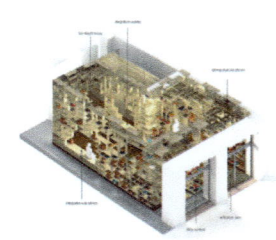

Figure 2.23 Exterior context of Camper shop – photo Zeno Zotti Wrap around shelf diagram. Computer-generated axonometric of the interior – Kengo Kuma Associates

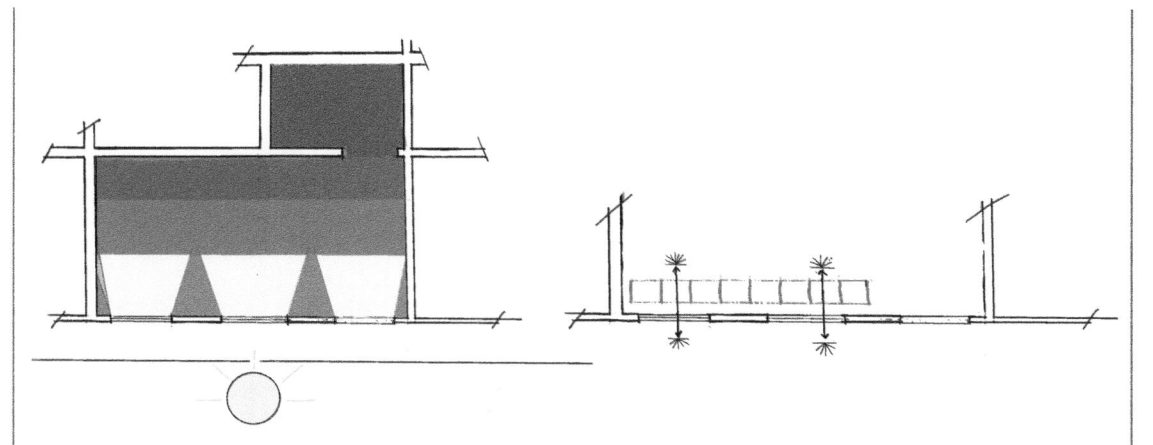

Figure 2.24 Limited light into back of the shop diagram; shelving helps to transmit light and display products to the interior and exterior

> *We have conceived this wooden board system to appear in elevation as a simple 32×32 cm grid, a dimension that simply follows the standard shoe size to display on stores.*
>
> *Though, it is due to the different position of its vertical boards, that the system suddenly becomes a very complex and random three-dimensional construction once seen in perspective.*
>
> (Kengo Kuma Associates)

The Introduction of a Grid

The first and most striking feature is the employment of a grid into the whole shop interior where it provides both the lining of the space and the display strategy.

Repetition and Duplication

The grid is organised around a 32cm box arrangement that gets broken down, doubled or tripled depending on the functionality of the wall element. Working with this as an initial concept helps maximise the clarity of the project's 'grid' concept and also allows the flexibility to respond to the specific functions required in the retail space.

> *It can be a useful starting point to grid out a space or entire building to get a good idea of the architectural and interior rhythm. In larger projects this is often set up with a structural grid such as columns and beams. Use a trace overlay to work out the composition.*

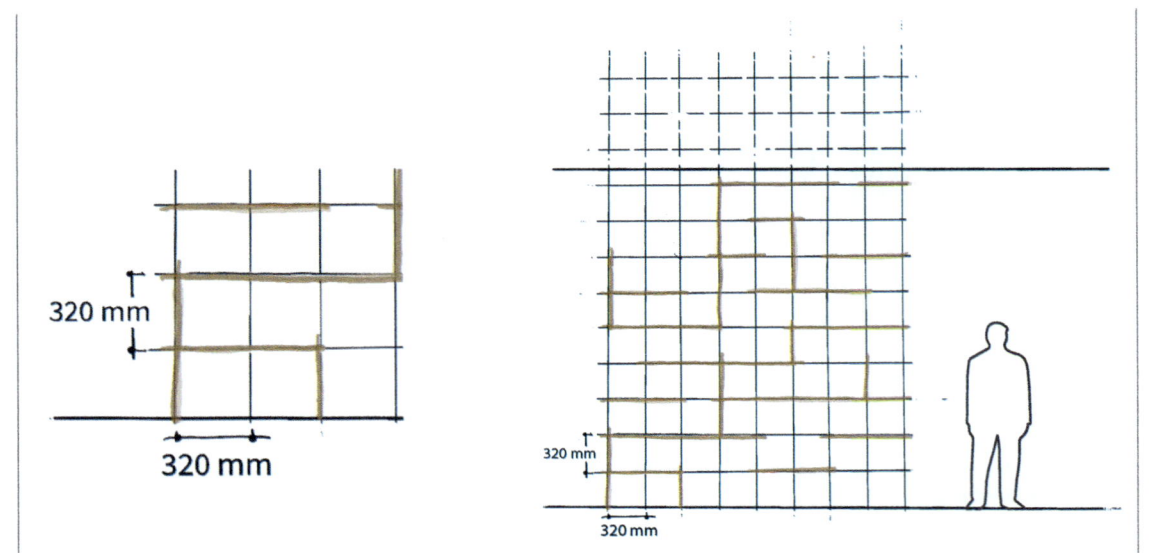

Figure 2.25 A 320mm grid/320mm grid with the shelf inserts indicated

Spatial Concepts

Organisation and orientation/a set of organisational rules are introduced to control the project development. All the display and program elements are wrapped around the shop within the shelving element, thus freeing up the main volume. The depth of the shelving responds to the activity such as the bench seating being 50cm deep and the window display being double the depth at 64cm, to allow the products to be displayed in the window and within the interior. In elevation the rule set is always kept to multiples of 16, 32 and 64.

Integrated Program Elements

Program elements such as the retail counter/reception and seating [to try on the shoes] are integrated into the wall structure to maximise the floor space.

Materials, Details and Light

By the very competitive nature of the highstreet shops the interiors are often short-lived; especially in this environment the interior designer should be thinking about the after-life of the materials used within the interior. From the outset this project has considered materiality by using 'very humble plywood boards' which can be easily recycled or repurposed.

To cut down on further material such as metal fixings a simple intersection joint is created in the plywood. A fully integrated lighting system is integrated into the plyboard by routing a channel into the board.

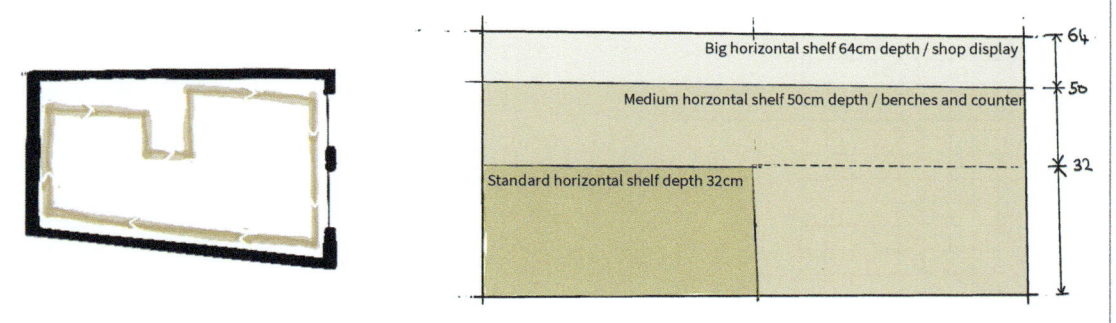

Figure 2.26 Shelving strategy wrapping around the space/different depths of shelving with particular functions

Figure 2.27 CGI image showing the integrated seating and reception – a visual highlighting the key concepts of integrating the seating elements and the retail 'counter' into the main structure. Shop interior photograph. Photo Credit: Zeno Zotti

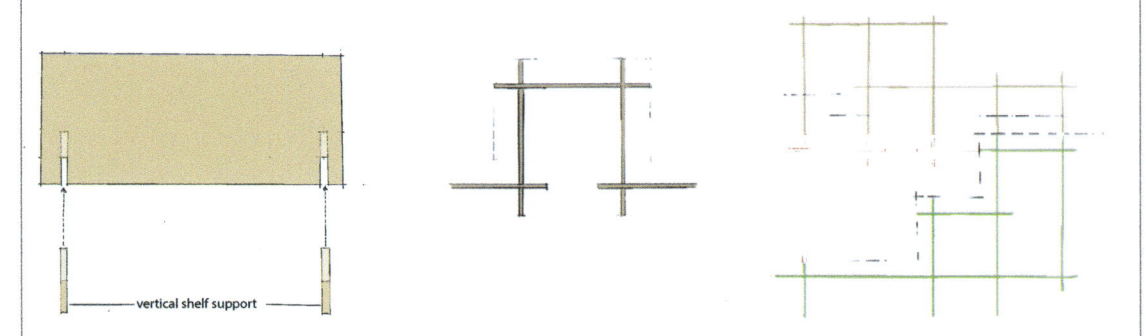

Figure 2.28 A simple slot detail cuts down on the need for fixings in construction. The shelves are cut at 80 mm from the joint's axis for stability/a simple rule set that all horizontal boards should be connected to at least two perpendicular boards ensures structural integrity to the grid construction

It's notable that the natural materials in this store such as the stone floor, plywood shelves and hemp-covered seats provide a highly complex and sophisticated shop interior that does not cost the earth [see Chapter 5]. It was also prefabricated off-site and took two weeks to install.

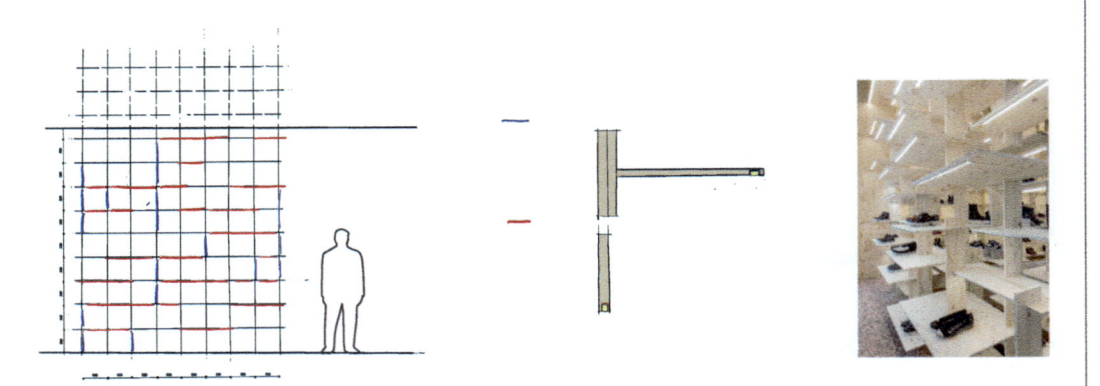

Figure 2.29 Colour-coded drawing to indicate where the shelf lighting [in blue], display lighting [in red] is located/ interior detail showing the integrated lighting strips and shelf details – interior photo of the shelf detail. Photo Credit: Zeno Zotti

This coexisting duality, between simple/basic at first sight, and complex/sophisticated when deeply observed, is what more fascinates us from Camper's attitude towards design… and is indeed this dual attitude what we have tried to imply with our design here in this Camper shop in Monte Napoleone.'

(Kengo Kuma Associates)

CHAPTER 3

3D

INTRODUCTION

Chapter 3 starts with the premise that drawing in 3D and modelling by hand may be more appropriate at the initial stages of a design, whereas using 3D CAD may be more appropriate when a design concept has been realised. The process of exploring design through 3D design principles is broken down to be sequential/logical with the appropriate scales set to match the design process along with an understanding of when to move into detail development.

3D volumes are introduced to define the key principles of 3D 'creation.' Shape and volume are diagrammatically explored to define the key 'spatial' relationships of simple and complex 3D configurations [subtraction, addition, etc.]. Sketch modelling and 3D analytical drawing are defined as conceptual design tools [complementing Chapter 2], reinforcing that the process of conceptual development is a complementary 2D and 3D process. A guide is provided for the development of a design from the concept stage.

3D Overview

3D drawing has become more accessible and easier for the draftsperson. Programs such as SketchUp actively encourage the designer to go straight in with the 3D drawing, which is great to a point. As with all CAD processes, the Infinite scale can cause a lack of design prioritisation; being sucked into detail where detail is not required or the use of the 3D warehouse to dress a space with predefined objects [thus rendering the design process null] are common mistakes. As a budding interior designer there is a lot of temptation out there for a quick 3D fix using a software-based approach. In this chapter, the focus is on 3D drawing by both hand and computer as a spatial design aid, to enhance the design process.

The 3D environment is the natural home of the interior designer. 3D spatial design defines the profession past the perception of surface treatments and the dressing of spaces associated with interior decoration. Working between 2D and 3D environments develops a holistic design process – much of the decision-making process of whether to be working in 2D or 3D will come with experience.

In this development sheet you see the full tool kit of design exploration using sketch modelling and orthographic drawing studies.

DOI: 10.4324/9781003120650-4

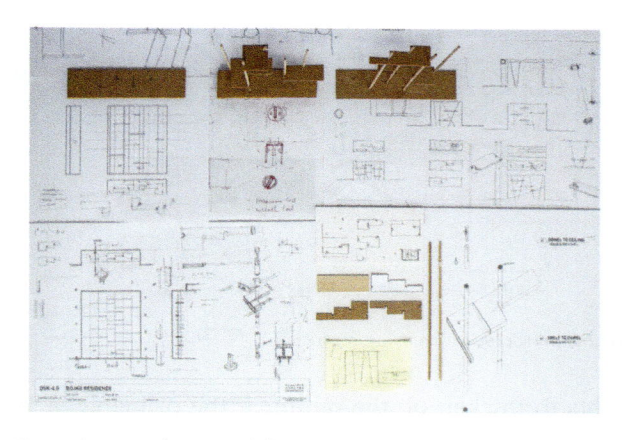

Figure 3.1 Developmental sketch models and drawings. An interior furniture study – Shelving Forest, 2020/VladimirRadutny Architects, Chicago, USA

3D ENVIRONMENT

3D represents three dimensions: in a mathematical context they are referred to as X and Y to indicate length and width with Z representing height. This is also the location system adopted by CAD software. A 3D drawing can be orthographic [parallel] or in perspective [distorted].

3D Environment: Drawing Board

The most common 3D drawing on the drawing board is the axonometric or the isometric. It is a measured drawing that can be scaled and should in most cases be to scale. It is a parallel drawing, so all the vertical height is parallel, but the plan information is set at varying degrees, the most common being 45/45 or 60/30.

Set the 2D plan drawing at the correct angle on the drawing board – 30/60 or 45/45 – using a set or adjustable square.

Draw in parallel height lines, make them a little longer than needed – scale off a height measurement.

Use the set square to carry around the measurement [no need to measure each one].

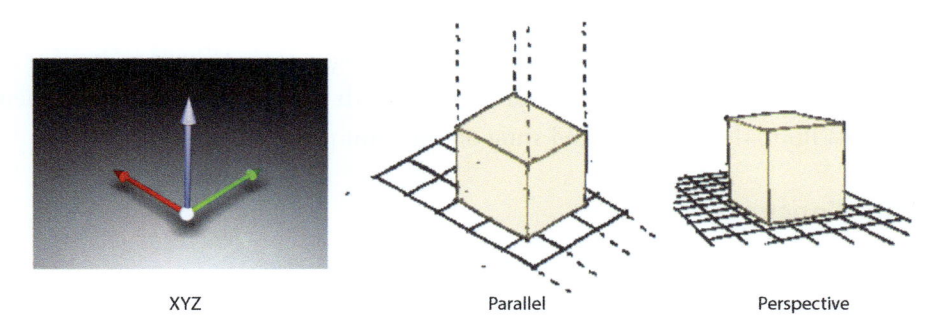

XYZ   Parallel   Perspective

Figure 3.2 *XYZ* 3D axis: the difference between parallel and perspective projections

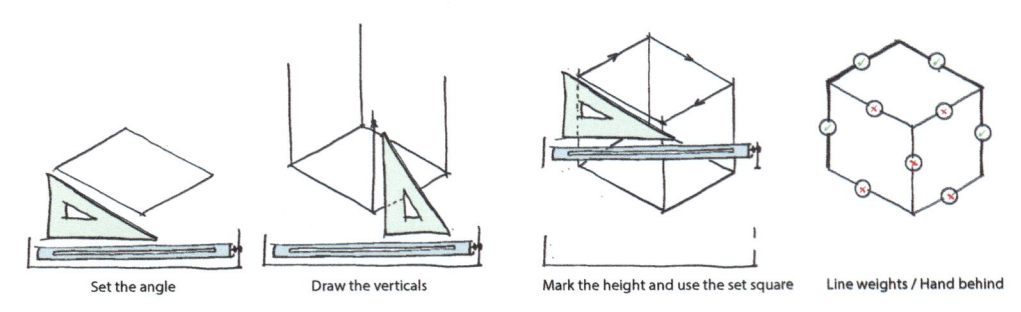

Set the angle   Draw the verticals   Mark the height and use the set square   Line weights / Hand behind

Figure 3.3 Axonometric drawing process diagram/*line weights principles for an* axonometric

To give the illusion of depth use line weights to thicken up the outline – the principle is to thicken any lines you can get your hand on.

PRIMARY FORMS

The Cube/Rectilinear Prism

The cube is the building block of 3D forms; it is a stable form that can be multiplied, combined and modified to create complex spatial relationships.

You can develop more complex forms using the topological levels of the cube; it can also be broken down into more complex forms using subdivisions.

Within volumetric forms there are defined topological points that can be referenced:

Points/vertices
Lines/edges
Planes/face

Design Principles

The cube and rectilinear prism are the most widely utilised 3D form when setting up spaces and enclosures. They signify a mass object that can be significant as an entire building or as small enough to represent an internal enclosure.

Fokkema & Partners Architecten, Loft Lensvelt, 1998. In this project three cube volumes are used to reduce all the necessary program elements [bathrooms, bedrooms and a kitchen] to a minimum. Leaving the original structure and the double height space to express itself as an open plan environment – the plan is also turned on its head with the living room and kitchen being located on the first floor, the bedroom and snug on the ground.

Cube Spatial Concepts

A space within a space – Insertion/interior architecture
Setting up an enclosure – Wall ceiling and floor thickness
Corner articulation – Expression of edges and corners
New additions/subtractive forms

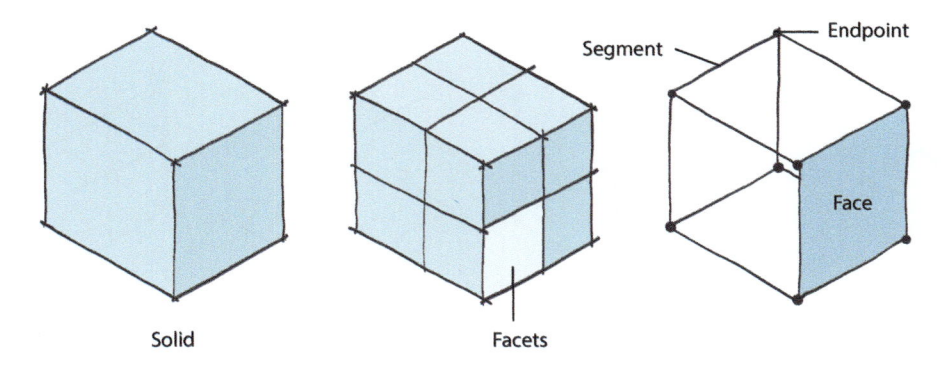

Figure 3.4 A cube with subdivisions/facets diagrams/cube edge, segment and face diagram

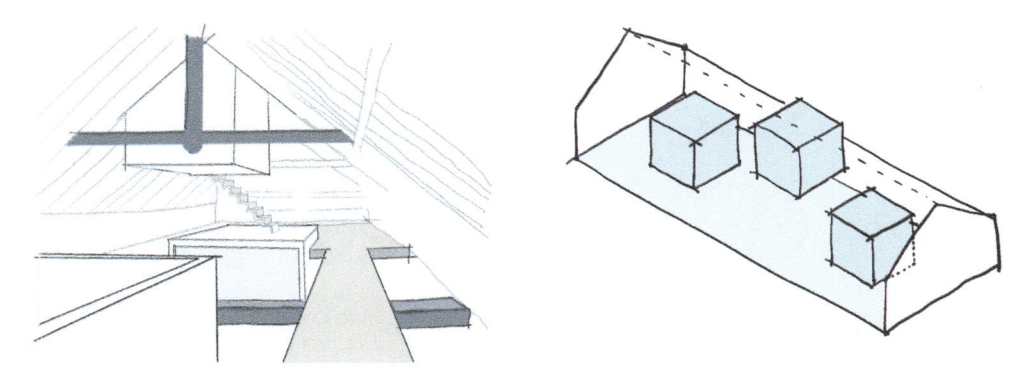

Figure 3.5 A series of cubes setting up a double height space. Fokkema & Partners Architecten, Loft Lensvelt, 1998

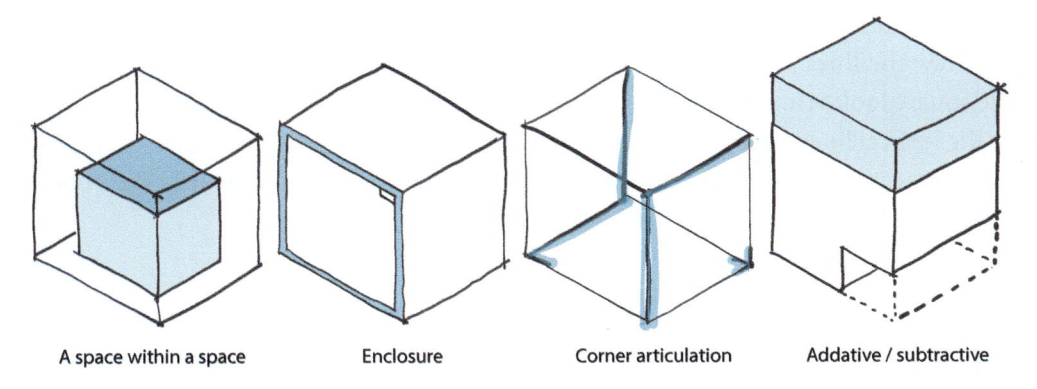

Figure 3.6 A diagram of the different spatial concepts that can be applied to a simple cube

3D Primary Forms – Drawing an Analytical Cube Freehand: Orthographic

When representing a 3D form the cube should be the starting point in the design process; it can define a spatial envelope; the floor, walls and ceiling – or the mass of a building form. At the initial stages, a simple cube can be used to define more complex forms such as a curved, faceted, detailed or organic forms.

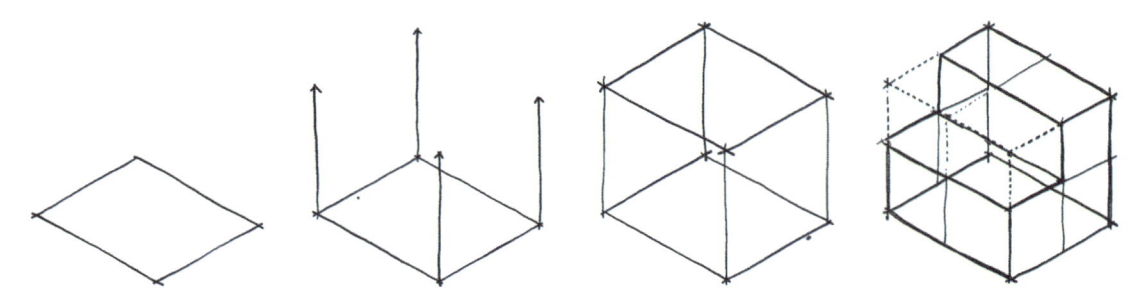

Figure 3.7 Analytical construction; a 3D cube – technique

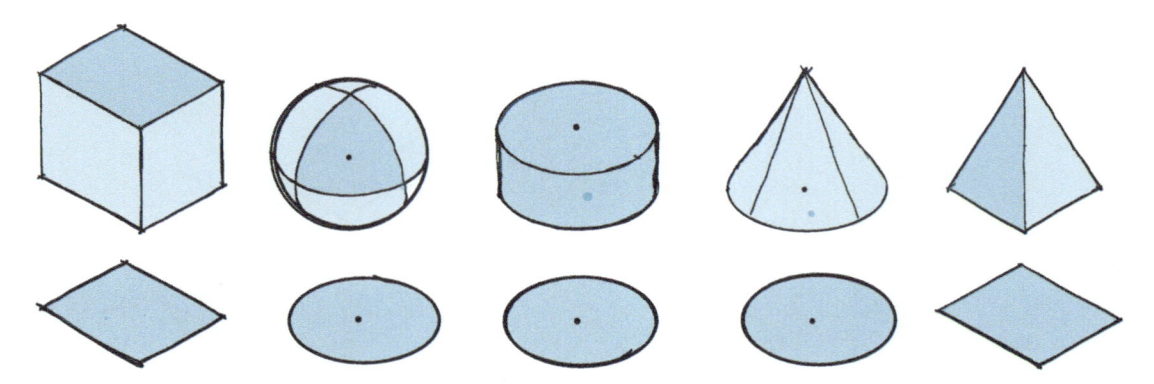

Figure 3.8 Basic 3D forms and 2D shapes. Cube, extruded square rectangle; sphere, a centralised form, from any view it remains circular; cylinder, extruded circle; cone, a circle extruded to a single-point pyramid – a rectangle extruded to a single point of a 3D form from a 2D shape

Start by drawing a square at a 30/60 angle known as an isometric. Graph paper can help keep lines straight [avoid a ruler if you can].

Try to draw the lines a little longer than you need; crossing corners are a good thing as they make the square look visually squarer.

Draw the vertical lines, keep them parallel, try and draw them a little longer than they need to be.

Finally connect the upper lines 30/60 angle to form a square; crossing lines the cube can be further broken down by adding facets/subdivision.

Shape

Following the same trajectory as the 2D definition of shape a volumetric object can take on different primary forms. They are complete objects, platonic solids derived initially from a 2D shape.

Design Principles: Primary Shapes

Primary 3D forms are often used as an initial interior and exterior architectural expression. At an architectural scale the basic forms represent the mass of a building within the landscape or the city. Within the interior environment a simple volume can represent a space within a space, an enclosed space or furniture elements furniture elements – it's all dependent on the scale of design you are working on. In all cases it's a way to test out a conceptual composition 'before' developing detail.

In the initial 'conceptual' design stage do not worry about creating complex forms – use a simple form to represent the volume, develop more complex volumes and shapes when you have a better understanding of how it all works together. It will save you having to resolve difficult junctions or dead space.

The Delft University of Technology Library by Mecanoo Architects, 1998, uses a cone form to create an intimate reading space where you are visually in contact with the other readers. It utilises and expresses the convex nature of the cone architecturally.

Design Principles: Complex Forms

In this interior intervention by Office dA a series of wooden slats set up a series of complex 3D organic forms using a sectional/contour approach to gain a sophisticated spatial intervention. The sectional approach can be a clever way of developing complex forms; it can be left open as a structural expression or covered to create a smooth form. The form is either sliced up into sections similar to an MIR scan or made up of a series different sectional profiles – conceptually and spatially the 2D sections form a 3D form.

The reading room – visual contact is always maintained in the space through the spatial characteristics of the cone form.

  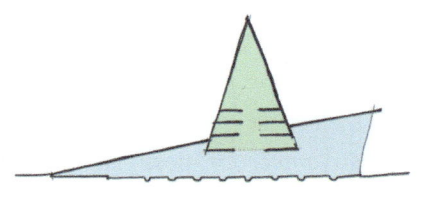

Figure 3.9 Exterior and interior of the Delft Library by Mecanoo Architects. Photo Credit: Mecanoo

 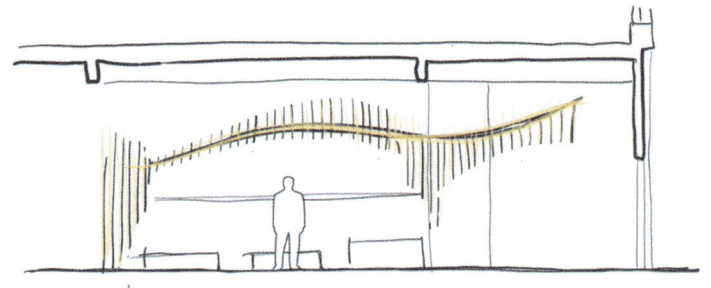

Figure 3.10 Multiple slatted wooden profiles – Restaurant NADAAA, Boston, 2008. Photo Credit: John Horner courtesy of NADAAA 2008/section diagram showing how the 2D planes form the complex canopy

It is easier to draw complex forms as a 2D drawing first rather than as a 3D drawing – a badly constructed drawing is unhelpful to sell a design so use 2D plan and section techniques if you're not sure.

3D Properties

Shape, size, colour and texture are the key properties of both 2D and 3D objects.

Shape – relates back to the origin of the 2D form.
Size – defined by the width, depth and height.
Colour – the surface colour, tonal value.
Texture – the bump, surface texture, light reflective qualities.

Design Principles: Properties

Colour – There are many references [too many to cover here] to the importance of the use of colour within interior design. Your personal interaction with colour depends on many factors.

Hue and nuance
Amount and location of the colour in space
Paint colour and spatial function
The effect of colour over time in the space

The Danish architect and designer Verner Panton (1926–1998) ranks among the most prominent and innovative designers active during the second half of the 20th century. In the course of his long career, he created an extensive and multifaceted oeuvre in which his preference for mostly bold colours and his skilful play with basic geometric forms and figures manifested itself.

(Verner-Panton.com)

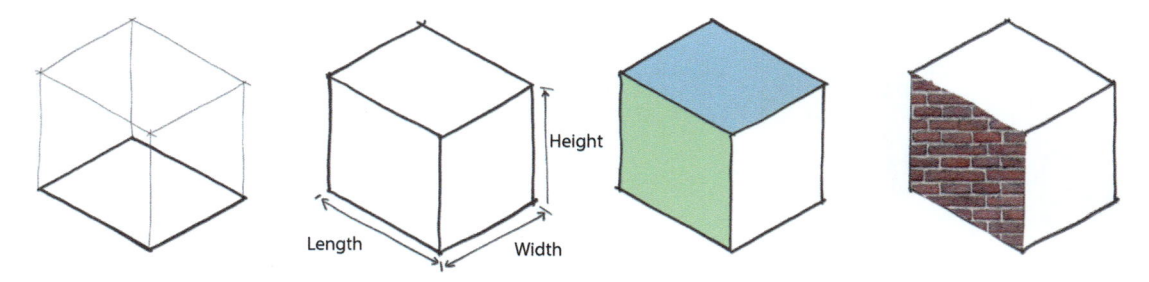

Figure 3.11 The properties of a 3D cube

Figure 3.12 Intense colour and pattern – Spiegel Publishing house in Hamburg, Hamburg Verner Panton, 1969/The Light and Colour, an exhibition by Verner Panton at the Trapholt Museum, Kolding, Denmark, 1998

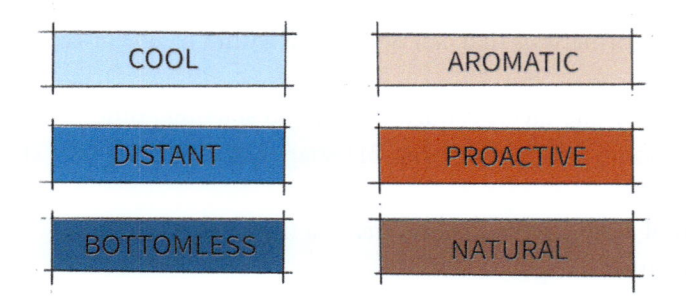

Figure 3.13 Colour chart example of the 'possible' effects/mood of colour. Reference: colour – Communication in Architectural Space. Gerhard Meerwein

Texture – colour, texture, material, surface and light all play a part in the development of a holistic interior design proposal. Those considerations can be brought in too early in the design process or be given priority at the incorrect design stage. It may be appropriate to focus on texture and colour if they are part of a bigger material approach [structure] or a project that is at a smaller scale, a singular space/plane or object.

Central Beheer, Herman Herzberger, is an early example of the use of 'honest materials,' where the interior construction is exposed rather than clad in additional material surfaces or paint finishes. With the premise of a sustainable future this way of working with construction materials is becoming more acceptable [and should be encouraged] within contemporary interiors.

Mac house by La Errería Architecture Office is a good example of honest material being used to clad interior space. OSB [Oriented Strand Board] is a wooden-based sheet building material with structural properties. Whilst used in construction it is increasingly being accepted as the interior finish [not painted and not clad with additional materials such as plasterboard].

Figure 3.14 Central Beheer, Herman Herzberger, 1970 – Kantoorgebouw Centraal Beheer, Apeldoorn, the Netherlands (1968–1972), architect: Herman Hertzberger. © Willem Diepraam./Mac House Alicante – La Errería Architecture Office, 2018.

TRANSFORMATIONS

There are various transformations that can be develop within a cube or rectilinear prism to create complex solids.

Breaking down a cube into facets is normally a good starting point.

The plotting of a point will help develop 3D shapes that extrude to a single point such as a pyramid.

The introduction of a 3D grid can help develop a framework.

Corners can be rounded by geometric divisions.

3D Formal Transformations

Formal transformations follow a set trajectory such as moving from one location to another or rotating by a specific angle. Move, rotate and scale are common transformations that you will use in CAD to develop a drawing or 3D model.

> *3D formal transformations are related directly to the transformations listed in Chapter 2 with the addition of the Z axis for vertical movement.*

Design Principles: Transformations

Transformations in design are normally related to the movement, kinetics or the transformation of an element into another [see Chapter 4 for more details]. In this precedent by Peter Ebner and friends a built-in bed is tucked away inside a central furniture element – allowing it to transform into a bench in the daytime. It's one of many transformations incorporated into a central furniture element inserted into this apartment design.

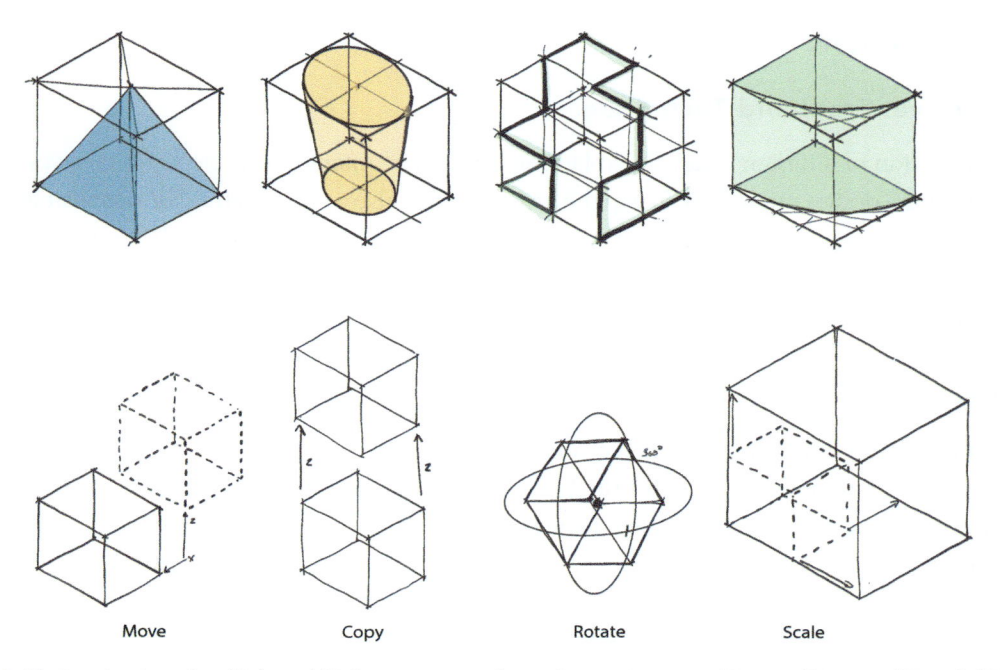

Move   Copy   Rotate   Scale

Figure 3.15 Creating formal and informal 3D forms using a cube as the starting point; 3D move/3D rotate/3D scale/3D array

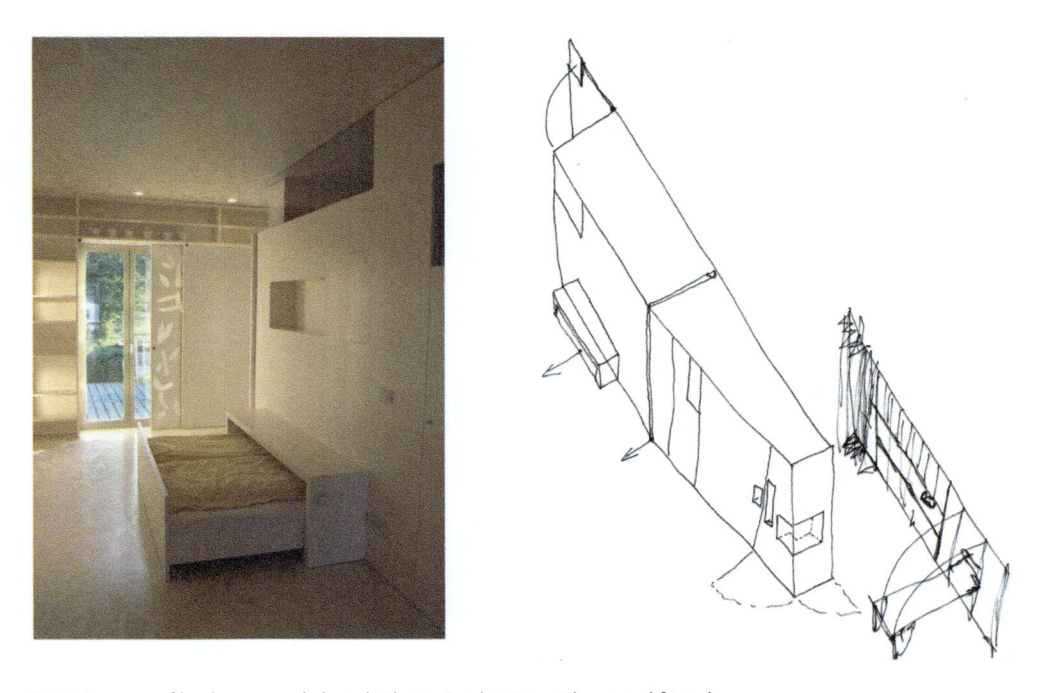

Figure 3.16 Storage of bed open and closed. Photo Credit: Peter Ebner and friends

VISUALISATION

Perspective: Freehand Technique

Communication of a design is key to explaining the project intentions. A perspective gives a good idea of what the design might look like in the given space; it also a good method of visualising the design intention. A perspective is a 3D view that has distortion to give a visual depth. They can be especially useful when trying to communicate the composition of an interior space or elements in space.

This is a quick method you can use to sketch a perspective:

Perspective: Freehand Method

Draw in a horizon line @ about eye level and a back wall.

Add viewport perspective lines for the four corners.

Draw in the enclosure and then use the viewpoint to help you draw in elements.

Drawing in a person will help 'scale' the space.

Perspective: Drawing Board Method

Drawing a perspective on a drawing board is similar in process to the sketch version:

Draw a horizon line.

Set a viewpoint and draw in the enclosure.

You can use a 'draft' sectional drawing to help plot out the elements in the scheme; if it is 'to scale' it will help you understand the proportions.

> *Follow the basics of hand drawing a perspective – use a long ruler to set up the grid. Use the subdivide rule to create a graduated grid. You can push the grid back from the section if you want to create more depth.*

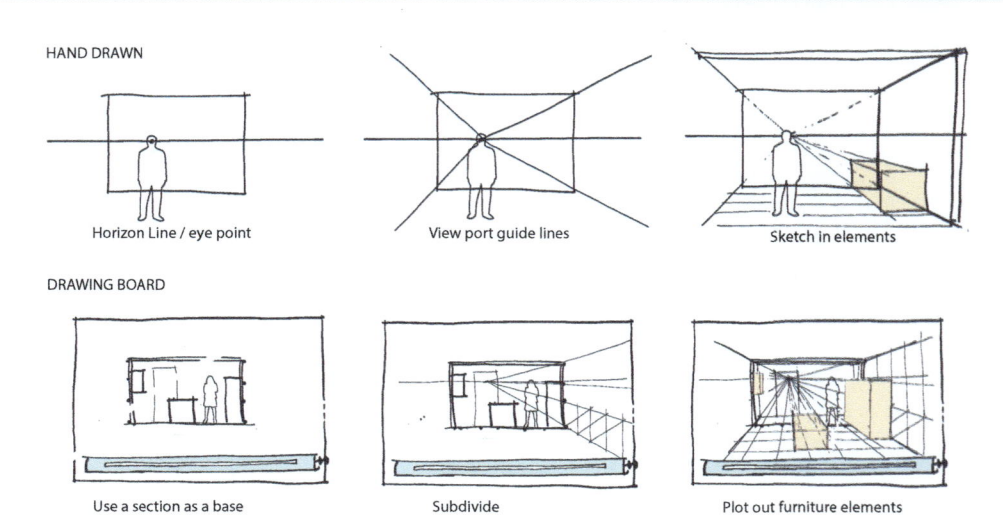

HAND DRAWN

Horizon Line / eye point   View port guide lines   Sketch in elements

DRAWING BOARD

Use a section as a base   Subdivide   Plot out furniture elements

Figure 3.17 Hand-drawn perspective principles/drawing board method

CONCEPTUAL DEVELOPMENT

Model Development

Model making is by far the most productive 3D conceptual design process in interior design practice. In the preliminary stages of a design a series of quick sketch models will go a long way to exploring and communicating spatial concepts.

A common mistake is to think that concept model making needs to be created using card or mount board. One of the problems with using mount board is it is hard stuff to work with, requiring heavy-handed cutting or multiple cuts just to get through the substrate.

> *Using stiff, hard-to-cut card inhibits the conceptual design process as the time [and struggle] involved forces the user to finalise a model. Hard modelling hinders an iterative design process, which is important to explore at the conceptual design stage.*
>
> *In the initial stages stiff paper, 300mg or more, will provide ample volumetric sturdiness. It can be easily cut with a pair of scissors, folded to create volumes, glued and taped very quickly – so leaving you much more time to explore your design options rather than struggling with the material.*

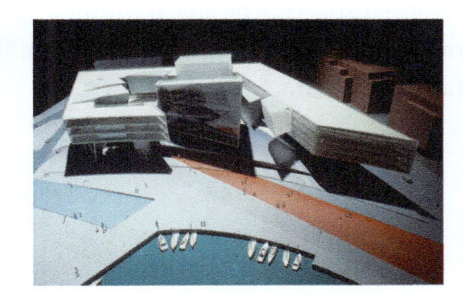

Figure 3.18 Paper model at the Venice biennale 2012/student paper model, Abigail Newton/crystal necklace, Zaha Hadid. Image Credit: Cardiff Opera House by Zaha Hadid Architects, © Zaha Hadid Foundation

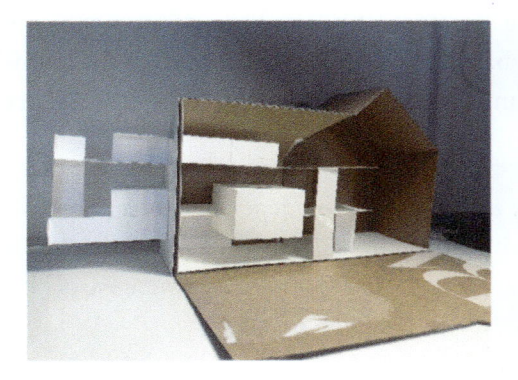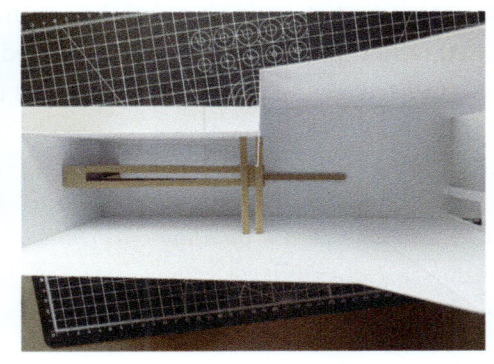

Figure 3.19 A model in varied materials pulls apart so you can read the elements in and out of context. Photo Credit: Abigail Newton. The change in modelling card is used to signify a different material [wood]. Photo Credit: Eve Sturmey

Sketch Model Making – Mass Models

In the first instance try not get involved in too much detail such as furniture or material surfaces as your model can become 'doll's housey', which will detract from the higher-level conceptual design moves.

A detailed 3D model effectively communicates all levels of design in a singular object; it is the plan and section in one object. When introducing design concepts to a lay person the model can be useful in communicating key design moves. You can further enhance any main design moves by modelling them in varied materials and pulling them apart so you can read the different elements individually.

Design Spatial Concepts

3D spatial concepts follow those described in Chapter 2 – one of the clearest 2D relationships is that of the section which deals with vertical spatial relationships such as floor levels and height ratios. Many spatial concepts come alive when implemented in 3D space.

A Space within a Space

Mac House in Alicante by La Errería Architecture Office; here three spaces have been inserted into the existing building. The private functions of the bedrooms and bathroom are housed in the enclosed spaces. The space within a space approach allows you to experience the whole volume rather than separate it with traditional floors. It is a key concept in interior architectural practice [a space within a space].

> *An insertion in space is a key principle of interior architecture and interior design, creating a space in a space.*

In the mezzanine office insertion by AMAA Studio a freestanding structure is inserted into the space, 'a space within the existing space' that celebrates the existing fabric of the industrial building. The unfinished 'stripping back' of the original structure [the demolition of interior elements] is exposed rather than covered up. The stripped back interior is complemented with unfinished materials utilised for the new elements, such as unpainted steel work and raw concrete stairs.

> *A clear space left between the old and new; it's important to adopt this type of approach when dealing with a building of architectural significance. Often interiors are short-lived, but the architectural structure will live on. It is also an opportunity to juxtapose the old and new eloquently.*

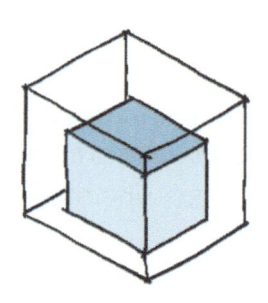

Mac House in Alicante by LA ERRERÍA architecture office 2018

A space within a space

AMAA Collaborative Architecture Office for Research and Development 2019

Figure 3.20 Mac House in Alicante by La Errería architecture office. Image Credit: La Errería architecture office, 2018/ AMAA Collaborative Architecture Office for Research and Development, 2019. Photo Credits: Simone Bossi. Model Credits: Francesca Vinci

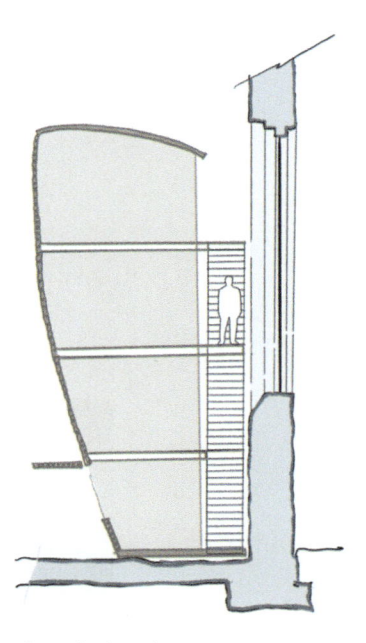

Figure 3.21 Library and community centre in the parish church of Müncheberg, Klaus Block Architects, 1998

The church was founded by the Cistercians in the 13th century. It was rebuilt in 1817 according to plans by KF Schinkel, destroyed down to the foundations in 1945, rebuilt in 1992 and in 1997/98 was given the working title 'Ruins under the roof' for use as a pure worship space also to be used as a city library, community, and cultural centre. Klaublock Architects the diagrammatic section expresses how the stair element separates the old and new structures, leaving a clear readable gap for the user to experience as they move through the floors.

Subtractive

Subtractions – Subtractions from solid volumes offer the designer many development opportunities in terms of functionality and spatial compositions. Utilising both horizontal and vertical subtractions can provide complex spatial relationships – when introduced horizontally equal access can be an issue due to the change of level [disabled access].

Wall Volumes – Thick wall elements can be subtracted to provide many functional properties such as seating, tables, steps and hidden storage.

Depressed Floor Plane – A depressed floor plane within an open plan environment [or single enclosure] creates an intimate space without the need for walls. It can also help define different areas in the same way a rise in floor level can.

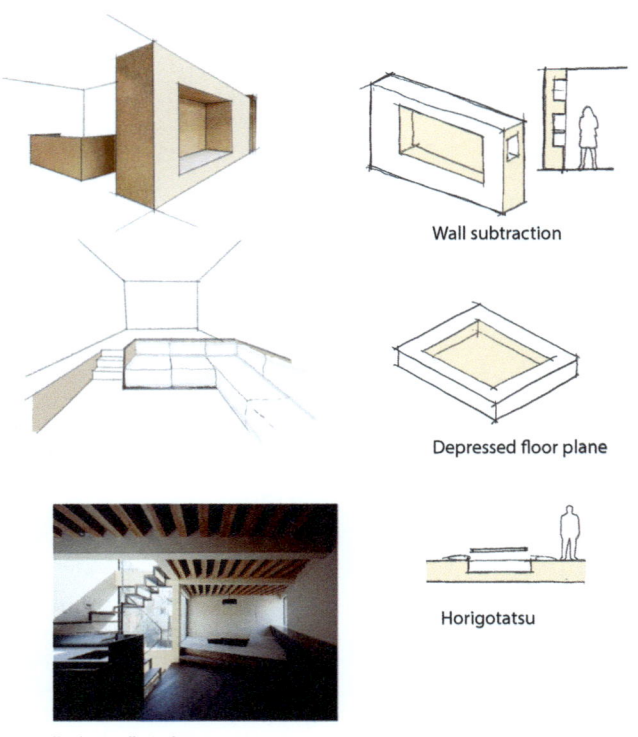

Wall subtraction

Depressed floor plane

Horigotatsu

Alley by Apollo Architects & Associates, 2013.

Figure 3.22 Subtractive wall element depressed floor plane; horigotatsu table – Alley by Apollo Architects & Associates, 2013. Architecture: Satoshi Kurosaki/Apollo Architects & Associates. Photo Credit: Masao Nishikawa

A wall setting up a reception whilst providing an intimate sitting space on the reverse. It retains its volumetric mass whilst still being functional.

A depressed floor plane sets up the living room area and seating of an open plan space, utilising the difference in levels to provide an integrated seating element.

Horigotatsu – A Japanese table that is low to the ground and recessed.

Horigotatsu is a traditional style of Japanese seating that is integrated within the floor plane [through a subtraction] to provide a seating area. In this project by Apollo Architects the horigotatsu table is integrated into the interior architecture and finished in the same material as the floor.

Additive

New Additions – New additions are 'typically' architectural additions to an existing building. They can be an extension, a new building or a significant design element that is new to an existing building. In successful interior design and interior architecture schemes there is a clear definition between the old and new whilst retaining a symbiotic relationship.

> *Two penthouses were converted out of tank rooms on the roof of a former multi-storey research building which had been altered in the mid-1990s into luxury flats. A modular steel-framed system was used, allowing the units to be assembled and fully fitted out in the factory, transported by truck to London and installed by crane in a few days. The two ends of each unit are fully glazed, framing panoramic views over the Thames River, while the remaining facades are solid with smaller windows and clad in stainless steel mesh, which catches and shimmers in the light.*
>
> (Pierre d'Avoine Architects)

Interlocking Volumes

Interlocking Volumes – They help to set up different spaces within different areas in an open plan environment. The overlap can provide the spatial opportunity to assign specific functions, such as a dining area or study; it also maximises the floor space within a constrained site. The introduction of floor planes helps to develop the detail of the volumetric concept.

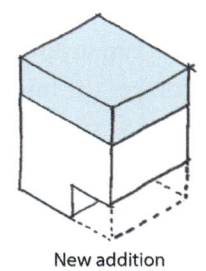

New addition

Figure 3.23 Piper penthouse, Pierre d'Avoine Architects. Photo Credit: David Grandorge

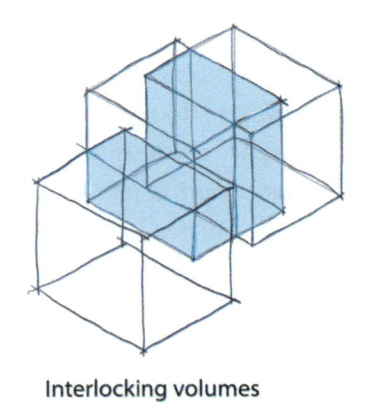

Interlocking volumes

Figure 3.24 Takatsuki house, Tato Architects, 2017. Yo Shimada, Team/Yo Shimada, Akira Yasuda. Photo Credit: Shinkenchiku_Sha

> *The spaces between different floor levels were left open to create a floating effect, allowing the floors to be used as desks and shelves where objects could be stored. At the same time, this design allowed us to visually emphasize the relationships between various rooms.*
>
> (Tato Architects)

3D Organisation

The introduction of a simple 'thick' wall element can help set up a scheme spatially and functionally. By raising the front profile up off the floor and away from the ceiling a spatial impression of a floating element can be achieved, which helps to reduce the impact of a mass object.

In plan you can see how this simple 'thick' wall element sets up the galley kitchen, bathroom, bedroom and living space. The wide doors in the bathroom area act as walls to give some privacy. The shelving unit in the main space is on wheels and can be moved; it sets up the bedroom space and provides storage for clothes (Scheme Reference: Barbieri Apartment, Simon Conder Architects).

Mezzanine Space

Mezzanine – The introduction of a mezzanine into a single space provides an efficient use of space where you can utilise the under or over space for multiple uses. Depending on the activity, sleeping or storage – it might even help work with restrictive heights – do you need full head height to sleep or to store equipment?

In this small scheme from EBBA Architects a mezzanine insertion sets up a series of functional spatial responses. The mezzanine sets up the kitchen space below, while allowing the living area to bathe in light in the double height space.

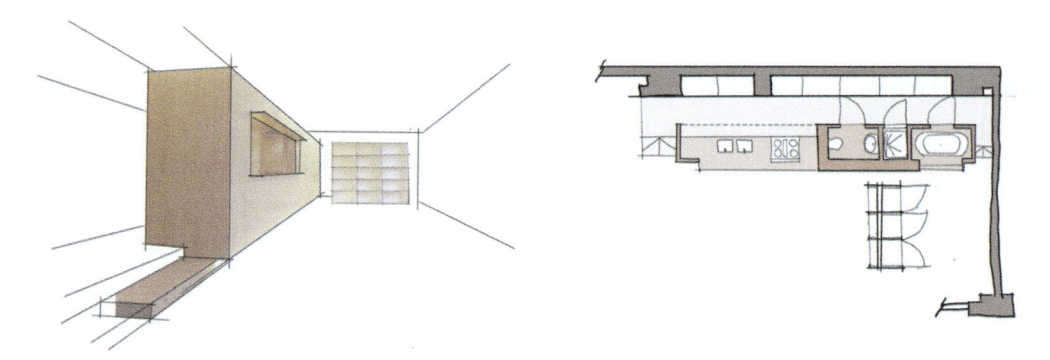

Figure 3.25 A single 'floating' wall element sets up the kitchen, bathroom and storage space/the thick wall plan

Figure 3.26 A mezzanine insertion sets up the program elements of the flat over two floors. Warehouse conversion, EBBA Architects, 2020. Photo Credit: Benni Allan

Upstairs there is a single bedroom and an en-suite bathroom; in the darker space towards the back of the mezzanine there is a dressing room and snug that also acts as an additional bedroom, separated with a curtain.

The introduction of a mezzanine can help to spatially organise a scheme as well as maximise floor space – where you have double height space, they can be pulled back to celebrate the drama of the volume.

DESIGN DEVELOPMENT

Recognising the next stage of detail is an especially important attribute to a designer, taking a project from a basic to a more developed stage. Through this process the design concept is tested to see how it works. Scale plays an important part in design development. The sequential movement up in scale means the designer can add more detailed information in sequence. In the initial stages this should be a holistic process rather than just a section of a drawing. Later in 'detail' development an area can be developed to give a better idea of the construction and materiality.

Developmental Tasks/Checklist

Thickness – Defining thickness to ceiling, roof floor and wall substrates.

Initially when developing a design in concept, a simple form is used to represent the spatial relationship. Depending on the scale sometimes it is layered with circulation and structural information.

When starting to develop a design past the conceptual stage one of the best places to start is to add thickness to the plan section and/or 3D model. Every wall, floor, roof carries a thickness, so it is a good place to start adding detailed decisions. The type of structure construction will often dictate the thickness – in the initial stages you can use rule of thumb calculations.

Passageways – Ensuring that the flow and circulation work with appropriate passing spaces; 900 mm minimum and 1100 mm to pass comfortably.

Stairs – Checking that the correct number of steps are drawn in to get from A to B and the opening between floors is enough to allow a person adequate headroom. The average commercial step size is a 170 mm riser × 270 mm tread. The head room when in a space should be no less than 2100 mm.

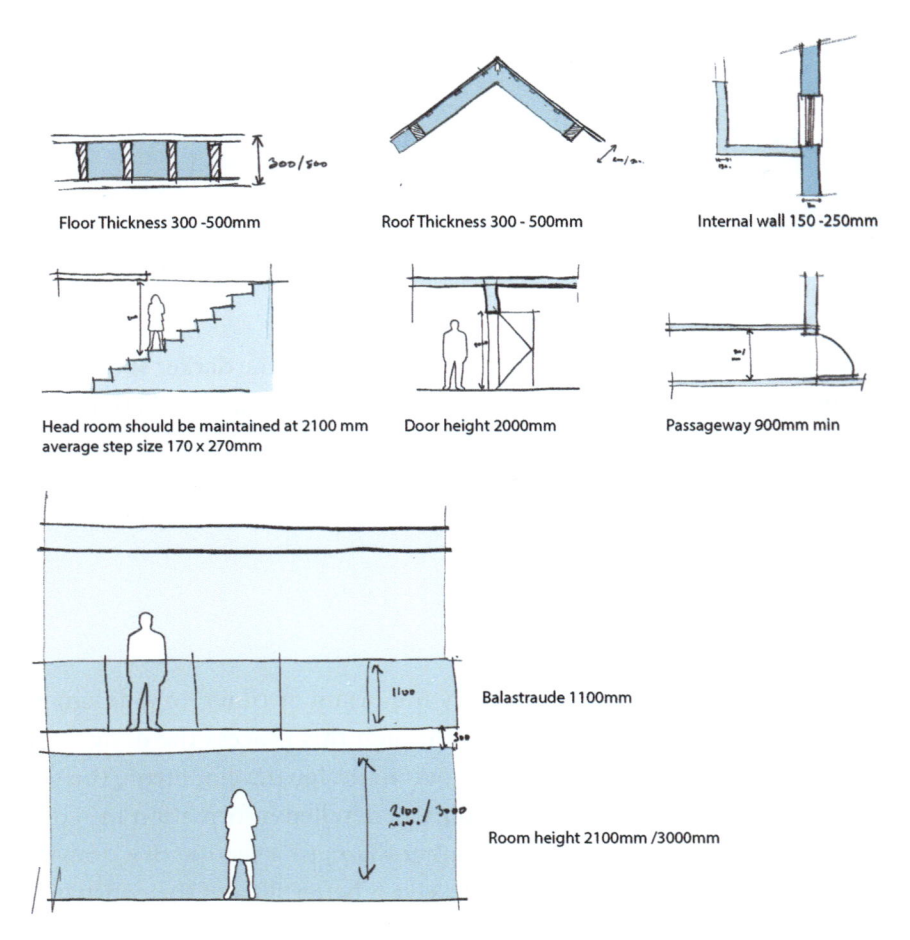

Floor Thickness 300 -500mm   Roof Thickness 300 - 500mm   Internal wall 150 -250mm

Head room should be maintained at 2100 mm average step size 170 x 270mm   Door height 2000mm   Passageway 900mm min

Balastraude 1100mm

Room height 2100mm /3000mm

Figure 3.27 Route, circulation and head height – Looking at route and circulation is an area that is good to work up. Ensuring you have enough headroom or passing spaces in corridors

Doors – The average door height is 2000 mm and the width at least 700 mm [900 mm for good disability access].

Enclosures – Develop openings that demonstrate a proficient level of spatial proportion – head height between floors is a good place to start along with the introduction of balustrades in stairs and mezzanines. You should ensure that a minimum head height of 2100 mm is maintained throughout the scheme.

Lighting

Lighting – Consider artificial and natural lighting. While a lighting plan will give specifics you might want to design integrated lighting [similar to Chapter 2 case study] or incorporate natural light into a scheme by making additional openings. A lighting feature can be a good statement of design intent when selling a scheme proposal.

Recessed Fixtures – Recessed fixtures are any indoor lights fully contained inside your walls, ceiling or floors.

Types of Artificial Lighting – Track lighting, pendants, wall sconces, ceiling lighting, ambient lighting, task lighting, accent lighting.

The beneficial properties of natural light are well documented – hospital buildings from as early as the 19th century were constructed with a narrow plan and tall windows to maximise the amount of light that could enter the building, thus aiding patient recovery. In the recent years building technology has focused deep plans to maximise floor space combined with a reliance on building services such as artificial lighting and mechanical ventilation, the type of spaces many interior designers will encounter even today despite the drive towards more sustainable buildings, of which naturally it environments would surely be one of the main priorities.

Natural Light Sources – Windows, skylights, clerestories, light shelves, solar tubes.

Figure 3.28 Different types of lighting in symbol form

Figure 3.29 Banquet seating built as a 'fixed furniture element' with a Tip Ton chair and table [loose furniture]/William Morris wallpaper Design 214716 Morris Seaweed Ebony poppy

Fixed Furniture

Fixed Furniture – At the development stage it's good to consider fixed furniture [built-in]. Many of the spatial design principles in the previous section employ the principles of fixed or transformative furniture as a key architectural move to set up the functionality of the space.

The Final Finishes – Material finishes might relate to an earlier stage of concept development such as structural choice – in most cases they refer to the final finish = decoration.

Further Surface Finishes – Wallpaper/paint/varnish [covered in Chapter 5].

> *Specification of loose furniture, fittings and surface treatments should be the finishing touches and not a consideration at the conceptual stage of a project.*

CASE STUDY – INSERTION

Pinterest HQ – San Francisco, IwamotoScott Architecture, 2017

> *'Pinterest is about a grid that structures all the ideas and images, and architecture provides the grid in building,' says co-founder and chief creative officer Evan Sharp, who studied architecture at Columbia. 'We wanted to set up the right architecture to shape circulation and the qualities of the working environment to reinforce collaborative behaviour.'*
>
> (IwamotoScott Architecture)

Reading of the Space

Remodelling of a Building

The site is an existing building in San Francisco's south of market neighbourhood, a tractor factory built in 1911. It comprises a grid framework of concrete columns and floorplates.

The ground floor is a double height space followed by three additional levels. Original design features of the building are a central atrium and mushroom column details.

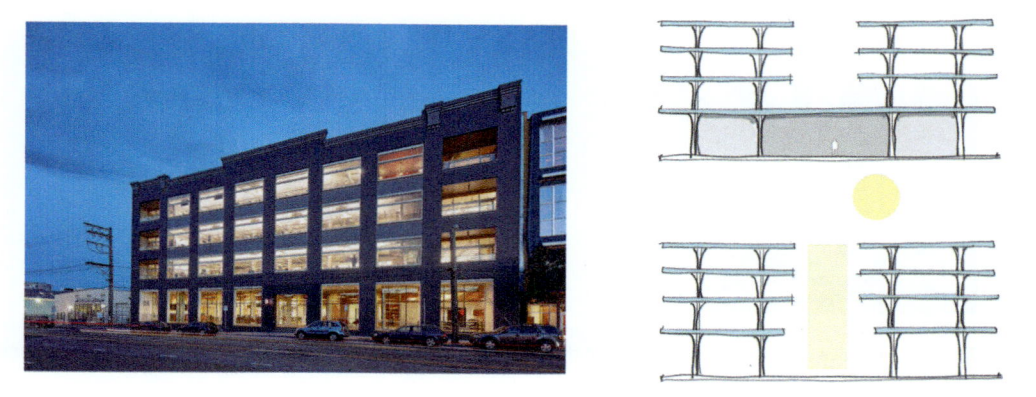

Figure 3.30 Exterior view of tractor factory. Photo Credit: Bruce Damonte. A diagram of the opening up of the atrium space to bring light into the ground floor of the building

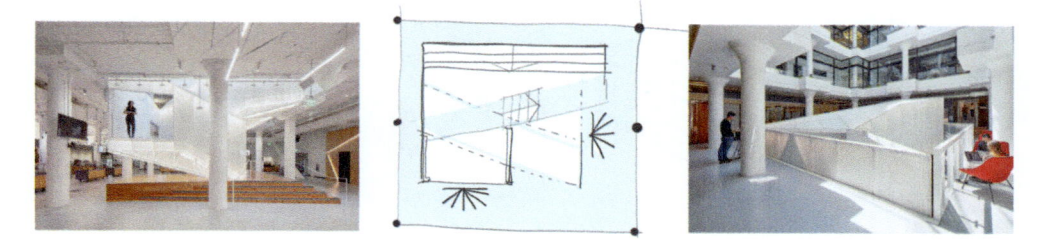

Figure 3.31 The sculptural staircase on ground floor level leads to a light-filled atrium. Photo Credits: Bruce Damonte

Initially the atrium only came down to the first floor. As a main remodelling strategy, the designers opened the atrium up into the ground floor so light could penetrate through the building.

Insertion [Major Element]

Inserted into the central atrium is a twisting transparent staircase that sits away from void space, setting up views at various levels into different spaces. The stair elements knit through the void space linking the ground floor to level 2.

Simple Materials

Colour, Material and Texture

The reception area is set up by a contemporary coffered ceiling made of plywood slats.

Throughout the design there is a use of 'honest materials' that are recyclable – to create a rich interior through the creative use of materials [see Chapter 5, Materials, for further information].

 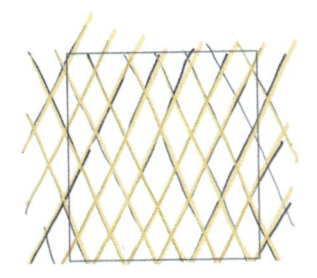 

Figure 3.32 A new lattice ceiling structure helps with the acoustics of the large open space. Photo Credit: Bruce Damonte

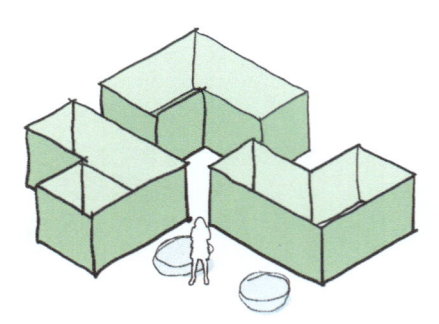 

Figure 3.33 Meeting rooms are sited centrally in the plan to maximise the daylight for working spaces. Photo Credit: Bruce Damonte

Adaptable Workspaces

The general workspaces are set to the perimeter to take advantage of natural daylight.

The meeting rooms are arranged as a patchwork quilt of enclosed and open spaces, which reinforces Pinterest's building's grid structure and informal meeting spaces.

Pinterest HQ, San Francisco, CA

IwamotoScott Architecture, Design Architect

Brereton Architects, Executive Architect

Bruce Damonte, Photographer

CHAPTER 4

MODIFICATION AND MOVEMENT

INTRODUCTION

In Chapter 4 flexible and inventive design concepts are at the centre of the chapter, the transformation of space is introduced as the thoughtful adaptation of existing space [Schröder house principles], with further emphasis being given to 'multifunctional' design and storage elements. Also covered are kinetics [moving parts], a recent 'digital' consideration to interior design practice; within this practice, there is a movement to relate digital environments back to natural environments as experienced in nature and vice versa.

Overview

Through this chapter a series of possibilities are introduced that may be layered into an interior design project strategy. Often the approach is a problem-solving one such as the lack of space, a response to a particular contextual issue or technologically driven.

When developing the functionality of space, pragmatics can often take over such as a table being a table or a wall being a wall [static objects in space]. It is through this chapter that the discussion is about the possibilities of using flexible design strategies to enhance our perceptions of space, such as a wall that can move and transform a space from open to enclosed, or 'thickened up' to provide extra layers of functionality. These are often simple elements that if approached differently in conceptualisation can add extra layers of design inventiveness.

Kinetics is discussed as a wider primer to what part technology might play in the future of interiors and architecture. While it may seem complex, quite often microcomputing kinetics are built on a series of quite simple actions and principles.

About 90% of the time the process of design is pragmatic to maximise the output through a set of hierarchical steps, context, concept to design development. At each stage of the design process there is always the opportunity to embrace further spatial or programmatic concepts suggested in this chapter that have the potential to add an additional dynamic layer to a design project proposal.

> *How will we live together? Beasley and his collaborators offer a vision of a transformed world where future architecture seeks communion with plants, animals and inert matter.*
> (Philip Beesley Studio Inc.)

DOI: 10.4324/9781003120650-5

Figure 4.1 Grove, Venice Biennale, 2021. Photo Credit: Philip Beesley, Jordan Prosser and Mac van

TRANSFORMATION: WALLS

The following are a series of projects that exemplify the simple transformation of space through movement in walls or walls that move. They move in a lateral or horizontal direction or rotate and swivel, adding a duality functionality. All the precedents reconfigure space, modify it from one function to another or maximise the available floor space.

Walls

The Rietveld Schröder House is the archetypical example of a transformative interior. It is the most important precedent of the transformation of interior space from over 100 years past [along with it being an iconic De Stijl structure].

The house itself is a complex piece of furniture that goes well beyond the sliding partitions to provide a wonder of interior and architectural interventions, such as the transformation of the skylight, the floating corner window detail, bespoke fixed furniture, lighting and radiators.

For this section on transformation of space/walls it is the first floor that is of specific interest – a series of sliding walls reconfigure an open plan environment to a series of partitioned bedrooms.

The Diller, Scofidio and Renfro Brasserie is an iconic interior design refurbishment in the basement of the Philip Johnston Seagram building. The project has a series of inventive spatial and functional key moves and an attention to detail that is unsurpassed from the 2000 period of interior design.

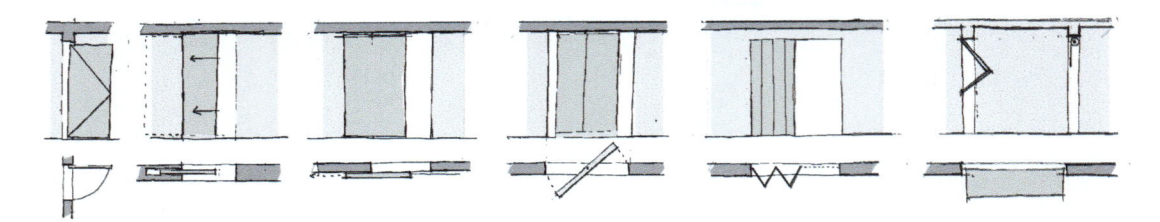

Figure 4.2 Diagram of sliding door types: swing/pocket/sliding/pivot/bifold/overhead fold/roller

> *This type of strategy has a level of duality of function which can maximise or resolve spatial/ circulation problems often encountered when planning out space to be functional.*

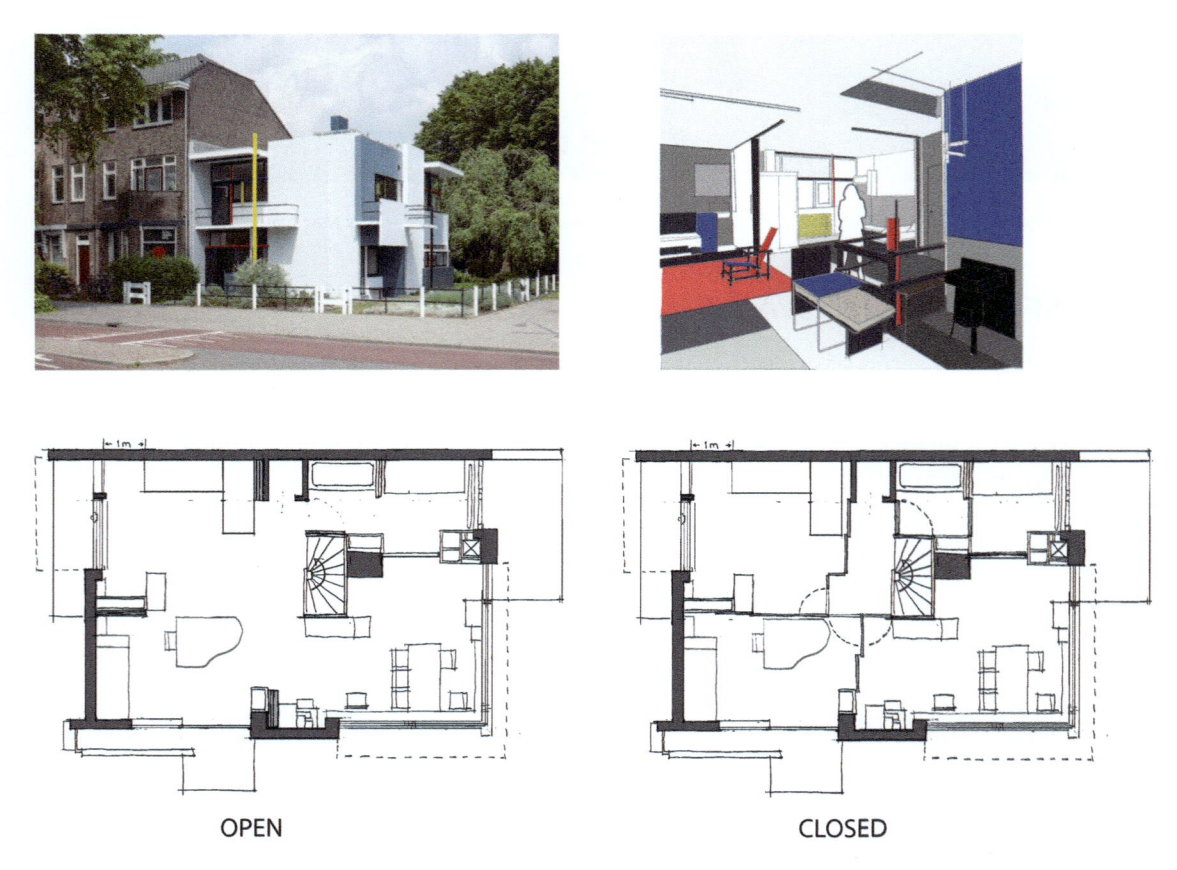

OPEN   CLOSED

Figure 4.3 The Rietveld Schröder House exterior in Utrecht, 1924 – an unusual addition to an end terrace in Utrecht. Photo Credit: Stijn Poelstra. The Rietveld Schröder House Interior visual, furniture and architecture integrated into a transformable space. Plan drawings of the first-floor space open and closed to create bedroom spaces and a hallway

While static as a plan it has had an element of transformation within the design proposal in the second dining room that flanks the main space. A wall equal to the width of the space swings across on a pivot and stainless-steel track to create a large 'private' banqueting space.

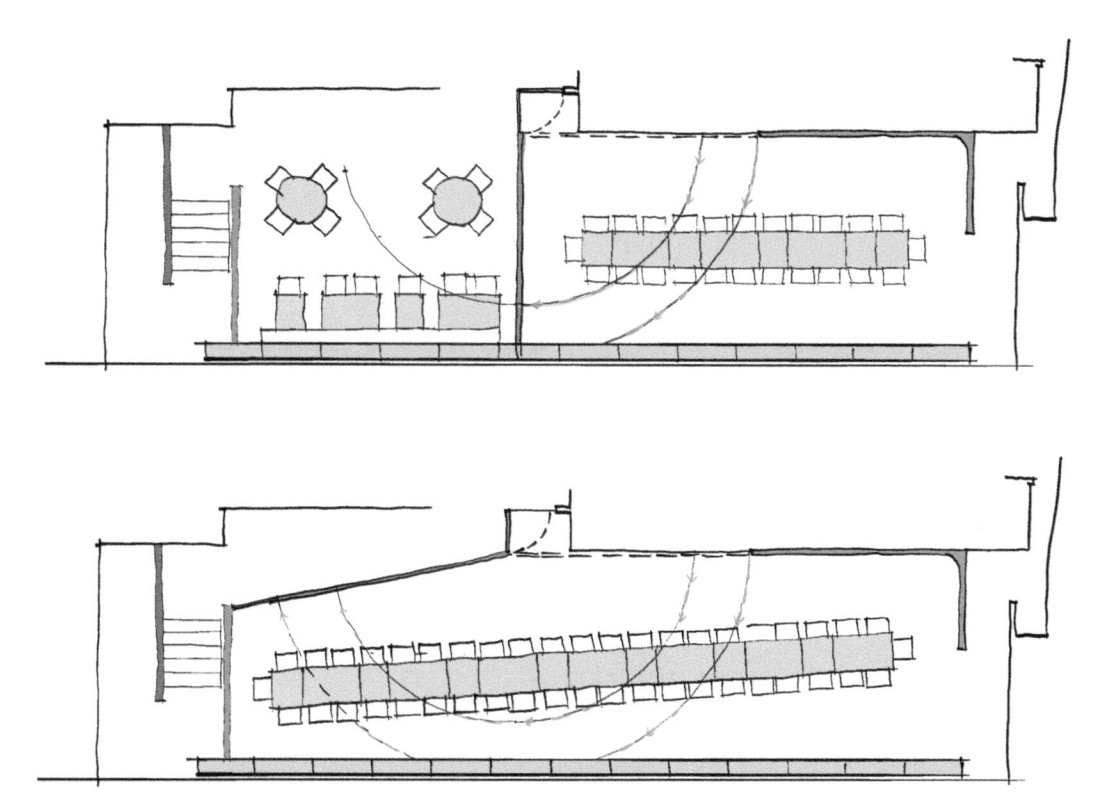

Figure 4.4 A plan showing the transformation of the private dining room to a private banquet space – pivoting door [which remains closed after the pandemic]. The Diller, Scofidio and Renfro Brasserie, NY, 2000

> *In restaurant design an adaptability of space for multiple configurations is an especially useful concept to embrace.*

Swivel/Moving Façades

On a difficult tight corner site in NY Holl and Acconci slotted in a new façade wall that stretches the full length of the triangular site. The hinged panels open horizontally and vertically providing exhibition panels for drawings and models. The façade breaks down abruptly the division between the inside and outside space using the planar panels. The seemingly random openings add a dynamic breakdown of the formal façade; when closed the concrete and recycled fibre construction forms an impenetrable, bunker-like façade. The store front for architecture is a well-documented interior architectural project; it exemplifies an abrupt sculptural juxtaposition between indoor and outdoor space/openings and closure.

> *In functional terms it is good to think about the transformation of planar surfaces in horizontal configurations as well as vertical.*

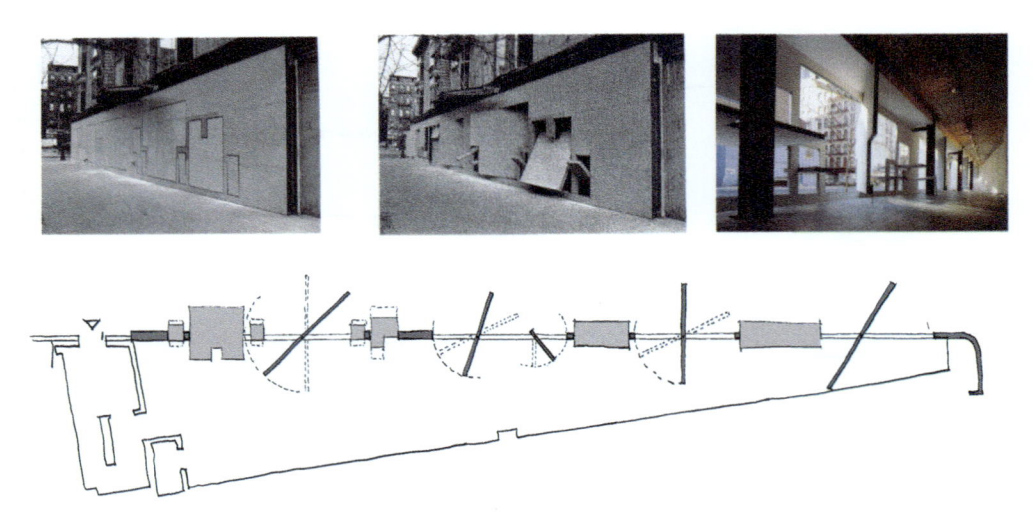

Figure 4.5 Storefront for architecture [open and closed], Steven Holl Architects, 1993: Photo Credit: Paul Warchol – interior space showing the façade element open, providing hanging space for exhibitions. Photo Credit: Paul Warchol – plan of the open pivot façade

SPACE – STORAGE AND LIVING

Space storage and living is a series of design interventions that maximise the functionality of constrictive spaces. From freeing up space with clever storage strategies to the maximising of small spaces to become habitable, efficient use of space is paramount to most, especially with the future needs of affordable housing. The third precedent focus is on moving 'robotic' furniture, which takes to a new conceptual level the transformation of the interior living space.

Interior Storage

This recent precedent from RUST Architects, a studio for an artist, 2014, demonstrates the thickening up of walls to facilitate maximum storage possibilities. The bed is tucked away for daytime storage to maximise space and there is plenty of utilisation of overhead space, which is a perfect strategy for longer-term storage.

> *The thickening up of walls is a key strategy to implement when you have limited space to work with – thickened walls can often accommodate multiple programmatic functions such as seating, kitchen, beds, etc. Using the 'higher' space within a single floor in tight spaces maximises storage potentials freeing up floor space.*

Underfloor Storage

Japanese design is no stranger to the efficient use of space and storage – the futon mattress being a prime example of efficient use of space, where it can be folded and stored in a cupboard to allow you to use the space during the day for relaxation, working and eating.

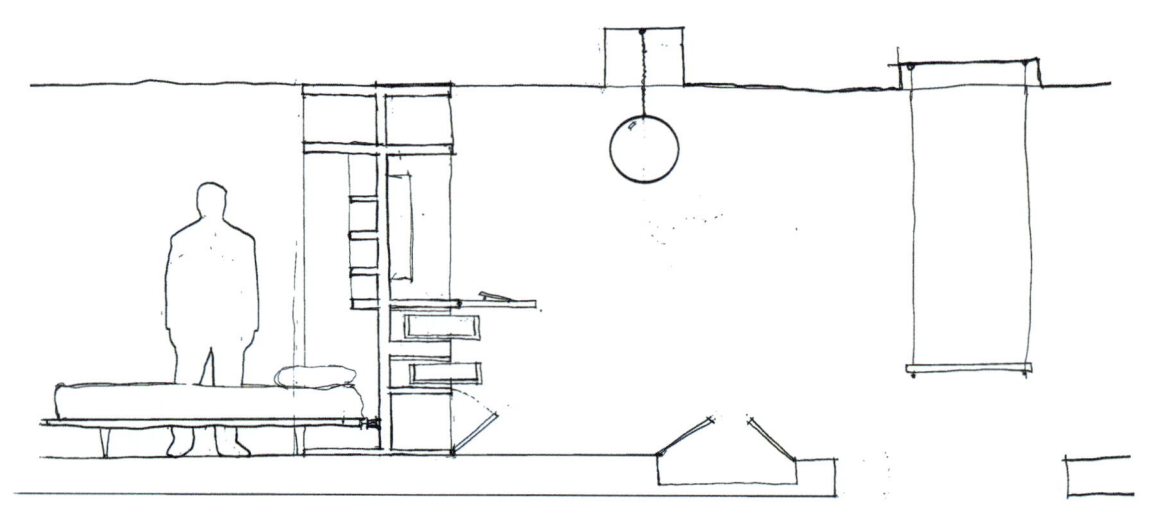

Figure 4.6 Walls as storage/walls as beds/using height/floors as storage

Figure 4.7 Studio for an artist, tucked-away bed storage for the daytime, multiple drawer storage for efficiency of space – RUST Architects, 2014, Family Apartment 4, effective overhead storage, RUST Architects, 2016. Photo Credit: Gidon Levin

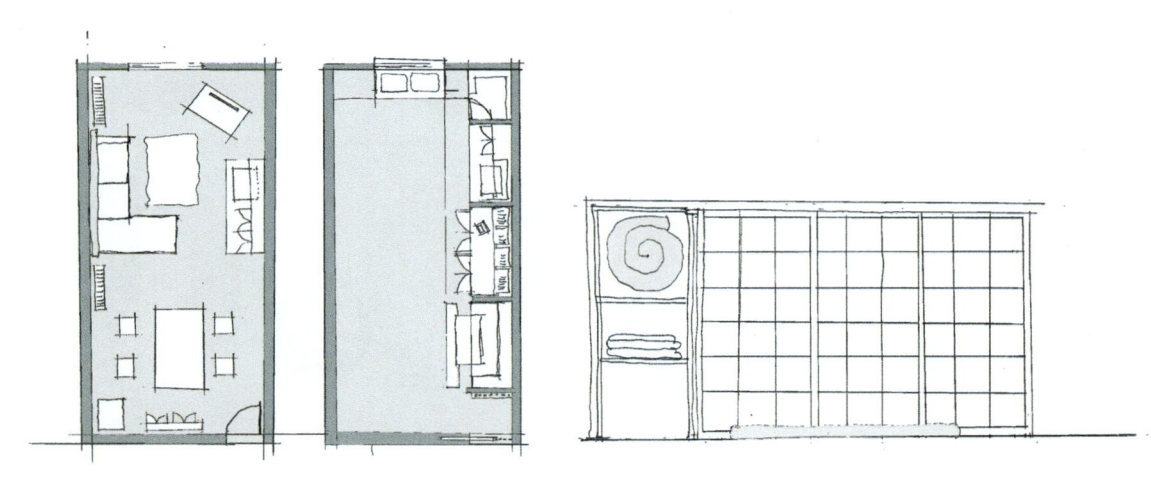

Figure 4.8 Two plan drawings of a living space demonstrating how space can be freed up by incorporating functional elements into a thickened wall element. Diagram of cupboard storage of the bed 'futon' in a traditional Japanese room. Allowing the space to be used as a living area in the day

Smart Zendo is an interior developed by simplex design for a 45 m^2 apartment in Hong Kong – the space is a typical limited space scenario in the city's high-density environment.

In this scheme you see an unusual underfloor system of storage and furniture elements [dining table] along with screen partitions and floor to ceiling storage. Underfloor storage and smart integration of technology allow the space to be open as possible to the mountain view.

> *The owner of the apartment is a busy young couple, Eric and Lory. Sim-Plex uses the concept of the Zendo to bring the view of the scenery outside the window into the house. The integrated TV cabinet wall and the wooden floor platform are plain and warm, but yet there were a large number of intelligent devices hidden by. The design is also integrated to the traditional Feng Shui doctrine, to create a spiritual space where tradition and technology, people and scenery are combined.*
>
> (Sim-Plex Design)

Moving Robotic Furniture

Ori Living started as a research project at the MIT Medi Lab, whose focus was on responding to the challenges of urban density – ORI has designed a series of 'robotic' furniture elements that are in production and have been implemented in high-rise urban environments in the US. The key

Figure 4.9 Living space open with a mountain view. Bedroom having raised bed with underfloor storage. Retractable screen – automated sunken horigotatsu table, Smart Zendo, Sim-Plex Design, 2019

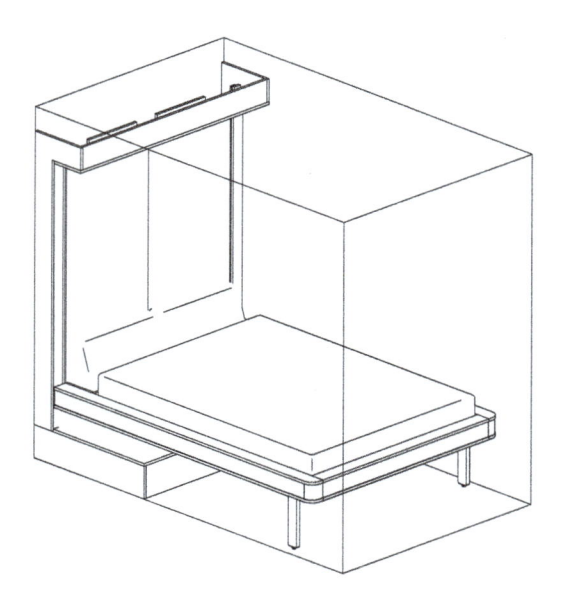

Figure 4.10 Cloud bed – axonometric drawing; the cloud bed stacked away into the ceiling element.
Credit: ORILiving.com

concepts are the transformation of space from sleeping, living to working. The furniture elements themselves are 'robotic'; they move and stack and are controlled by a smart phone, console or smart speaker.

TRANSFORMATION: BUILDINGS

These architectural precedents are unusual responses to indoor-outdoor relationships. One has a bedroom that can be extended outside and the second reveals a bathroom area that can be either inside or outside when the architectural structure is peeled back, heightening the indoor-outdoor relationship of interior and architectural spaces.

Moving Buildings – Interiorsa

The Living Room House by fomalhaut is a new construction in a limited medieval site in Germany. It has an amazing 52 windows checkered into 3 façades, with the conceptual premise that you can see into the building and out of it, reinforcing the indoor-outdoor relationship. A strategy of employing a thick wall containing programmatic elements is used to free up the three façades [as described in storage]. The interior is custom-made 'Washbasins come from the pottery, banisters from the smithy and a stone tub/boat from the sculptor.'

This clearly restrictive site is elevated to provide a drawer on the third floor to enjoy the 'outside space.' The concept allows the free flow of traffic and people through the dense medieval site.

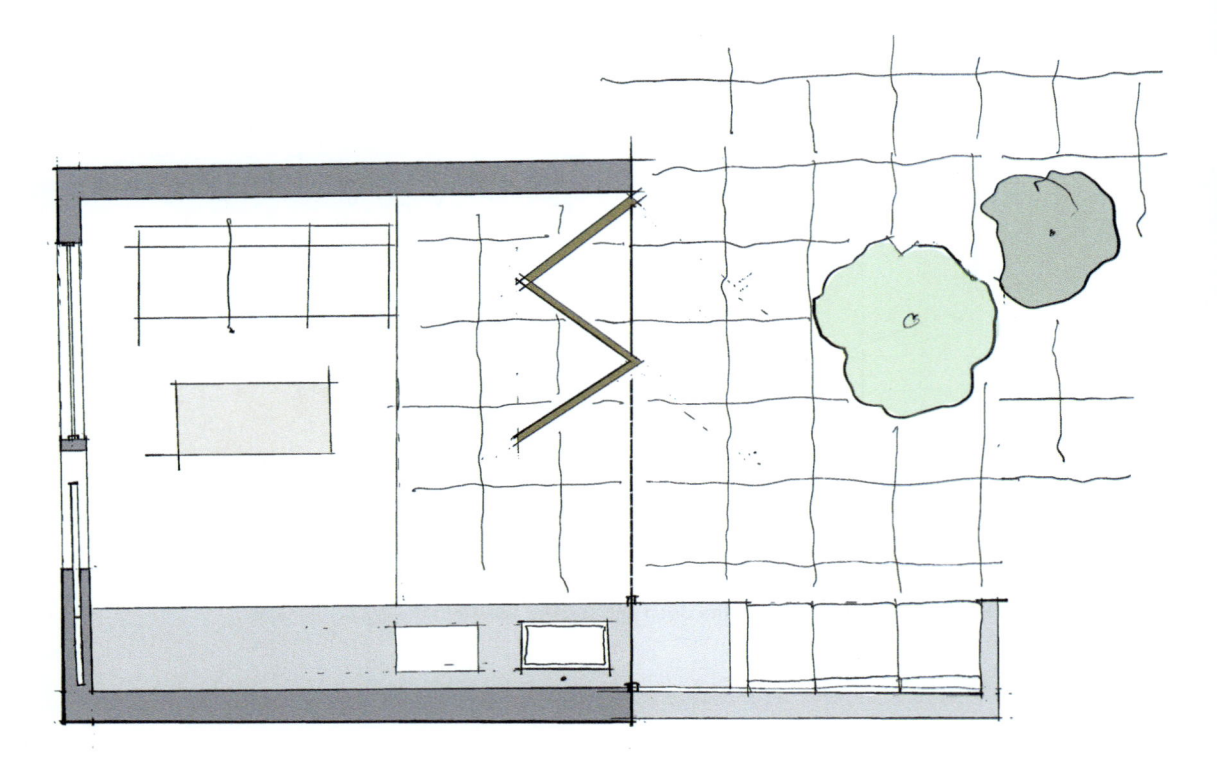

Figure 4.11 Diagram indoor space – garden spaces. The introduction of a glass bifold door along with bringing the external paving into the kitchen space accentuates the indoor-outdoor relationship

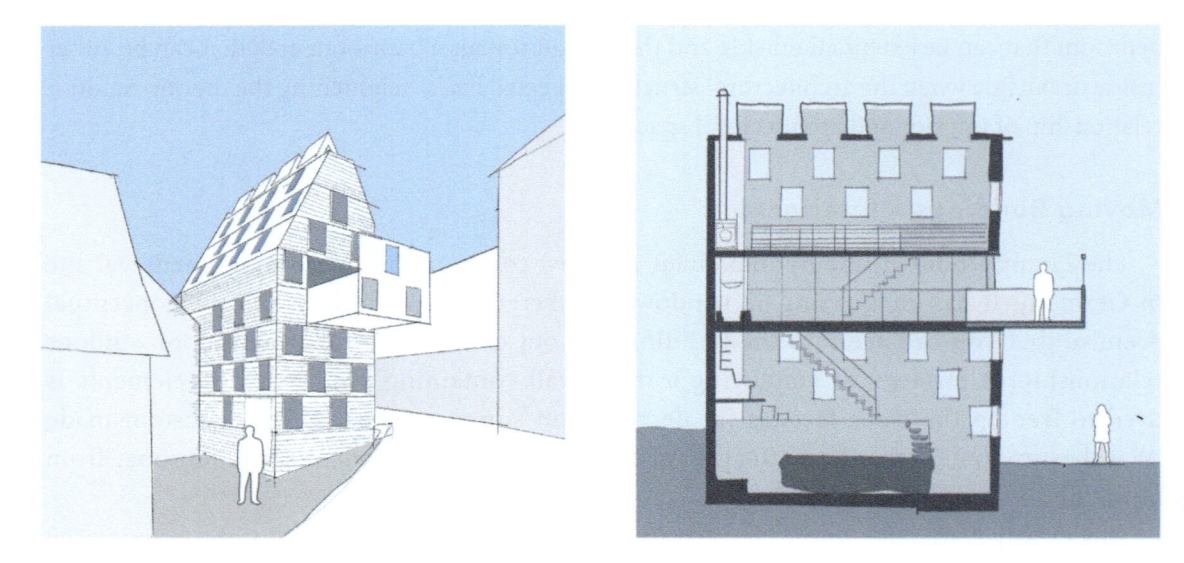

Figure 4.12 The Living Room House by Fomalhaut, 2005. IA section through the building expressing how the draw bedroom element opens out into the open air

> *The bedroom can be extended outwards to project like a drawer some 2 m outside the box. A key-operated switch turns on two 360V electric motors that set the 24 m² large 'drawer' in motion, causing it to travel outwards along its axis on two racks. Automatic switches at the ends of the rails shut off power after the 3-minute journey. The 'drawer' rests on six roller bearings.*
>
> (Formalhaut)

Sliding House

Sliding House by dRMM studio is a fantastical but simple realisation of a transformative building structure. A building that can respond to the climate, open to enjoy the sun or close to shelter from the elements. The technology is simple, employing a self-supporting 20 tonne enclosure [structure] on a linear rail track. The workings of the electric motors and wheels that drive the structure [and stop it] are incorporated into the 'thicknesses of the enclosure structure.'

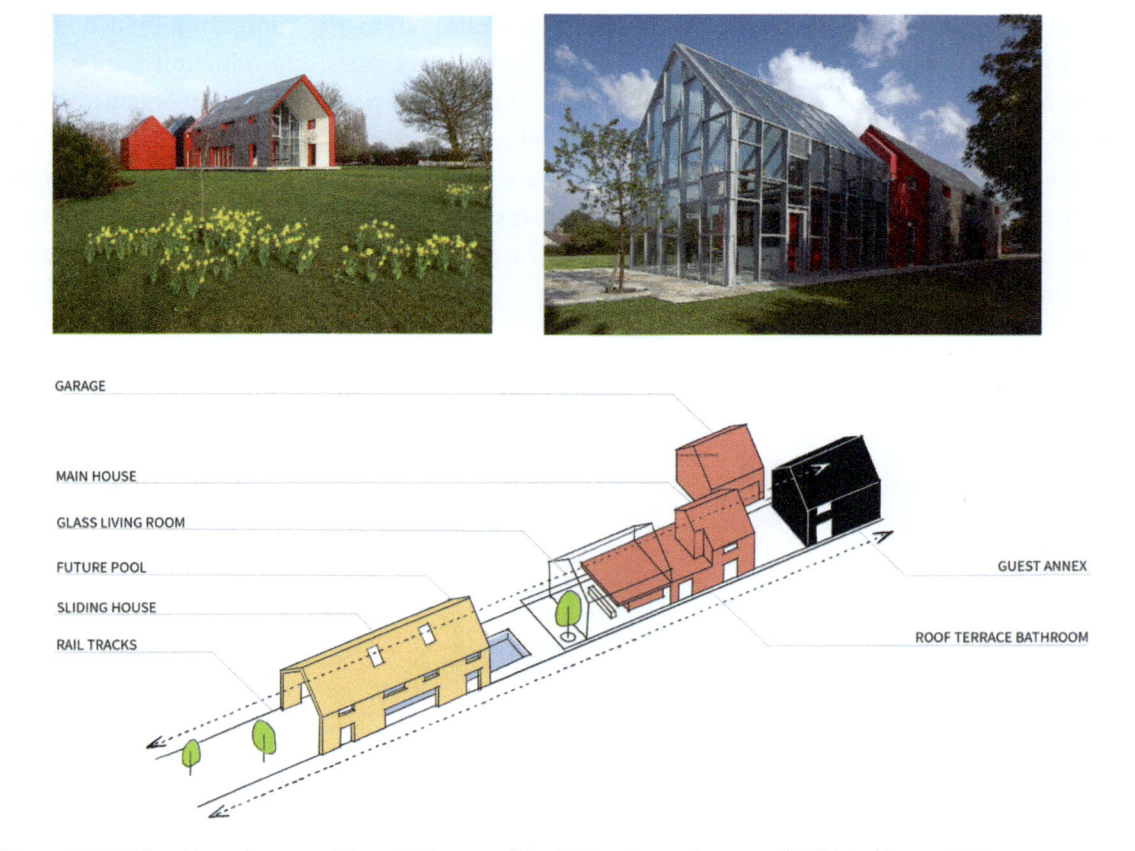

Figure 4.13 Sliding House [open and closed]. Diagram of the Sliding House elements. dRMM Architects, 2009

> *Sliding House offers radically variable spaces, sunlight, and views through its innovative, responsive design. The effect of the dynamic change as the roof moves is difficult to describe in words or images. It is about the ability to alter the building's character, sunlight, and openness according to season, weather, or a remote-controlled desire to delight.*
>
> (dRMM Architects)
>
> *The thickness of wall structure enabled the moving parts/services to be concealed within the enclosure.*

REACTIVE ENVIRONMENTS – KINETICS

Moving Parts/Surfaces

Since the conception of computing in architecture and design there has been a strong interest in digital environments – initially a visual immersive proposition there has been a push over the last 25 years to create physical environments that we can engage with or participate with, such as Phillip Beasley's How will we live together?

Initial research/installations focused on Utopian ideals, parametric computing [which allows you to control and modify complex objects] and links with natural reproduction such as bio-morphic [naturally occurring patterns or shapes reminiscent of nature and living organisms], for which computer computational capabilities are well suited.

The following series of kinetic interventions are from architectural to sculptural. Despite the technological focus they are quite simple forms of kinetics, uncomplicated using today's technology – engineered in clock-like mechanisms, orchestrated through basic coding and man-ufactured with CNC engineering processes.

Figure 4.14 Jean Novel Institute de monde Arabe, 1987. Jean Nouvel, Gilbert Lézénès, Pierre Soria, Architecture Studio. Photo Credits: © Georges Fessy. Diagram of the camera-like diaphragm

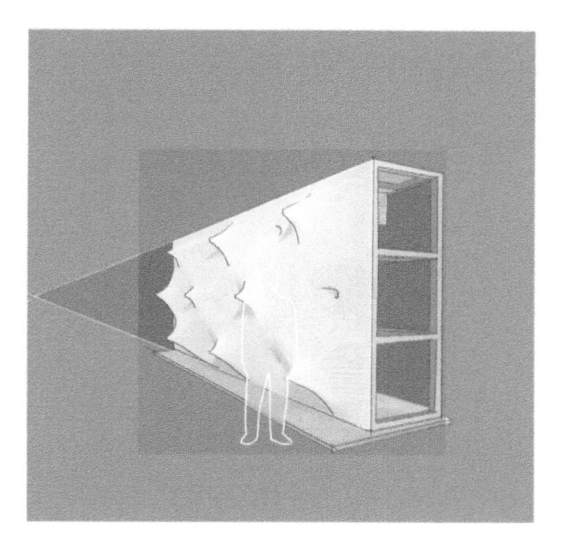 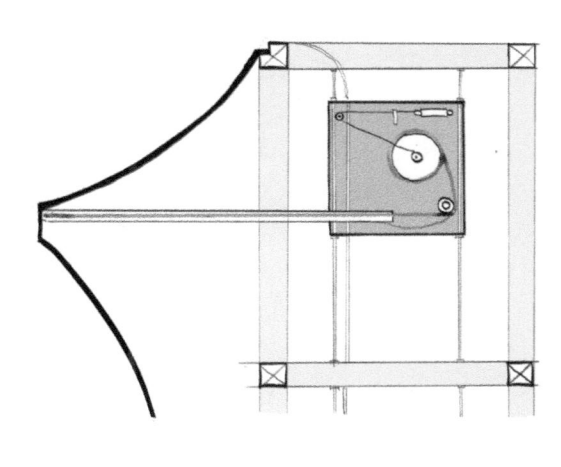

Figure 4.15 The Kinetic Wall, 2014, by Barkow Leibinger – diagram section drawing of the working elements/visual of the wall element

Kinetics Façade

Jean Nouvel's Institute de monde Arabe is an early example of kinetics in contemporary architecture that predates computing in design by quite some years with it being built between 1981 and 1987. On the south façade, which faces the predominant sun direction, a kinetic façade is installed, a series of motorised camera-like diaphragms open and close through the day in response to the level of sunlight. The motorised diaphragms are highly detailed objects with a watch-like precision.

> *The kinetic façade provides solar shading; often in architecture and interior design a kinetic transformation and movement will provide a functional purpose.*

Kinetic Wall

THE KINETIC WALL, 2014, by Barkow Leibinger was an installation piece at the 14tharchitecture biennale. Exploring the 20th-century architectural ideal that architecture need not be a static form, it is a simple wooden form that supports tensile fabric and a series of rods. Digitally controlled regimented motor and rod assemblies are choreographed to create a kinetic surface that undulates through a series of programmed topological patterns.

While the Kinetic Wall is part of Barkow's investigations into the 'new' technological processes of architecture, there is also the wider investigation into the surface, which looking forward should be very much part of future interior design digital and physical integration.

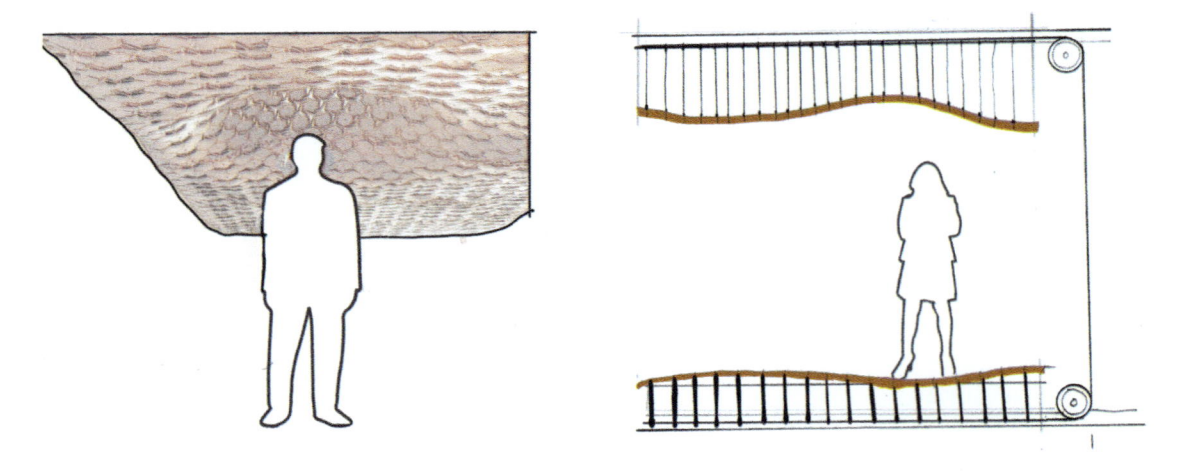

Figure 4.16 Visual of the kinetic canopy structure. Diagram of floor pulley relationship

Kinetic Floor and Overhead Plane

> *URBAN IMPRINT is how we design a piece of this new urbanism, an augmented materiality, as we define it. An environment that is a 'blank canvas' to be reshaped by the future self.*
> (STUDIO INI)

URBAN IMPRINT, 2020, is a recent kinetic installation from Studio INI. It is set up between the parameters of a sensory floor plane and a reactive overhead plane. An immersive kinetic experience is set up between the two planes as you walk through the defined space. Imprint is a highly engineered structure through the process of computational design, pulleys, weights and CAD fabricated panels. To create an internal enclosure that is described as an 'Argumented Materiality,' bringing to reality one viewpoint of the physical engagement with parametric CAD computing.

MOVEMENT: CAPTURE – SURVEILLANCE

Cameras – Surveillance

Cameras and surveillance have been part of our lives for over 50 years. Since the introduction of video tape VHS in the 1970s [the ability to record and rerecord video footage] there has been a fascination in the appropriation of it within interior practice.

D+S+R was the first practice to appropriate the technological advancements in recording technology through a series of installations – to date it is still here but it is ever more sophisticated with the use of AI facial recognition and automated 'visual' algorithms.

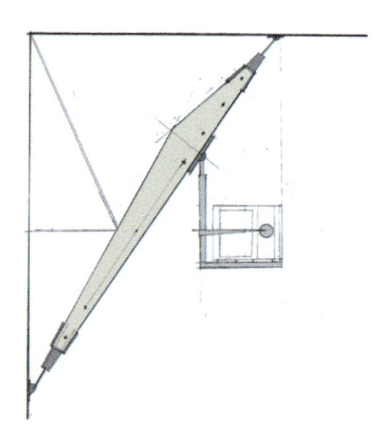  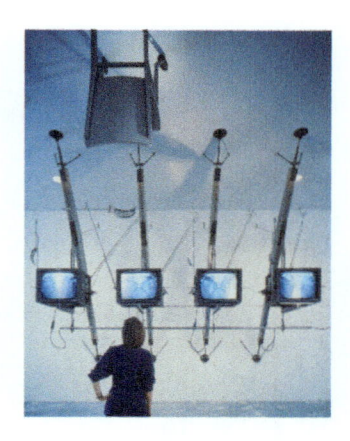

Figure 4.17 Diagrammatic drawing of the monitor structure. Parasite entrance structures, parasite gallery installation – courtesy of Diller Scorfidio + Renfro, 1989

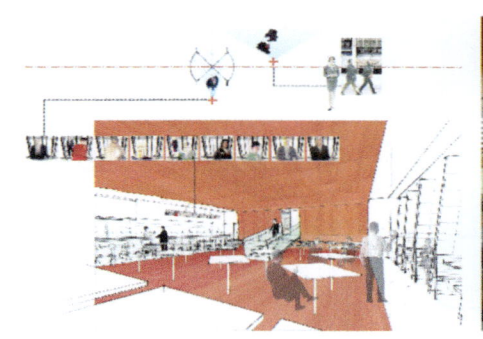 

Figure 4.18 Rendering of the brasserie – courtesy of Diller Scorfidio + Renfro, 2000. Image of the grand stair entrance to the brasserie. Photo Credit: Michael Moran

Para-Site/Brasserie, 1989

Diller and Scofidio have had a long relationship with surveillance technology. Parasite, 1989, was an early example of technology being employed to create an immersive environment – to make the participants part of the artwork. Several cameras were installed at the entrance to the museum, set to a time delay and played back in the installation room on a series of what are now regarded as archetypal interior architecture structures.

Conceptually, the same strategy was employed in Brasserie, 2000, as visitors to the restaurant were recorded as they entered the building to be played back in a series of time-lapsed screens above the bar as they took the central promenade staircase into the restaurant.

Zoom Pavilion, 2015

The Zoom Pavilion is an installation that features 12 computerised surveillance cameras, programmed with facial recognition software. As you enter the Pavilion live recordings focus on the visitor – focusing on specific groups or individuals. It is an exciting, self-gratifying space to be in

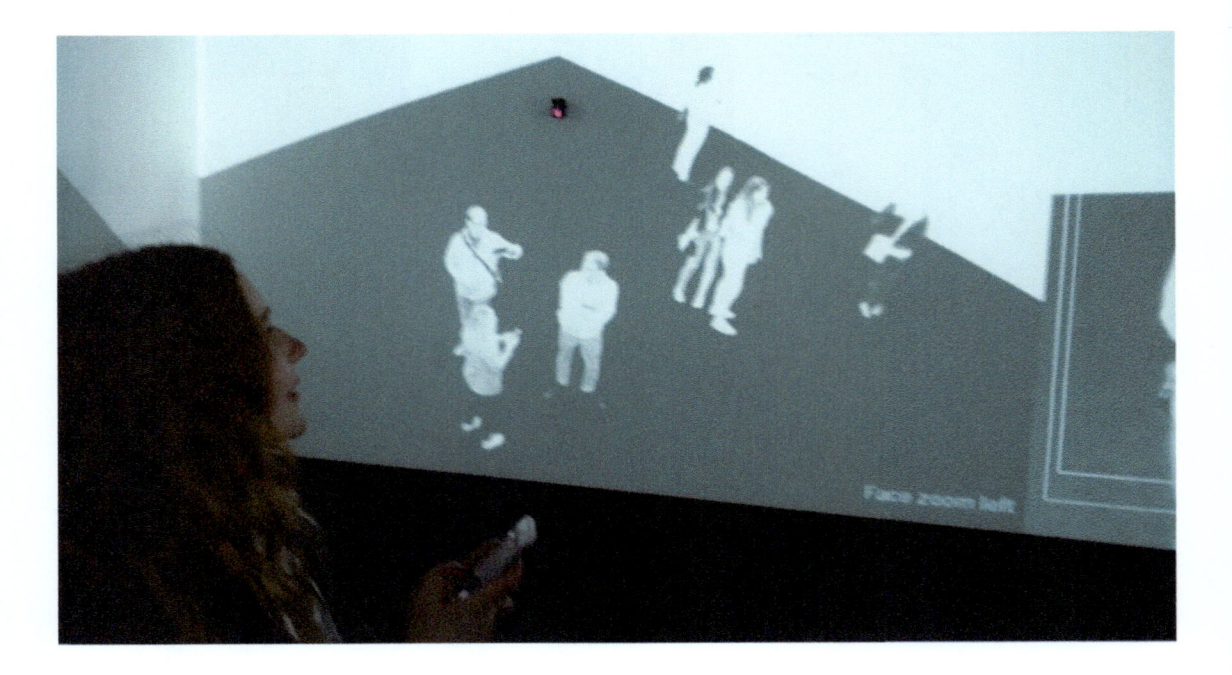

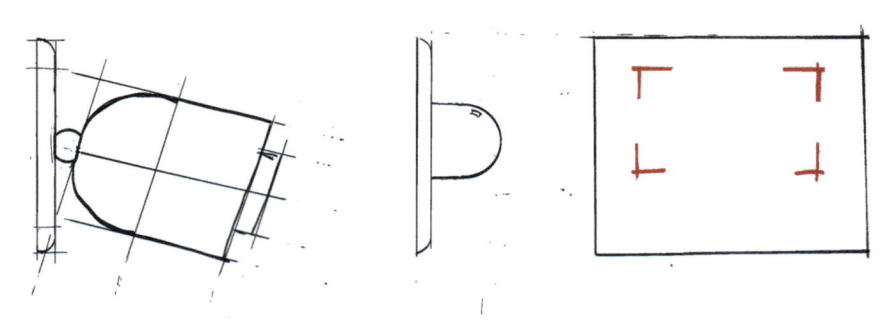

Figure 4.19 Zoom Pavilion – collaboration between artists Rafael Lozano-Hemmer and Krzysztof Wodiczko. Diagram of the capture and sensor elements used in the installation set-up. CCTV camera, movement sensor, facial recognition

that explores further our relationship with surveillance and projection, with the added model of people and artificial intelligence (AI) being layered into the surveillance narrative.

Pom Pom Mirror, 2015

The Pom Pom Mirror by American artist Daniel Rosin uses simple technology to create a reactive environment. An Xbox Kinect motion sensor captures the movement of the mirror viewer and plays back instantaneously through a series of 464 choreographed motors – all driven by specialist software and a Mac Mini.

> *In this artwork you see the potentials of how in the future reactive wall surfaces may well play a part in interior design futures.*

 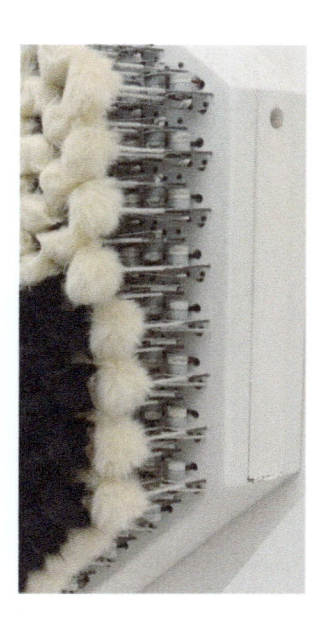

Figure 4.20 Gallery installation of the Pom Pom Mirror. Close-up of the Pom Pom Mirror: steel kinetic shafts, 928 faux fur pom poms, 464 motors, control electronics, Xbox Kinect motion sensor, mac-minicomputer, custom software, wooden armature

MOVEMENTS; LIGHT

The section is focused on the digital future of light.

Light is an integral element within the process of interior design, such as the introduction of daylight into spaces or the development of internal space to have sufficient artificial light so that they became habitable workspaces. Within interior design practice you will make multiple conscious decisions about immersive lighting – to make the space feel cosy, dim or cold.

Whilst looking forward to digital environments we already have a good level of automation in most new built interiors such as movement-sensing light switches [some that do not let the user switch them off!] and LUX sensors that can dim or increase light levels. The section looks towards the future of lighting technology, with reference to light kinetics and art practice.

James Turrell

James Turrell is an American-born artist that has been practising principles of space and light for over half a decade. His work features the use of both natural light [sky rooms] and artificial light, the perception of space often playing a part in spatial trickery.

> *My work is more about your seeing than it is about my seeing, although it is a product of my seeing. I am also interested in the sense of presence of space; that is space where you feel a presence, almost an entity – that physical feeling and power that space can give.*
>
> (James Turrell)

Figure 4.21 James Turrell, open sky, Naoshima, Japan, 2004. James Turrell, the light inside, the Museum of Fine Arts, Houston, 1999. Photo Credit: Ed Schipuil

Random International

Random International runs a collaborative studio in the UK. Founded in 2005 by Hannes Koch and Florian Ortkrass, their swarm series of installations focus on LED light installations mimicking patterns found in nature such as rain, birds and fish.

> *Swarm Studies explore the intelligence in motion of self-organising systems through increasingly dematerialised, sensory environments. Evolving from this, the piece invites an experience of architecture as something animate and responsively integrated with surrounding natural phenomena and human activity.*
>
> (Random International)

The technology behind the swarm sculptures is commonplace – microcomputers and addressable LEDs. Addressable LEDs allow you to address a 3D array [multiple LEDs in a 3D grid] and simple micromodules [or computer script] can add to sequence the array [see raspberry pi in Chapter 6].

> *Based on principles of particle and swarms found in programs such as Maya and 3dS Max this kinetic light installation is becoming increasingly a reality in interior space due to the miniaturisation of lighting elements [LED] and microcomputing.*

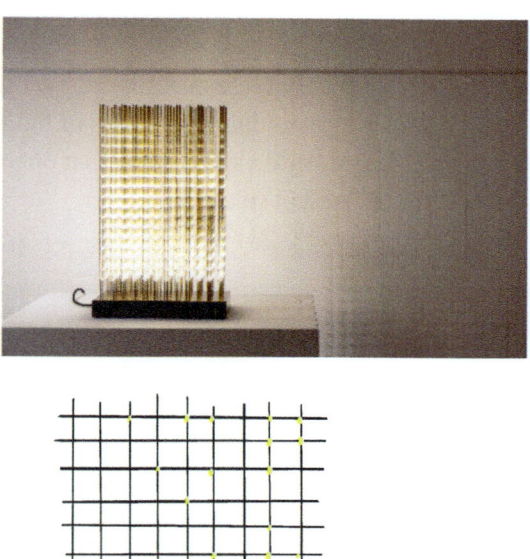

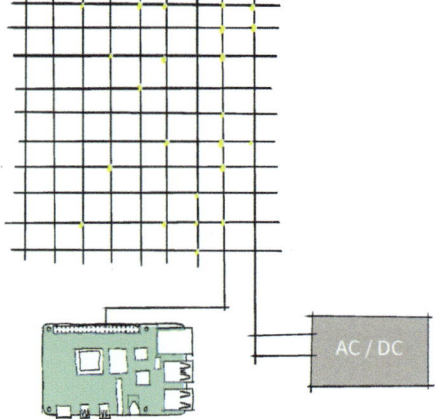

Figure 4.22 Random International Swarm Study/VI, 2014, Random International Swarm Study/III, 2011. A shift in complexity and sophistication in the installations from early exploratory art works. A diagram illustrating the main components of the swarm studies

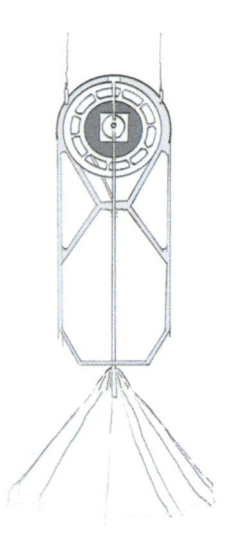

Figure 4.23 Flylight installation. Photo Credit: Dutch Design Week. Diagram of the cog wheel mechanism

Studio Drift: Flylight

Flylight is one in a series of kinetic light sculptures [luminaires] that have been explored by Studio Drift. Now part of a permanent display in the Rijksmuseum Amsterdam, the series of lights have been in research and developed over a five-year period. They feature a silk canopy that opens and closes in response to the complex string and steel micromechanical structures.

CASE STUDY – TRANSFORMATION

Didomestic – Madrid, Elii Architecture, 2013

Architects: elii – Uriel Fogué + Eva Gil + Carlos Palacios
Team: María Sole Ferragamo, Miguel Galán, Pablo Martín de la Cruz

---

Didomestic is a clever use of a 57.60 m² attic space in Madrid by Elii Architecture.

In the primary volume there is only enough space for one space, due to the height of the space and the angle of the roof. In normal practice any additional level would be reserved for general storage as it does not have adequate head height. In this project the practice has maximised the potentials of space through creative spatial thinking along with integrating flexible design strategies.

Key Moves

The designers initially cleared the plan to free up the limited space available. They stripped back the original interior to a single volume.

 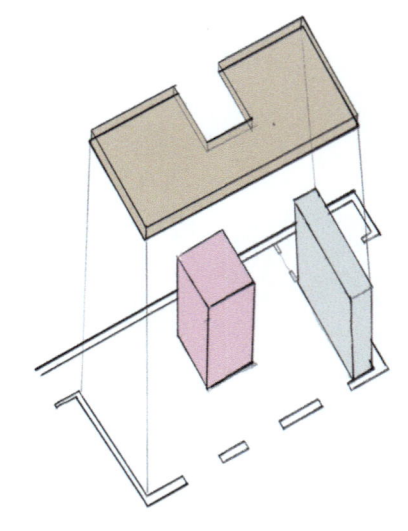

Figure 4.24 Central core and OSB mezzanine setting up the space. Photo Credit: elii (maquetas) Miguel de Guzmán (obra) axonometric of the core, mezzanine and the kitchen wall element

  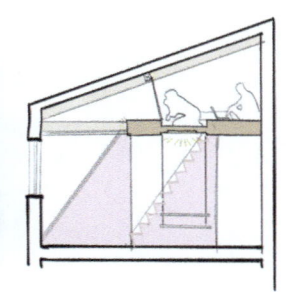

Figure 4.26 The retractable kitchen table that reveals the lighting for the dining space. Bathroom mirror concealed in the floor next to the sunken bath. Photo Credits: elii (maquetas) Miguel de Guzmán (obra); sectional diagram of the mezzanine space showing the limited head height being used

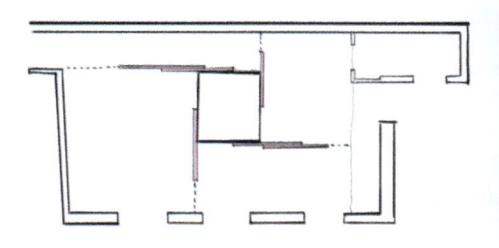  

Figure 4.25 Plan drawing of the partitions that divide up the space. Photograph of the open space. The space with a partition pulled out. Photo Credits: Elii Architecture. Photo Credit: elii (maquetas) Miguel de Guzmán (obra)

The central core was introduced to the plan; the core has a staircase that links the attic and main space. It acts as a storage element and sets up the plan below into a series of reconfigurable spaces using sliding partition screens. A skylight above the central core lets daylight penetrate into the central plan of the building.

A mezzanine was inserted into the roof space; it wraps around the thickness of the existing beams.

The functional 'programmatic' elements, that is, the kitchen, bathroom, storage space and domestic appliances, are housed in two side strips 'thickened walls.'

Flexible Strategies

The flexible screens can create a guest room, separate the kitchen from the dining room or can be retracted to open up the whole space.

The moving panels that are integrated into the core and run along guide rails. These panels can be used to create different arrangements, such as adding an extra room for a guest, separating the kitchen from the living room area or opening the whole floor for a party. The panels have transparent sections so that the natural lighting coming through the mansard roof can reach this space.

(Elii Architecture)

 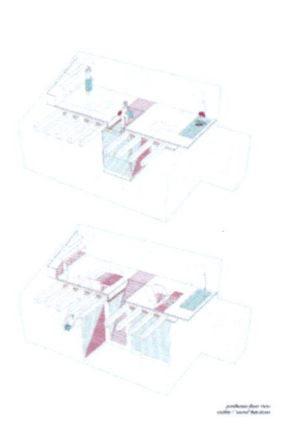

Figure 4.27 Simple palette of materials, letting light into the space. Photo Credit: elii (maquetas) Miguel de Guzmán (obra). Isometric highlighting the different transformational elements in the scheme design

A traditional Japanese room [washitsu or Tatami room] uses lightweight screens [Shoji Blinds] to divide rooms into separate spaces. It been a Japanese interior practice for many centuries.

The attic floor space [which is a thicker structure] houses multiple functional elements both below and above. Functions that are normally placed in a plan, furniture elements such as a table and chairs, dressing table, bookcase are all slotted into the floor thickness.

Simple Kinetics

Handles mounted on the wall connect the elements in the floor structure by pulley systems, allowing the ceiling elements to be lowered or retracted into place.

> *The secret trap doors that are integrated into the ceiling of the access floor and into the floor of the mezzanine and that house the rest of the domestic functions. The ceiling doors are opened with handles fitted on the walls. These handles actuate pulleys that lower part of the furniture (such as tables and the picnic benches, a swing or the hammock) or some complementary functions and objects (such as the disco ball, the fans to chill out on the hammock or an extra shelf for the guest room).*
>
> (Elii Architecture)

Materiality

The panels have polycarbonate sections so that the natural lighting coming through the roof can filter into the downstairs space. OSB is used to clad the new mezzanine space. There is a sense of eclectic fun in the use of materials and colour that even includes an integral disco ball for parties!

CHAPTER 5

MATERIALS

INTRODUCTION

Chapter 5 introduces traditional materials, contemporary finishes and surface treatments. There is a focus on interior design construction materials and applied materials. A material directory defines common interior substrates [OSB, etc.] and newly developed materials available to the designer. Throughout the chapter examples of 'material design' are used to illustrate creative interior design schemes that have material qualities.

Overview

Regardless of how small or big the space is that you are dealing with, materials are integral to every aspect of interior practice. As a designer entering well into the 21st century there are serious issues that arise from the environmental impact of materials used in interiors and architecture. From short-lived interiors to landfill, to the use of plastics and vinyl for cost and convenience, interior design is a major contributor to unsustainable practice.

Within this context we have all seen a recent movement [trend?] to simplify and strip back interiors [Chapter 1] to be more honest in terms of revealing rather than covering up standard building materials, such as the acceptance of OSB and ply as an interior finish.

The honesty of materials within interior design practice has never been more important for playing an active role in sustainability. This chapter has an unapologetic focus on honest materials and is away from material stereotypes such as wallpaper and fabrics.

Happier Café, designed and built in Taiwan from 2016 for a six-month installation inside an old air force library in the middle of Taipei. A series of different spaces to inhibit are created using paper off the roll [which is readily recyclable]. It demonstrates a creative response to 'temporary' interiors with a responsible approach.

DOI: 10.4324/9781003120650-6

Figure 5.1 The Happier Café paper interior. JC Architecture, 2016. Photo Credit: Zach Hone

FUNCTIONAL MATERIALS AND CONSTRUCTION

One of the first material considerations is its function and that often starts as a structural consideration. There are six core materials that are likely to be used in architectural and interior construction: wood, metal, concrete, masonry, glass and plastic. Moving to a more sustainable future we must consider an additional factor, the impact the material choices have on the environment.

Wood – It is a sustainable building material taking CO_2 from the atmosphere and storing it.

Metal – The manufacturing process adds CO_2 to the atmosphere; it is a strong material and can be recycled.

Concrete – It is a common building material that has less than favourable eco credentials but is widely used in all scales of construction.

Masonry – Brick and stone masonry [brick, stone, concrete block] is made from natural elements; so it has a low environmental impact. It also has good structural and thermal mass properties.

Glass – It is made of natural materials and can be readily recycled multiple times.

Plastic – It is derived from oil and used widely in construction. It can be recycled a maximum of ten times; if not recycled plastic it can take up to 500 years to decompose.

These materials [along with others] are also used widely as applied interior surfaces [as a covering rather than structural], so the chapter covers this application along with a further subset of material definitions, including insulating materials [sound and heat], wall and floor finishes such as plaster wall coatings, floor screeds, ceramics, rubber and vinyl – and not to forget the use of fabrics within the interior environment!

Six Core Materials

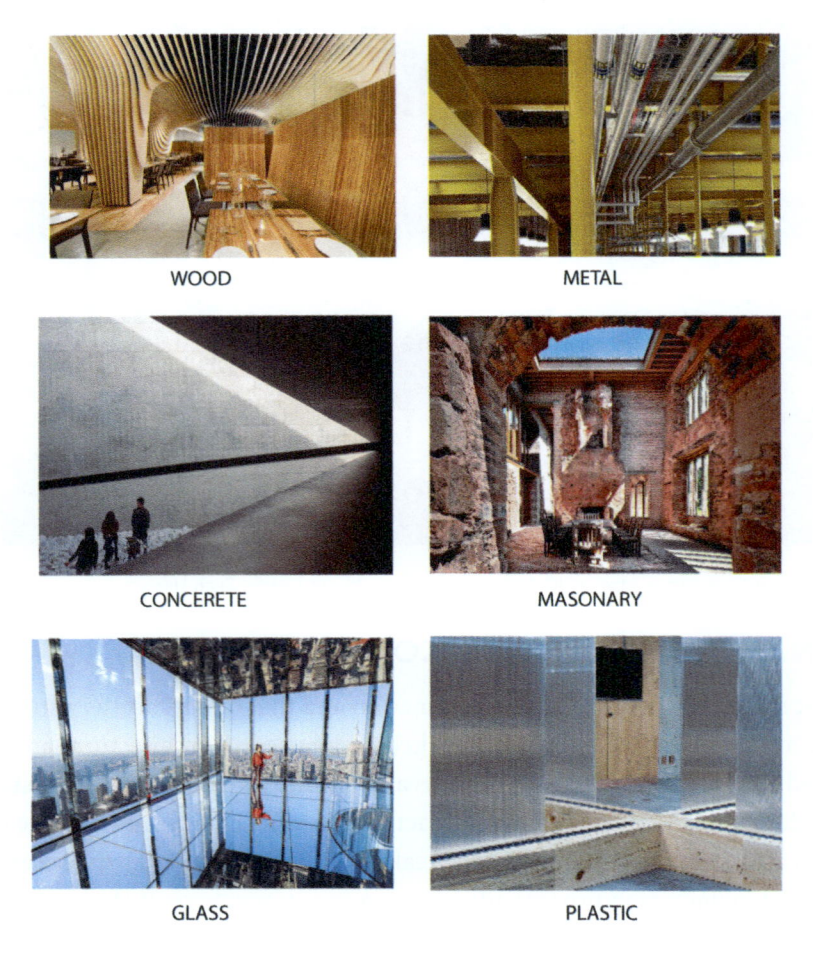

WOOD   METAL

CONCERETE   MASONARY

GLASS   PLASTIC

Figure 5.2 Wood-based product: plywood. NADAAA Architects. Photo Credit: John Horner. Steel-framed structure: Grimshaw Global, Locksbrook, UK. Concrete cast in situ: Tadao Ando – Naoshima Historic Masonry structure: WWM Architects, UK, Astley Castle, 2013. Photo Credit: Héléne Binet Glass acting as a structural component, NY, USA. Plastic: polycarbonate as an interior screening. Coop 3, Domino Architects, Tokyo/Shibuya, 2017

WOOD

Wood is formed from carbon dioxide, water and elements from the soil. It is made up of up to 50% carbon [from CO_2 in the air] which remains stored in the tree or timber until it is burned or decomposes [which releases the carbon captured back into the atmosphere]. In a built form it is a carbon store; so it has a positive carbon footprint, taking CO_2 from the atmosphere. When in built form timber buildings and interiors can reduce a carbon footprint of a project or offset it to become carbon neutral.

The recycling of wood into wood-based products can extend the CO_2 storage life of wood or in other cases it can be turned into a biomass fuel, so in principle adding the same volume of CO_2 back into the atmosphere – carbon neutral.

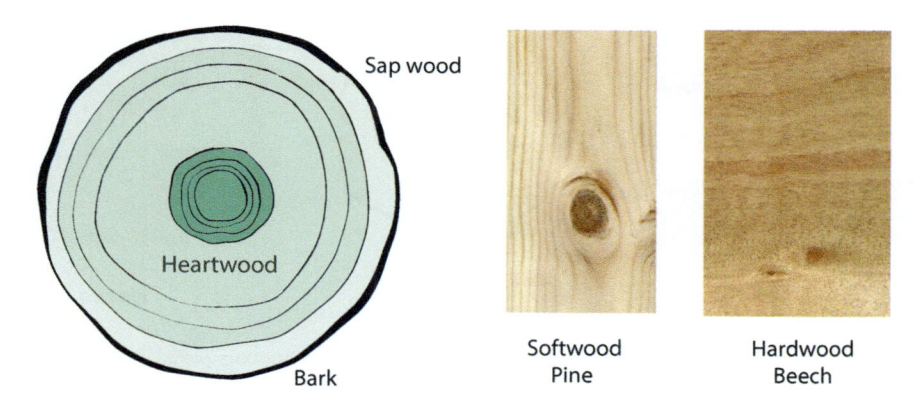

Softwood
Pine

Hardwood
Beech

Figure 5.3 Diagram of the core components that make up wood. Softwood example: pine; hardwood example: beech – the grain tends to be tighter in hardwood

Types of Wood

In its raw state there are two types of wood: hardwood and softwood. Softwood has a more open structure and hardwood a dense structure.

Common types of wood with abbreviations:

Softwood

Douglas Fir (DGA)
Pine (PIP)
Western Red Cedar (WRC)

Hardwood

Beech (BE)
Oak (OK)
Larch (EL)
Teak (TEK)

Structural Timber – Exterior structural wood is often treated with a preservative; it is in a sawn state [not planned] so it can have a rough surface, though construction timber today is eased edge/smooth.

Untreated Timber – It is used indoors where it is protected from the elements – used to create interior stud walls. You can often tell the difference between treated and untreated through the colour of the wood – treated is greenish or purple in colour and untreated is a natural colour.

Common timber sizes
$2 \times 1 = 50 \times 25$
$2 \times 2 = 50 \times 47$
$4 \times 2 = 100 \times 50$

Treated / Untreated

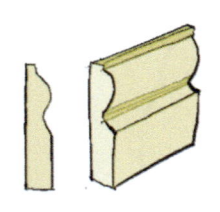

Moulding

Planned wood

Figure 5.4 Untreated CL16 [structural] and treated wood for outside applications [bottom plank]. Diagram of skirting board moulding. Planned softwood

$4 \times 3 = 100 \times 75$
$5 \times 2 = 125 \times 47$
$6 \times 2 = 150 \times 47$
$6 \times 3 = 150 \times 75$
$7 \times 2 = 175 \times 47$
$8 \times 2 = 200 \times 47$
$9 \times 2 = 225 \times 47$

For structural purposes there are two common grades of wood: C16 and C24. C16 is kiln dried and commonly used for internal construction such as walls, floors and roofs. C24 is higher in cost, has less defects and can handle bigger loads and spans.

Softwood comes in standard lengths: 1.80 m, 2.10 m, 2.40 m, 3.0 m, 3.60 m, 4.80 m, 6.0 m and up to 6.30 m [available in other sizes as well].

Planed Timber – It is used where a smooth finish is required, such as a window frame, door frame, skirting, etc. It will take paint, stains and varnishes to create a smooth finish. PAR redwood timber is often used for a quality interior and exterior finish. It can also be routed to create complex interior and exterior mouldings.

> *Planed timber is often quoted in terms of its 'nominal' sawn size – it is likely to be 3 to 5mm smaller than the quoted size.*

Wood-based Products

Most wood-based 'composite' products come in sheet form – wood-based boards. Other composite wood products are engineered products such as glue-laminated timber (GLT)/cross-laminated timber (CLT) which provide a more stable construction material [resistant to shrinking and splitting]; they also allow for impressive spans in building construction.

Figure 5.5 Sands End Arts and Community Centre, MAE Architects, 2020. Photo Credit: Rory Gardiner

Engineered Wood

> *The building's frame is made from a mix of cross-laminated timber (CLT) and glue-laminated timber (glulam), two types of engineered wood that have slightly different benefits.*
>
> (MAE)
>
> *The main spaces of the building (main hall, cafe and nursery) are naturally ventilated = not air conditioned = using zero energy.*
>
> *The services in most places are discreet/invisible (distributed within a purpose-built and designed trench running within the ground floor slab) – to enhance the CLT structure and help the architecture shine.*
>
> (Max Fordman LLP)

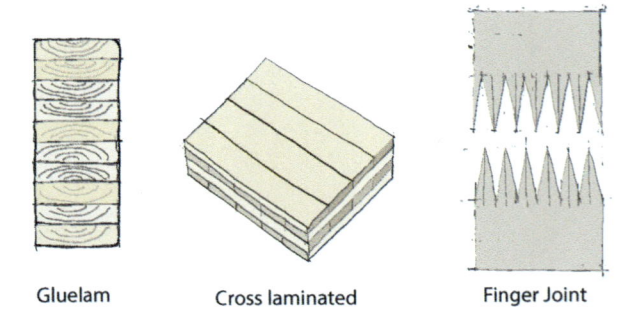

Gluelam   Cross laminated   Finger Joint

Figure 5.6 Glulam beam/cross-laminated timber/finger joint diagram of different types of engineered timber and joints

Figure 5.7 The Vilbert Chair, designed by Verner Panton in 1993, in production at IKEA in 1994. Refugee shelter, Günther and Schabert, 2016. Photo Credit: Micheal Heinrich. CNC sheet ply for temporary emergency accommodation

Glulam – glue-laminated timber: Multiple timber laminations 30–40 mm glued together to form continuous timber members – Finger joints were also developed to maximise the spans possible.

CLT – cross-laminated timber: The unwanted properties of solid wood, such as warping and splitting, are minimised in CLT.

Wood-based Boards

Wood-Based Boards – Commonly used both structurally and for interior fit outs, wood-based boards are a new product in construction terms. They have revolutionised the construction industry allowing for the rapid fitting out of interior fittings and furniture; they are also more widely being used as an interior finish. The sheet material can be cut by hand, machine and computer numerical control [CNC] machines; these wood-based boards along with CNC advances have transformed interior furniture into 'flat pack' self-assembly construction.

Common Wood-Based Boards

Plywood (PLY) – often with a veneer such as beech or melamine.

Particle Board (PI) – small sawdust type chips bonded together [with treated surface].

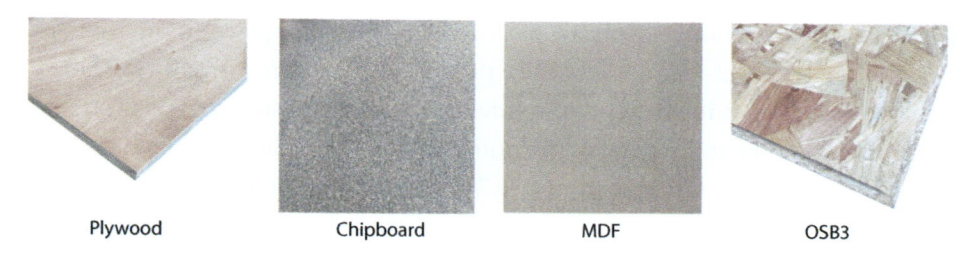

Plywood   Chipboard   MDF   OSB3

Figure 5.8 Beech plyboard; chipboard, MDF OSB 3

Medium Density Fibreboard (MDF) – fine wood fibres bonded together, a smoother finish that often has another finish, e.g., painted or rubber.

Oriented Strand Board (OSB) – shaped wood strands that are arranged in cross-oriented layers.

The typical size of wood-based boards is 2440 × 1220; they are available in smaller sizes and as big as 2620 × 5000 [OSB]. It is always useful to design with the standard sheet sizes to mind 2440 × 1220 as you can:

Minimise cuts – helping save on labour cost and production costs [see Chapter 2, laser cutting; same principles apply].
Minimise waste – by working with the sheet sizes.
Sustainability – you get more out of the material.

Wood for Interior Construction

Floors – The maximum single span of a traditional wood floor is 6+ m; this can be extended using intermediate supports. Typical joist spacing is 400–450 mm rule of thumb but can be increased to up to 800 with a thicker substrate; e.g., 50 mm floorboards.

Typical joist timber size [common construction]; 220 × 38 mm/span 4 m

The span and the thickness of the flooring will be a major factor in floor construction and in a professional context would be calculated by a structural engineer.

In recent years solid wooden joists have been replaced by web and I joists. An advantage is that they can span bigger distances and weigh less than typical wood construction; they also use less raw material. Web joists allow you to run services such as electric and plumbing through them; I joists are easily cut to size and web joists are prefabricated to size.

Flooring – Timber floorboards are common in interiors and range from 25 to 50mm thick. More commonly in new build applications is the use of OSB or chipboard that is typically 18 mm thick. The edges are tongue and grooved to slot together quickly and provide increased structural stability.

[See floor coverings for wood-based finishes.]

Interior Wall Construction – Wooden partitions are commonplace in interior design, providing a separation of spaces and a level of fire protection. They are typically non-load-bearing; the voids between are often insulated to provide some degree of sound insulation and thermal comfort and further cables and pipes can be routed through the voids.

Common timber sizes used in a partition are 75 mm × 50 mm or 100 mm × 50 mm sawn timber, fixed initially to the floor and ceiling; vertical timber studs are then inserted at set distances 400–600 mm depending on the thickness of the plasterboard [9–12 mm]. Horizontal noggings stabilise the construction.

> *When working out stud spacing it is useful to set studs out so that there are less plasterboard cuts. Within commercial interiors the use of lightweight steel partition systems speeds up the build process.*

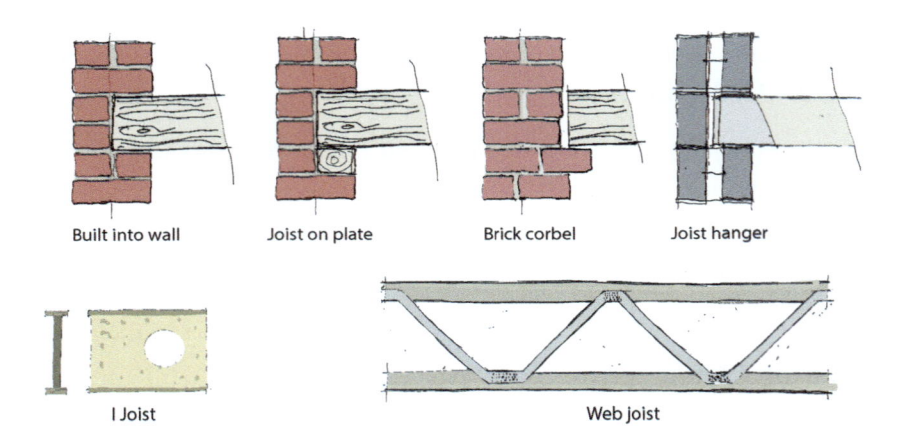

Figure 5.9 Standard wooden floor support methods I joist diagram with hole cut out for services/web joist diagram, wood and steel bracing

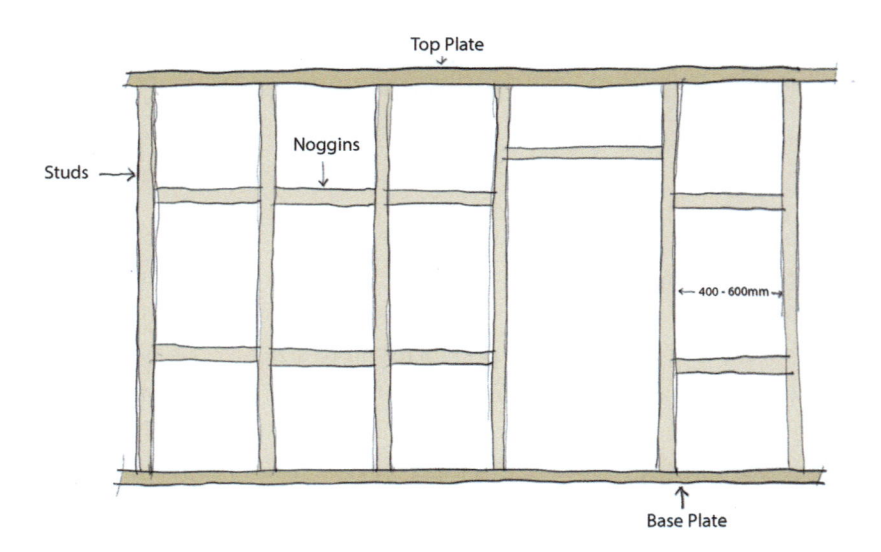

Figure 5.10 Typical components of stud wall – a base plate and top plate are installed and then the studs and noggings

Figure 5.11 A porous wooden liner defines the ceiling/enclosure within a bigger warehouse space. Bloomberg R+D Tech Hub design. iwamotoScott Architecture. Photo Credit: Bruce Damonte. Historical: Giles Downes' new hammer-beam roof in St George's Hall, completed in 1997 after a fire destroyed the original. Photo Credit: Ian A Gratton

Four Types of Typical Wooden Moulding Used in Interiors

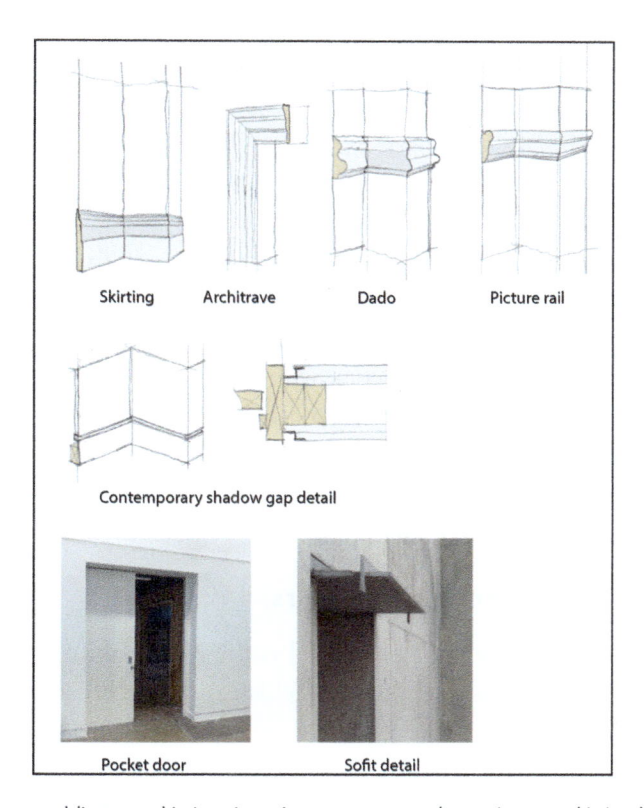

Figure 5.12 Typical wooden mouldings used in interiors. A contemporary alternative to a skirting board with shadow gap detail. Photos: a sliding pocket door that is incorporated into the wall void. Tadao Ando door soffit detail – Naoshima, Japan

> *Contemporary architectural and interior design diminishes the role of traditional interior mouldings in favour of a simplification of edge protection; it is integrated so it cannot be seen or simplified.*

Ceilings – Wood normally provides the substructure for common ceiling materials such as plasterboard or acoustic panelling. Wooden ceiling elements can provide an added level of detail to a design and were used widely in historical properties.

Interior Wooden Mouldings – The use of interior mouldings within period property can often be of significance and something that should be 'kept' when thinking about alterations. The mouldings as well as decorative performed a role in preserving the edges of an interior – such as skirting and dado rails that can take a knock from a chair or a picture rail so you can hang frames without drilling into the wall.

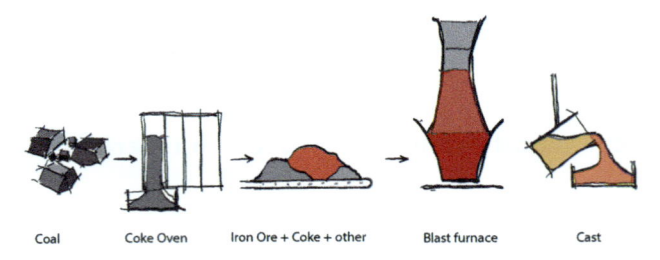

Coal   Coke Oven   Iron Ore + Coke + other   Blast furnace   Cast

Figure 5.13 The production process of steel manufacture – coal is turned into coke then combined with iron ore and fired in a blast furnace

METAL

Steel is made up of iron and carbon; other 'alloying' materials can be added to create several types of metal, such as chromium to create stainless steel.

Steel has mixed eco credentials in terms of its sustainability. Its production is energy intensive, and the raw material coke is derived from coal, which combines to add substantial amounts of carbon into the atmosphere. On the other hand, it can be readily recycled [and is] multiple times without degradation to its material properties – according to the American Institute of Steel Construction structural steel produced in the US contains 93% recycled steel scrap, on average. It is often referred to as a cradle-to-cradle material.

Types of Metal [Construction and Interiors]

Steel [available with different alloy configurations] is the most common metal produced. Steel must be treated as it is prone to rust – stainless steel is resistant to rust and used commonly for exterior fixture and fittings.

Figure 5.14 Olivetti showroom, Carlo Scarpa, 1958. Venice, brass detailing embedded into the stone finish. Lightweight aluminium ducting used for overhead services. Bloomberg R+D Tech Hub design. iwamotoScott Architecture, 2015. Photo Credit: Bruce Damonte

Iron (Wrought or Cast) is not commonly used in today's construction process.

Aluminium is used within construction and interiors for windows, façade systems, ducting and many other situations – its lightweight properties and resistance to corrosion make it the second most used metal in construction.

Copper is used externally as a high-end roof cladding; within the interior fit out it is usually used as piping in water and heating systems.

Brass and Bronze are used as a decorative element in the interior of buildings for door furniture, etc.

Zinc in sheet form is used as a high-end roofing and guttering material; in liquid form it is often used as a coating for steel to give it corrosion-resistant properties.

Metal for Construction

Metal is a strong construction material that can give extensive structural spans; combined with a low weight to span ratio it is a truly versatile material. It can be easily prefabricated and moulded

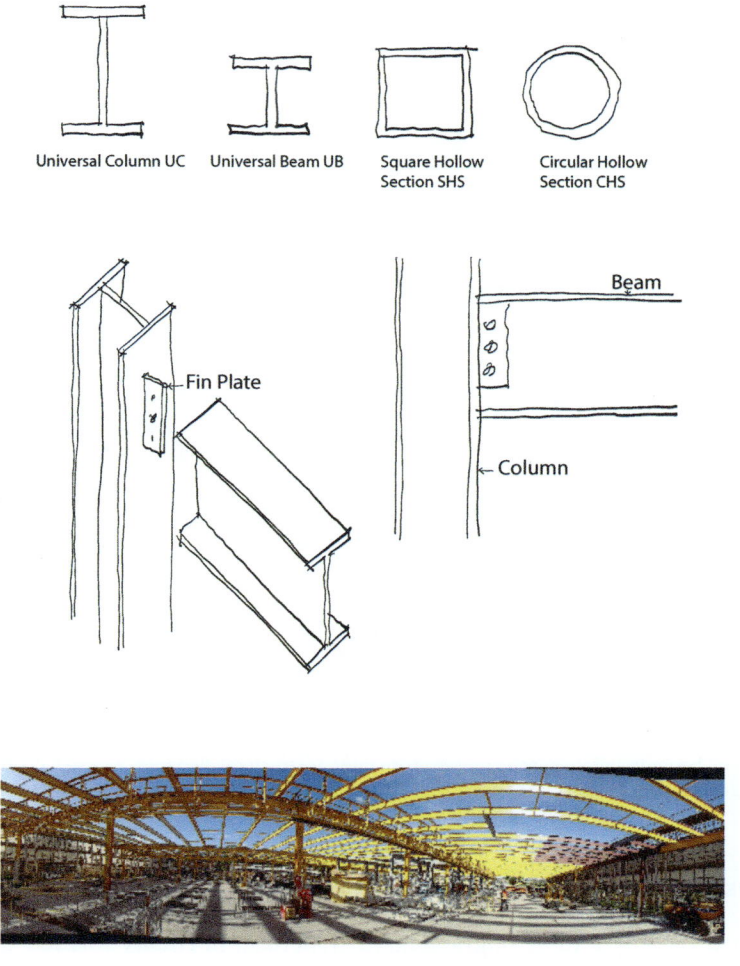

Figure 5.15 Common beam and column sections/type of connections. The impressive spans of the super room, steel framed I beam structure: Grimshaw Architects, 1972, Locksbrook, UK. Photo Credit: Grimshaw Global

into various profiles. Steel structures can be erected very quickly as they are prefabricated off site and use quick fixing methods [bolts] to assemble the structure.

Column and Beam construction is the most common type of steel construction; hot rolled steel sections [normally in I sections] are bolted together to create a gridded structure that can span multiple heights and widths.

> *Universal I Beams are often used to support an opening when removing a load-bearing wall from an existing construction. They are also sometimes referred to as an RSJ [Rolled Steel Joist].*

> *By placing the constructive crosses asymmetrically with a single column in each space, a different layout was created each time, with the cross as the centrepiece around which the space unfolds.*
>
> (Graux Baeyen)

Figure 5.16 Using the I beam to unfold space and set up an interior structural elegance. House C-VL by Graux Baeyens, 2021. Photo Credit: Jeroen Verrecht

Space Frames/3D Truss

Space Frames are visually a lightweight elegant structure, normally formed through members and nodes.

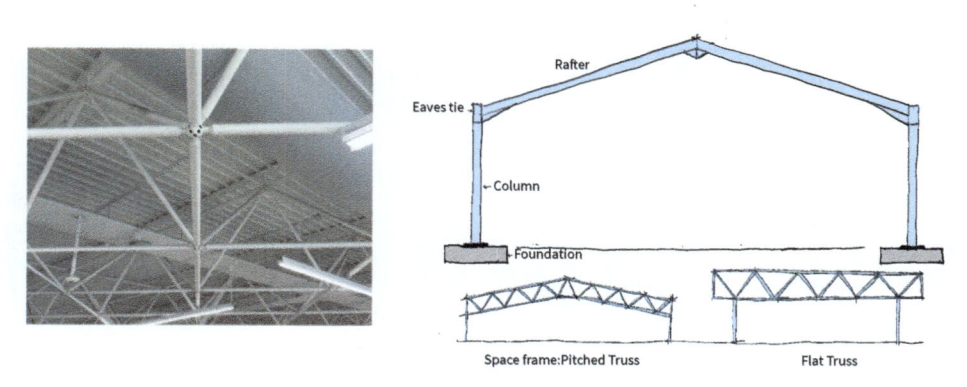

Figure 5.17 Mero space frame – elegant [strong] lightweight structure. FORMER CABINET MAKERS FACTORY– Mero space frame technology, one of the first widely commercially available space grid systems invented in Germany in the 1940s. PORTAL FRAMES allow the space to be opened up free of columns – typically utilised in commercial warehouse type constructions

Figure 5.18 Axonometric of Croft Lodge. David Conner design with Kate derby, 2017. Interior studio with ruined interior

Portal Frames have been adopted extensively in contemporary architecture and interiors, with origins in industrial architecture. The frame maximises the spatial envelope to be column free. Truss systems can also play a part in the portal frame – visually low impact and good to feed services through 2D; often seen in industrial architecture such as supermarket buildings and factory buildings.

> *The ruin is protected from the elements within a new high performance outer envelope. this means that in most places there are two walls, two windows and two roofs, a **STEEL PORTAL FRAME** was erected over the ruin, this was infilled with timber, sheeted with osb board, insulated, wrapped in a waterproof membrane and internally clad in black corrugated iron.*
>
> (David Connor design with Kate Darby)

Figure 5.19 Steel house, Zecc Architects, 2021. Juxtaposed wooden interior. Photo Credits: Stijin Polestra

The Steel Craft House is a fine example of self-building. In a period of ten years, a former garage was converted into a wooden residence with a Corten steel façade.

(Zecc Architects)

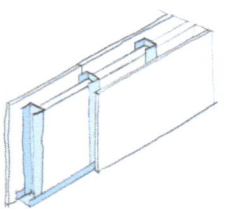
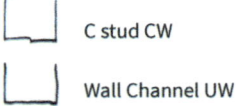

C stud CW

Wall Channel UW

Corner channelCW

Figure 5.20 Steel stud wall construction. Axonemetric detail of a single skinned metal stud partition/different types of steel stud profiles. C and L channels

Steel Cladding is not normally structural; it provides protection from the elements or a final decorative finish within the interior. It will often be combined with an insulating material if used on the exterior.

Corten Steel is used widely in contemporary architecture and interiors as a cladding; it has a treated surface that develops a rusted patina over time and is 'maintenance free.'

Metal for Interior Construction

Walls – Metal Stud Partitions are becoming more common in interior fit outs, especially in the commercial sector. They are non-load-bearing and are used to divide up space. The voids can be utilised in the same way as in wooden partitions with services.

A greater level of sound and thermal insulation can be achieved by doubling up the construction; it can also improve the fire rating. A single construction is quicker and easier to assemble.

Ceilings – Suspended Ceiling Systems typically non-load-bearing, attached to the underside of a suspended floor. Other systems can be self-supporting with no need for suspension fixings.

> *Suspended ceiling grids allow you to hide services in the void space; they have fallen out of fashion within contemporary interiors in favour of exposed services. Not installing a suspended ceiling saves on materials but does require a different fire proofing strategy.*

Floors – Steel Floors are found within industrial buildings; they are often part of a bigger structure such as a gantry or stairwell.

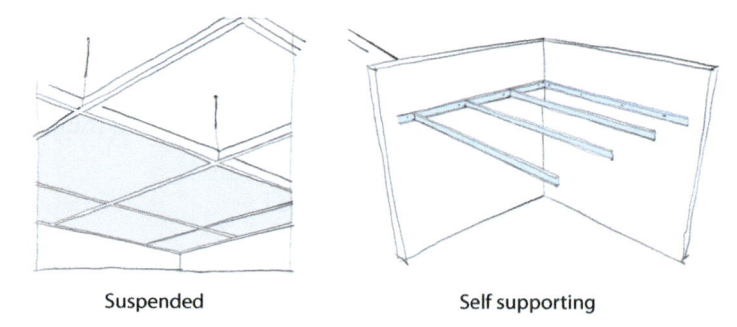

Suspended   Self supporting

Figure 5.21 Suspended ceiling/grid – hung from steel wire fixings attached to the ceiling substrate. Self-supporting ceiling fixed to the wall of the enclosures

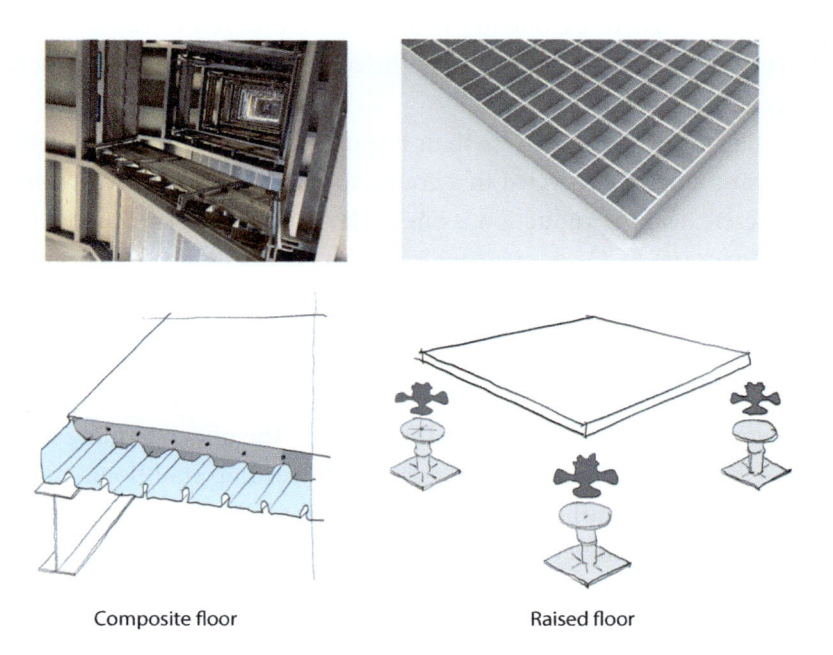

Composite floor   Raised floor

Figure 5.22 Steel floor and stair construction. Baltic Arts Newcastle. Welded steel grating. Image Credit: Staco gratings. Composite steel floor [reinforced concrete and steel tray]. Raised floor system, allowing service to be run underneath

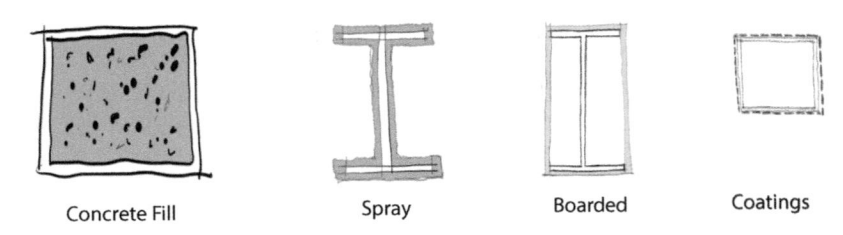

Concrete Fill Spray Boarded Coatings

Figure 5.23 Different types of fire protection. Concrete fill sprayed coatings. Boarded [such as plasterboard] specialist coatings.

Steel Composite Floors are used widely in larger steel-framed constructions; they are a combination of concrete and steel in slab form, normally slotted into the steel frame.

Raised Floor Systems provide a subfloor that can be tiled and services can also be run through the void space such as electric and data points. They are adjustable so can take a deviation in floor level.

Fire Protection

Intumescent Coatings are used to protect steel from heat/fire damage; they expand in the event of a fire to insulate the material for a given period [fire rating].

Interumesetant coatings can be sprayed or board based.

CONCRETE [INC. MASONRY]

The main components of concrete are cement, water and sand. The use of concrete in construction can be traced back 2000 years. It is within the 19th and 20th century that concrete was adopted widely for large structures, due to the development of reinforced concrete, which integrates the high tensile strength of steel wire with the compressive strength of concrete. It also has a good level of fire resistance.

The eco credentials of concrete are less than favourable, topping an estimated 5–8% of total global CO_2 emissions. It can be recycled in a cradle-to-cradle manner but always needs cement to reconstitute concrete, whose production is one of the major CO_2 contributors. There are many efforts being made to create ECO concrete, which normally involves a partial substitution of key ingredients.

Concrete for Construction

Concrete Framework – In 1914 le Corbusier transformed the understanding of traditional domestic buildings with the Dom-Ino building concept. It freed up traditional mass construction approaches to architecture and utilised reinforced concrete to develop a concrete framework; this is the most common type of concrete construction that we see today.

In Situ Concrete – It involves making a mould, adding reinforcement and pouring concrete – all completed on site. In multistorey buildings a 'climbing formwork' is used.

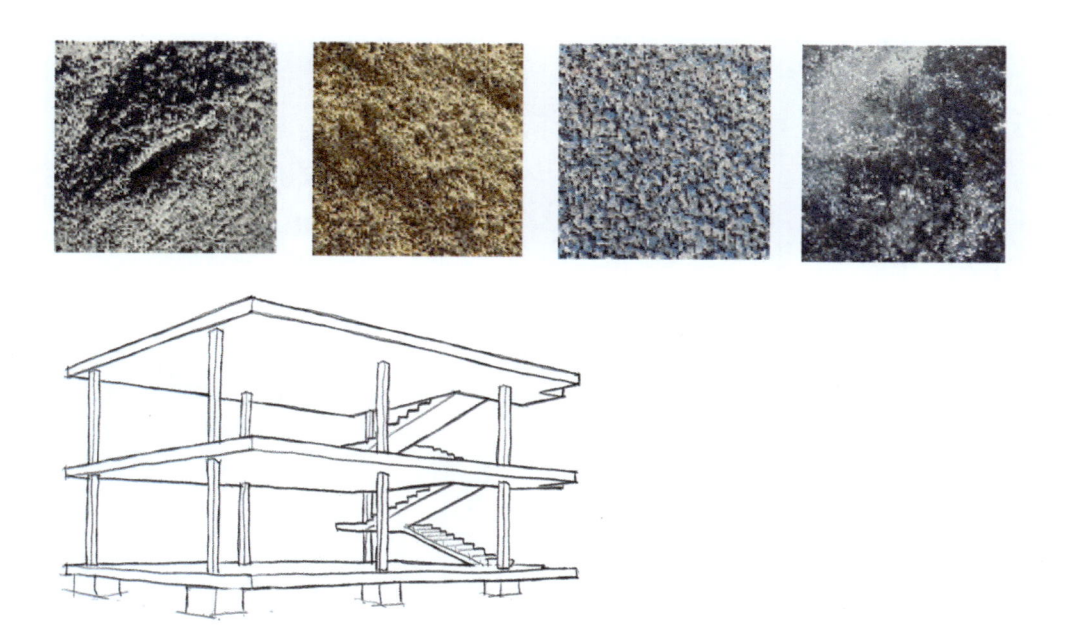

Figure 5.24 Components of concrete – cement, sand, aggregate and water – the reinforced concrete Dom-Ino building concept, le Corbusier, 1914

Figure 5.25 Precast sewage pipes used to define an architectural enclosure, SUMMARY Architects Installation at Venice Biennale, 2016. Photo Credit: Tiago Casanova. Climbing concrete formwork. Photo Credit: Sensenschmied

Prefabricated Concrete – Panels are cast in a mould in a controlled factory environment and then assembled on site, which can be beneficial as the quality of the structure can be maintained in a controlled environment. Elements such as stairs, cladding and lintels are commonly precast.

Concrete Blocks – These are used in general construction work such as foundations, walls and wall support. They remain exposed in many 70s and 80s buildings.

Figure 5.26 Concrete blocks exposed: Central Beheer, Herman Herzberger, 1970 – Kantoorgebouw Centraal Beheer, Apeldoorn, the Netherlands (1968–1972), architect: Herman Hertzberger. © Willem Diepraam.

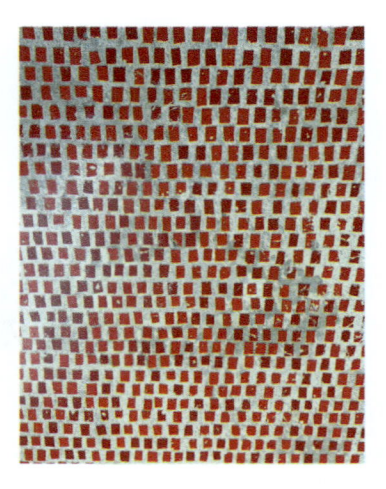

Figure 5.27 Polished concrete floor in Yoglar. School for early music and piano education, jerez. Architects: Enrique Jerez Abajo, Blanca Leal García. 2018. Photo Credits: Javier Bravo Jabato. Carlo Scarpa Terrazzo floor at the entrance to the Olivetti showroom, Venice

Concrete for Interiors [Finishes]

Floors

Polished Concrete is created by grinding back and polishing the substrate.

Floor screeds are a top layer added to a concrete subbase; there are many types of thin layers that can be applied. Screeds are often used to level a floor.

Figure 5.28 Fair-faced concrete exposing the grain of the wood and the shuttering used to form the concrete – Hayward Gallery, London. Chiselled finish applied to the concrete of the Barbican Centre, London. Photo Credit: George Rex

Terrazzo is traditionally poured; with a cement base and colourful aggregate it is then ground and polished in a comparable way to polished concrete. In recent years terrazzo has made a comeback in interiors utilising recycled materials in the mix. Today it is more commonly installed as a tile.

Treated Concrete

Fair-Faced Concrete – It is treated to create a decorative finish. Patternation in formwork, such as rough sawn timber, can create detailed surface patterns.

Acid-Etched Panels – A stencil is used to etch the surface of the concrete.

Chiselled – The concrete is chiselled to expose the aggregate. The finish of the Barbican Centre/London is machine finished.

Timber Formwork – It is used for creating wood grain detail.

Masonry and Brick for Interiors

Stone and brick have been used for centuries in the construction of traditional buildings. Within repurposing projects, the original stone or brick structure is often stripped back to reveal the history of the building. Contemporary stone within the interior environment is likely to come in tiles and as brick slips [applied materials].

Common Masonry Types

Stone

Granite, limestone, sandstone, marble and slate are the most common types of stone used in construction and interiors.

Sandstone is a commonly used stone; it is soft and porous and is often used to create architectural details. It is also used as flooring and paving.

Limestone is used to create architectural decorative features such as façades and pillars. It is also used as flooring and paving.

Granite is a tough material of high quality. It is also used for paving slabs, tiles, fireplaces and kitchen surfaces.

Slate is a durable material; it is highly resistant to water and cold. It is used externally as a roofing material, paving, coping and cladding. Internally it is used as floor and wall tiles, fire surrounds and worktops.

Bricks

Clay Bricks – Common bricks normally made of clay and kiln fired.

Facing Bricks – Also made of clay but manufactured to be weather resistant as they are generally used on the face of a building.

Engineering Bricks – Normally used in foundations or in a load-bearing situations.

Fire Bricks – Fired at a higher temperature they can withstand much greater temperatures, and are fire resistant and used in chimneys, hearths, BBQs, etc.

Air Bricks – They have holes in them to allow airflow in and out; normally inserted into a wall cavity or suspended floor.

Brick Slips – Used quite widely in recent interiors the brick slip gives the look of bricks without the bulk of the brick. Externally they can be combined with insulation to provide a better U value.

Sandstone Limestone Granite

Common Facing Enginneered

Figure 5.29 Sandstone, limestone and granite flooring. Common clay brick, facing brick and an engineered red brick

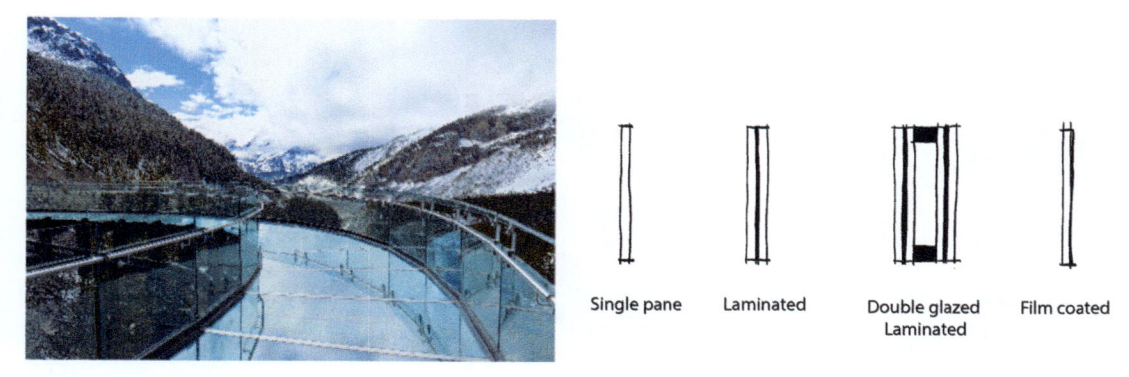

Single pane   Laminated   Double glazed Laminated   Film coated

Figure 5.30 Laminated glass acing as a structural floor/bridge component. Photo Credit: Jack Borno. Different types of commercial glass, single pane, laminated, double glazed and film coated

GLASS/PLASTIC

Glass

Float glass is the most common glass used in construction and interiors; it was developed in 1959 by Alister Pilkington.

> *Glass is a resource efficient material which is made of abundant natural raw material such as sand and glass waste (cullet's). Glass is a fully recyclable material that can be recycled in a closed loop over and over again.*
>
> (Glass Alliance Europe)

Glass does have good cradle-to-cradle credentials but both in new and in recycled glass a large amount of energy is used to melt the raw materials; in recycled glass this is reduced.

Laminated Glass is constructed of two or more layers of glass sandwiched between a polyvinyl film. It can be used as a load-bearing element but it is more commonly used for glass balustrades and floor to ceiling glazing [due to its safety credentials].

Glass Surface Treatments

Heat and Sun Coatings

> *Red-orange glass suggests the colour of cooling magma, referencing the site's geology and offering a warm approach. The glow extends to the interior, bathing the entry and central stair in light.*
>
> (Faulkner Architects)

Figure 5.31 Tinted glass used in the Lookout House, Faulkner Architects, 2018. Photo Credit: Joe Fletcher

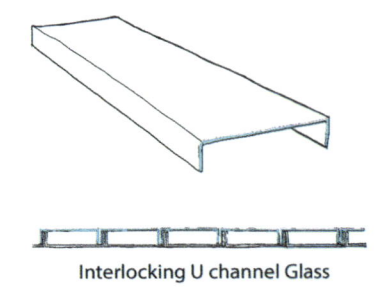

Interlocking U channel Glass

Figure 5.32 Different types of glass blocks used to create an immersive refractive environment. Glass art Gallery, Osaka, Japan, 2015. Jun Murata Architecture. Photo Credit: Images courtesy of Jun Muata. Drawing of U channel glass system

Tinted Glass can be used to reduce solar gain and it can also be used to create warmth and a juxtaposition of view.

Other Types of Interior and Exterior Glass

Glass Blocks originate from the early 1900s and were originally used in an industrial warehouse to bring in natural light.

Glass Profiles/Channel Glass Systems create an air void that helps develop better insulation/U values.

Plastic

The production of plastic involves **OIL** as a raw material and the use of energy. Many plastics can be recycled [10 times max?]; if not recycled plastic can take up to 500 years to decompose.

Polycarb – Polycarbonate is used widely in construction. Multiwall polycarbonate [extruded] has excellent thermal properties. Multiwall polycarbonate's thermal insulation coefficient can reach down to 1W/m² K. It can be fully recycled at the end of its life.

Figure 5.33 Sophisticated polycarbonate room divider screen. BAM Office, Berlin, by Gonzalez Haase AAS, 2019. Photo Credit: Thomas Meyer

PO   PVC   PU

Figure 5.34 Three common uses of plastic in interiors. **PO** polypropylene chair, Tip Ton Vitra chair; **PVC** 'dado' trunking for electrics and data; **PU** foam commonly used in seating and Upholstery.

> *Polycarb has good refraction qualities and can add to a contemporary look when used as an external façade material or within the interior environment.*

Plastic Types

PVC – Polyvinyl chloride can give off toxic gases both in situ and in the event of a fire [which is why you cannot use it on a laser cutter].

PO – polyolefin – It is not as flexible as PVC. Created with oil and natural gas by a process of polymerisation, it is used in garden furniture, microwave dishes and plastic plumbing pipes.

PU – Polyurethane is used widely in high traffic and industrial zones and in insulation products [SIP panels]. PU is available as a rigid or flexible material.

INTERIOR WALL AND FLOOR FINISHES

Wooden Floor Surfaces

Parquet Flooring – It comes in various geometric configurations, the most common being herringbone.

Bamboo – It is a sustainable and quick growing material that has good CO_2 absorption credentials and has a good level of oxygen production.

Cork – It is sustainable and quick growing [it can also be used as a wall cladding] and it offers a good level of thermal and noise insulation. It is biodegradable and its production is environmentally friendly/sustainable.

Laminated Floors – Either a wood veneer or in most cases it is an image of the material it is [printed on paper]. Laminated floors are difficult to repair; so they have a limited life span. Used in refurb work as can be laid directly over existing floor finishes due to typically being only 7mm thick.

Tiles

Stone – Common stone tiles for domestic and commercial interiors include marble, granite, limestone, travertine, slate and sandstone. Stone is a hard-wearing surface that is good to use in wet environments [when treated]. It also performs well with underfloor heating. Stone is also used widely as a wall cladding.

Figure 5.35 Parquet, bamboo, cork and laminate

Figure 5.36 Unconventional use of standard white glazed ceramic tiles as a wall cladding. DROP KHAWANEEJ. Photo Credit: design by roar – quartzite stone used 'structurally' externally and internally for the Therma Spa, Val, Switzerland, 2012. Peter Zumthor. Photo Credit: 7132 Therma Spa

Figure 5.37 The original linoleum floor in the Bauhaus Bernau ADGB Trade Union School, corridor, 1928–1930. Photo Credits: Eberle & Eisfeld Fotografie + Grafik GbR Rubber flooring in a classic rubber stud relief

Ceramics – There are three types of ceramic tiles: Glazed, Unglazed and Porcelain. Glazed tiles have a glass-like coating; unglazed tiles do not carry a surface treatment, such as terracotta tiles. Porcelain tiles have strength and can carry a translucence depending on their composition. Recently in interiors you see ceramic tiles fashioned to look like stone and wooden floors. Ceramics are also used widely as a wall cladding in bathrooms and kitchens.

Vinyl

Vinyls are used widely within interiors as they are a cost-effective choice, resistant to chemicals and knocks and are waterproof. They can be recycled the same as plastic but suffer from the same production issues as the raw material used to produce it is OIL. There is also growing evidence that they add to an unhealthy interior environment for a period after installing, emitting VOCs [Volatile Organic Compounds]. Vinyl floors are quite common and quick to install; vinyl is often used as a wall covering in clinical environments.

Linoleum – Modern 'Lino' is made up of flax seed oil, wood flour, pine rosins, pigment and jute as a backing. Linoleum is the most natural covering that is available to the designer. Flooring contractors prefer to use vinyl as it is more flexible to lay.

Rubber – Today's commercial rubber is rarely a fully 'natural' product; it is a combination of natural and industrial rubbers that are derived from petroleum. The rubber element is the sustainable ingredient.

Textiles – Carpet Natural and Synthetic

Carpet Tiles have long been a staple of commercial office design; they offer a satisfactory level of acoustic and thermal insulation, and are easy to install and cheap in flooring terms. Synthetic carpets are normally made of nylon, polyester or polypropylene; they offer good wear and stain resistance.

Natural Carpets are traditionally wool, sisal or jute; they tend to be more expensive and due to being a natural material are more susceptible to damage if not treated.

Recycled Carpeting is becoming more widely available and features recycled elements from fishing nets to PVB plastic in laminated glass car windscreens.

Wallpaper and Wall Textiles

Wallpaper comes in various finishes:

Lining Paper was traditionally used to line a room horizontally before the application of a horizontal finish paper. Today lining paper is widely used as a base for a painted finish; it is useful to stabilise existing walls that are of heritage construction [such as lath and plaster]. Woodchip is another basic wallpaper that is often used to disguise imperfections in walls.

Paper-Based Printed Wallpaper normally carries a pattern on the front, with a protective finish so it can be wiped clean.

Block Printed Wallpaper is traditionally printed on paper using a template block. The block is coated in ink/paint and then pressed onto the paper. Multiple colours and blocks make up the finished paper.

Flock Wallpapers are traditionally made with powdered wool, a waste product of the woollen industry, which is shaken over a fabric prepared with a design printed in varnish or size (a substance like glue). The powdered wool forms a rich pile that sticks to those areas covered by the design.

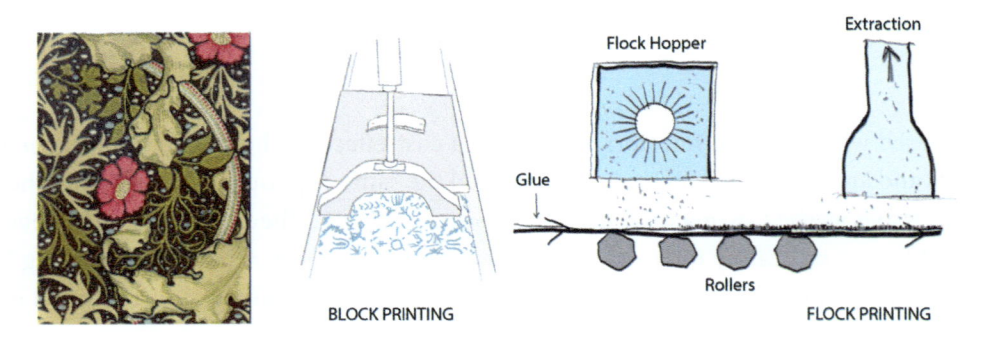

Figure 5.38 William Morris wallpaper design 214716 – Morris Seaweed Ebony poppy traditional block printing wallpaper. Flock wallpaper process

Figure 5.39 Digital texture. Image Credit: Tektura Wallcoverings Texture Linen wall covering – Linosa. Image Credit: Vescom 3D textured vinyl wallcovering – Shannon. Image Credit: Vescom

Vinyl Wallpaper offers a greater level of protection and is often used in high traffic areas as it can take multiple 'rubs or knocks.' It can be solid vinyl or a coating applied to a paper base. This type of paper offers bespoke options such as digitally printed images.

Fabric Wallpaper is a thin fabric sheet glued to a backing [vinyl or paper].

> *Most wallpaper/coverings come in a flat version or are embossed with a surface pattern. Fabric will normally carry the texture of the textile. Vinyl coverings can be moulded [blown] to represent 3D objects such as bricks or tiles.*
>
> *Traditionally wallpaper is applied to the wall using wallpaper paste; in commercial settings and with higher-end wallcoverings PVA glue is used, which creates a strong bond and limits the chance of staining on the covering.*

Coatings

Paint and Varnish come in interior and exterior formulas. Traditionally finishes are oil or water based but in recent years there has been a greater push towards water-based formulas as they are kinder to the environment and user. Oil-based paints and varnishes work better with exterior wood and are still often specified as a finish for new external timber.

Figure 5.40 WYBC RADIO STATION OFFICE, Forma Architects 2020. Powder-coated light: Light Flowers, design by Studio Tord Boontje, photography by Studio Tord Boontje

Paints and varnishes come in gloss, satin eggshell and matt finishes, gloss being the hardest in terms of wear and tear [it is able to take a knock which is why it is often used on skirting].

> *Bold colour blocking was used as an economical yet highly impactful strategy to create identity and provide space definition within the interiors.*
>
> (FORMA architects)
>
> *The stems and flowers are laser-cut from steel and then formed by hand in our studio. The parts are powder coated.*
>
> (Studio Tord Boontje)

Emulsion Paint – Paint can be used as a cost-effective strategy to define space on a low budget. Interior wall finishes are normally water-based emulsions and available in matt and satin finishes. They are applied by brush or roller but in industrial; commercial settings can be sprayed.

Powder Coating steel is the process of applying dry powder through an electrostatic process, then curing with heat – there are a series of RAL colours [European colour matching standardisation] that helps maintain consistency when specifying colours.

Curtains, Voiles, Wall Hangings, Blinds

Curtains come in many materials; some of the most common are cotton, silk and polyester. They offer good levels of acoustic and thermal insulation, especially when installed over windows and doors.

Voile is a sheer transparent fabric that provides a degree of privacy while still letting the light through. Voiles provide a contemporary take on curtains within the interior environment and are available in acoustic sound absorbing materials.

Figure 5.41 Traditional curtain entrance to restaurant creating a lobby area in harsh weather. Momo Grill, Studio Manikas Manike, 2013. Photo and Project Credit: Ramunas Manikas Movable curtain sets up an event space within a Tokyo fashion store. Pan Projects/Haruki Oku Design. Tokyo, 2020. Photo Credit: Kenji Seo Voile 'acoustic sheers' used to define space and absorb sound. Image Credit: Vescom

> *The use of curtains and sheers in interiors has myriad advantages. They can tell part of a holistic colour and material story, soak spaces in comfort and quietness, connect or divide a room, and block or dim natural light.*
>
> (Vescom)

Blinds, Shutters, Hangings

Blinds offer a more contemporary approach to black out and privacy as they tend to be fitted within the window element or even within glazing, thus retaining the opening and reveals of the interior architecture. There are similar material options as are available for curtains.

Shutters are often used to control solar gain into buildings, aid ventilation and provide shade – they can also help keep heat in when the climate turns cold.

Hangings have recently been introduced in the interior space as a way of defining space but also to add to the acoustic performance of space; they also add a contemporary decorative element to an interior scheme.

Figure 5.42 Plectere curve hanging wall panels, a combination of digital fabrication and natural sustainable materials. Design: Petra Vonk. Photo Credit: Filzfelt

Figure 5.43 Pleat system RSW, brand Caussa. Images courtesy of RSW Karuun raw material before working and finishing. Images courtesy of RSW

> *Braided wool felt strips come together to make a soft and three-dimensional hanging panel that comes in two standard sizes – Quarter Circle and Half Circle. The panels divide space and soften sound with their thick wool felt strips.*
>
> (Flizfelt)

OTHER INTERIOR FINISHES

Future Materials – Other materials derived from waste products and sustainable sources.

One of the fundamental questions around materials is how we use what we have produced rather than producing more.

Karuun* is a plastic alternative derived from the ratta plant.

> *Pleat is produced of the unique and future-oriented wooden material Karuun, based on the raw material rattan, which gains new color and surface characteristics by injecting natural fillers. Karuun is a sustainable alternative to conventional materials since the rattan palm needs healthy trees to climb on, which leads in the end to rain-forest protection.*
>
> (RSW)

Figure 5.44 Newspaperwood blocks. Image Credit: Newspaperwood. ORB waste sheet material prototype. Image courtesy of BIOHM Mycelium insulation panel. Image courtesy of BIOHM

NEWSPAPERWOOD – Newspaperwood reverses a traditional production process; not from wood to paper, but from (news)paper to wood.

> *NewspaperWood is the result of a 2003 project by Design Academy Eindhoven graduate Mieke Meijer. Since then a custom-made, fully automatic machine has been developed to produce a high-quality product from residual material from the paper industry. The material itself can be recycled again within the existing cycle of paper recycling.*
>
> (Newspaperwood)

Food Waste – Orb [Organic Refuse Bio-compound].
Naturally bound organic waste [food waste] formed into sheet materials for construction and interiors.

> *Orb is manufactured from difficult to reuse or recycle by-products; utilising resources that would otherwise go to landfill.*
>
> (Biohm)

Mycelium – Fucredit Fungus derived insulation panels; an alternative to PU 'SIP' panels.
Recycled plastic – Sheet panels made from chopping boards and plastic packaging – Smile plastics

Figure 5.45 Smile plastics recycled plastic sheet sample

We take waste plastics and other materials traditionally classed as waste and transform them through our unique processes into large scale, solid surface panels.

We tend to focus on single-use plastic packaging and other materials that would usually find their way to landfill. We chose these plastics to disrupt the unsustainable industrial ecosystems that have become the norm whereby finite and useful materials have very short, single lives.

(Smile Plastics)

CASE STUDY – RECYCLE

Discarded Things, Horumon Kappo Ryu – Hokkaido, Japan

Kamitopen Co., Ltd., Architects, 2019

Kamitopen Co., Ltd., Architects' restaurant design in Tokyo, Japan, is a forward-looking example of how materials from the built environment can be repurposed using materials that would normally be discarded in the refit process.

Figure 5.46 The reclaimed plasterboard, dry lined in an unusual fashion. Photo Credit: Keisuke Miyamoto. The plasterboard reversed to reveal the trade stamp. Photo Credit: Keisuke Miyamoto

Figure 5.47 Collected together, the steel studs combined to create a wall. Photo Credit: Keisuke Miyamoto wood and bamboo finish adds extra texture to the space. Photo Credit: Keisuke Miyamoto Reclaimed floor is left with the patina of the previous use. Photo Credit: Keisuke Miyamoto

Recycled Plasterboard

The unusual plasterboard finish is reclaimed from the existing interior and reassembled within the main restaurant eating area. The exposed plasterboard joints combined with the plaster board backing [and text branding] create a 'stripped back' interior that not only celebrates the raw material but signals a new level of repurposing.

Steel Studs

The steel studs that held the interior partitions have also been repurposed, used to create a steel enclosure. The inventive appropriation of this common building material is assembled to create a high level of finish [steel shine] that juxtaposes against the rawness of the plaster boarded wall and ceiling.

Figure 5.48 Bamboo tabletop constructed out of bamboo chop sticks. Photo Credit: Keisuke Miyamoto. Close-up detail of the tabletop. Photo Credit: Keisuke Miyamoto

Repurposing Wood

The floor is a repurposed existing wooden floor, not perfect in finish; the patina of previous use and machining helps to add texture and detail to the space.

Laminating old and new – Tabletops were sourced from reclaimed timber. They have a new layer of 'laminated' chopsticks added to the top surface, which provides a hard-wearing surface.

> *The new and the old work together to create a 'sustainable' interior that pushes to the forefront what is possible when designers embrace the repurposing of existing materials from a 'typical' existing project site. The project embraces one of the major questions around materials used in interior design and architecture; it does that within a commercial design context, which is notable as that is the sector of interior design that has a less than enviable record of specifying the 'latest' sustainable materials.*

Designed by Masahiro Yoshida and Tae Fukami
Photos by Keisuke Miyamoto

MATERIAL SIZING: RULE OF THUMB

When appropriate, rule of thumb calculations are useful for drawing up construction materials with appropriate sizes such as the typical spacings in a wooden/plaster stud wall or a steel/timber floor section in detail.

These are 'rule of thumb' and any structural alterations would be checked by a structural engineer or onsite by the appropriate tradesperson. A series of quick calculations can add an increased level of detail to a design drawing and demonstrate you have a good understanding of the construction being proposed.

Basic Wooden Construction

Basic wooden softwood construction [standard c16] – other wood types and engineered woods can increase the span and decrease the column size.

Columns – Wooden columns 1:20 ratio

Beams – Beams 1:20 ratio

Floor Joists – Domestic floor joists at 400 mm centres [standard c16]
220 × 38 mm/Span 4 m

Stud Partition – 400 mm centres + noggings for bracing [600 with thicker material]
Stud sizes: 75 mm × 50 mm or 100 mm × 50 mm sawn timber

Steel Construction

Columns – For three- to five-storey buildings' mezzanine structure
254 × 254 UC [Universal Column] column is the starting point
When drawing in a steel column in plan 254 mm UC is adequate

Beams – steel beams, sections with a span/depth ratio of 18–20 are typically used, i.e., for a span of 8 m, the steel beam will be approximately 450 mm deep
When drawing in a steel beam in section 450 mm is adequate

Stud Partition – 400 mm centres/50–70 mm width – different gauges of steel [thickness] dependent on application.

OUTPUTS

- **Introduction**
- **2D Drawing Sets, Conventions and Portfolio**
- **3D Representation – Conventions/Portfolio**
- **2D Prototyping – Laser Cutter**
- **3D Printing/CNC Milling**
- **Microcomputers**

INTRODUCTION

Chapter 6 looks at the physical and digital outputs that are utilised to present an interior design proposal. It maps along with the processes as set out in Chapters 1–5 with a focus on output, additional portfolio advice and digital fabrication. As an accompaniment to Chapter 4's digital transformation a more detailed account of microcomputing is also covered, the Raspberry Pi and its bespoke potentials in simple presentation and computing tasks.

Overview

The successful communication of a design proposal is one of the most important skills a designer needs to develop. You can have the strongest conceptual base but if you cannot communicate it visually using the correct mediums or the correct drawing conventions soon the academic or professional focus moves towards the illegibility of the project proposal.

One approach rarely fits all and judgement is required to work out what medium would suit best; for example, a model may be more effective than plans for a complex spatial communication or a key section may be better than a model, etc. The decision needs to be a strategic choice and should relate back to the design proposal.

Computers have their part to play in the communication of a design proposal but only a part [see Chapter 7]. Effective output is a designer's choice, something a computer will not be able to

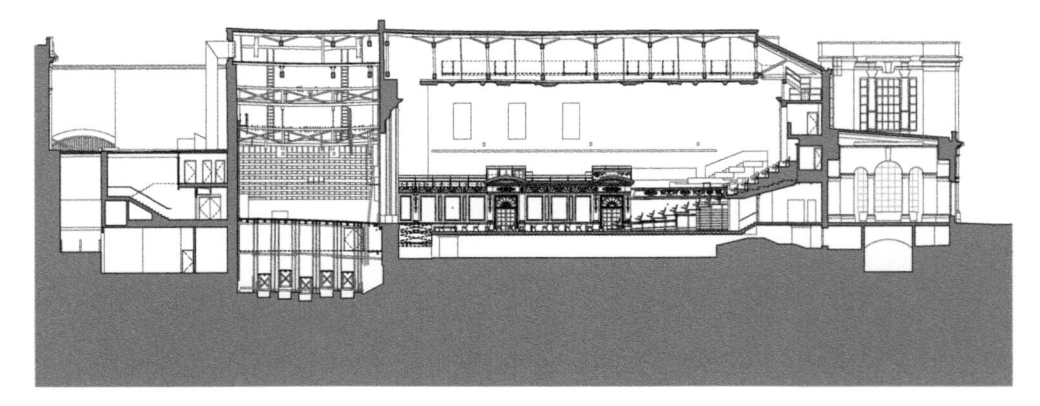

Figure 6.1 Long section of Alexandra Palace, London. FCB Studios, 2018. The historic background information has been included in this section to communicate the ornate context and detail of the existing building

DOI: 10.4324/9781003120650-7

Figure 6.2 Interior image of Alexander Palace, London. FCB Studios, 2018. Photo Credit: ©Feilden Clegg Bradley Studios

work out for you. For example, there is yet a computer program that can apply basic rule sets in annotation, drawing layouts and line thickness [including Revit].

> *We use the term 'arrested decay' to describe an approach of consolidation rather than restoration. In treating rooms as found spaces, the processes of deterioration have been addressed, elements that were unsafe or could not be viably repaired have been removed, added elements are legibly modern.*
>
> *These additions are informed by the grand scale of the Victorian palace and the ambitions it represents and are marked out by a scale and materiality that identifies them as new. At the same time, this is just one more layer added to many previous ones, another chapter in the history of Alexandra Palace.*
>
> (FBC Studios)

2D DRAWING SETS, CONVENTIONS AND PORTFOLIO

This section is an introduction to the final presentation of drawings, 2D print which is increasingly becoming a digital representation through screen-based methods such as Miro whiteboards, PowerPoints or PDF presentations.

In the case of printed or digital output the same rules 'should' apply when putting together a final presentation. Digital presentations suffer from scale issues as does CAD work (Computer Aided Design). The lack of editing drawings can be disruptive to the composition as it provides an infinite drop box where quantity can override legibility and quality.

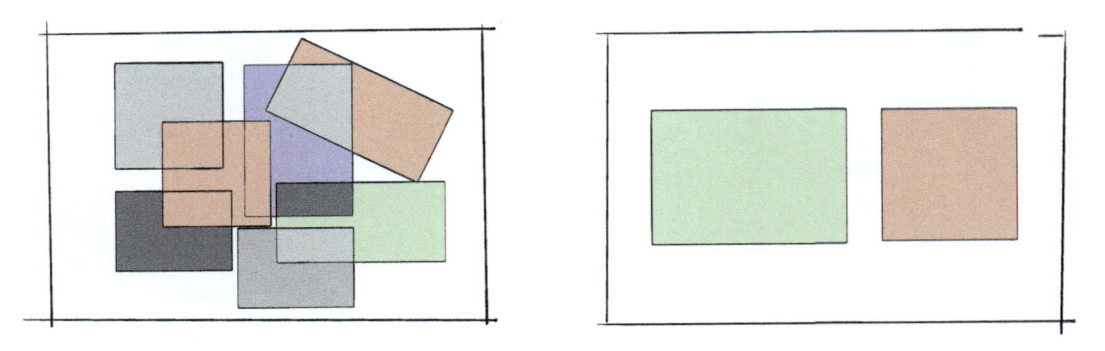

Figure 6.3 Image overload to the left – it's difficult to focus on the content when too much imagery is included; use the surrounding paper space, and follow a graphic grid

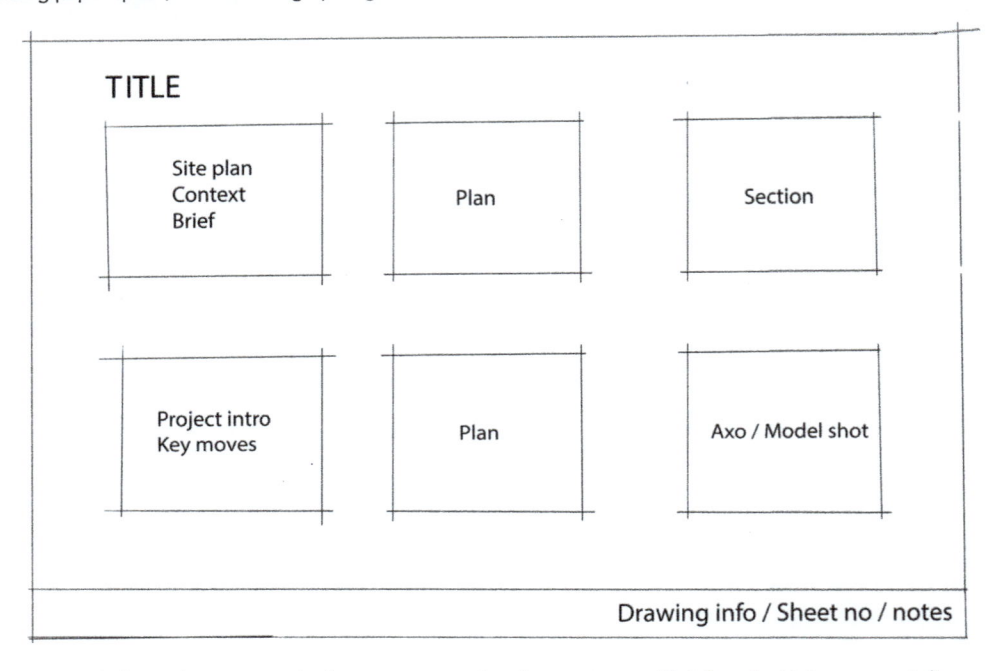

Figure 6.4 A typical one-sheet composite layout strategy: site plan, context and brief, project intro, concept diagrams, plans and section

Composite Drawings

Often you will present your design through a set of presentation drawings or as a composite sheet [a collection of drawings on one sheet]. Typically these will comprise:

A title for each page drawing
An existing site plan, contextual information, information on the brief
Project introduction/key conceptual moves
A set of plans for each floor
At least one key section so you can get the spatial relationships

A set of elevations if there are any alterations to the building

A 3D representation; an axonometric, isometric, physical model, perspective or perspective model shot

> *Legibility is not boring. It's an essential professional practice to effectively present and read a set of drawings. The creative content is the drawing's spatial design information and cannot be compensated for with graphics alone.*

Layout

Graphic Grid – Use a simple graphic grid when setting up your presentation sheet; this can be done well in advance of a final project submission.

Figure 6.5 Drawings are often accompanied by a 3D representation; an axonometric, isometric, physical model, perspective, or perspective model shot. Image Credit. Abigail Newton

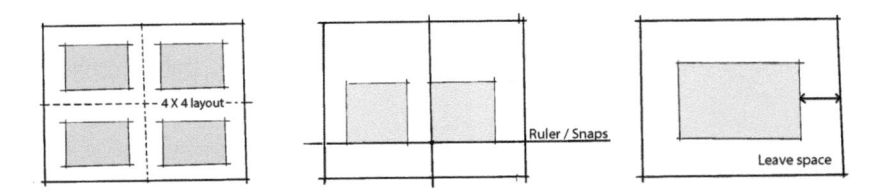

Figure 6.6 An A1 sheet prepared and subdivided into 4 × A4s. Use rulers and snaps so that drawings are lined up next to each other. Leave some paper space around the drawings

Use rulers or a grid if available.

Prepare scaled drawing boxes even before the drawing are finished so you have the composition set-up.

Avoid predefined overly graphic layouts [initially] as they can detract from your design drawings

A traditional sheet format is A1/a typical digital format is A3.

> *You can normally break down an A1 format into 4 × A3 sheets and use it to maintain the formal hierarchy [for portfolio submissions]; so it can be useful to set up an A1 sheet in this way.*

Space – Leave some 'white' space between the drawings and within the drawing frames – it allows you to read the individual drawings.

Scale – Pick an appropriate scale for your drawings; incorrect drawing scale can be counterproductive. Drawings at a scale of 1:100 or even 1:50 have an ambiguity that may be useful if certain areas have not been resolved in detail. If a drawing is set or drawn at 1:20 you expect sufficient detail to warrant the space being taken up in the presentation.

Introductory Information

Title – Title text is key to the initial engagement with your scheme proposal, and the font used has design intent in it. The use of inappropriate fonts can set the incorrect tone for a scheme proposal, so choose wisely. If unsure use a default architectural font such as Helvetica.

Serif fonts are more decorative; they have a small cap/tick at the end **T** and they can read better at a smaller scale.

Sans Serif fonts have no caps T; they work well for signs or where there is little room for text, and they are often viewed as more modern and are thus used widely by designers.

Font size should be proportionate to the paper size [even if digital]. You can normally read 24–40-point fonts from quite some distance so oversized text can look quite odd in any presentation especially when printed.

Existing Plan/Site Plan – It is important that the existing site plan/building plan does not override in scale and proportion the design drawings; depending on the scale of the building a smaller scale should be used such as 1:200 or 1:500 for a site plan.

 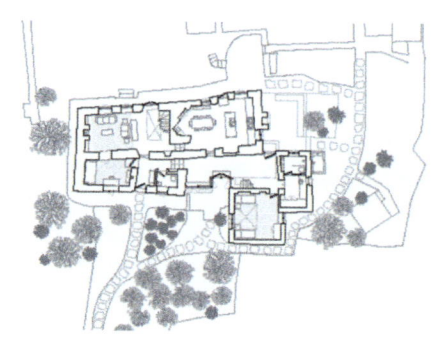

Figure 6.7 Cornish cottage, Jonathan Tuckey Design. A plan and model communicating the historic context of the 400-year-old cottage and reinforcing the environmental context

The site plan should not be too dominant.

It's ok to use a scan or OS map rather than draw it out as they can be quite detailed.

A site plan or existing plan should be at the introduction of a drawing set or composite sheet.

Any contextual readings/diagrams should also be in this 'initial' area.

You can annotate as site plan with site context such as sun path or elements of significance.

> *The design retains and adapts the original agricultural structure by providing organisation of spaces, improving its thermal envelope, and designates a new use as a rugged, dependable home.*
>
> (Jonathan Tuckey Design)

Project Introduction/Key Conceptual Moves – It is useful to have an introduction to the set brief, which should be summarised for the occasion – for example, if a client has set the brief or if the tutor has set up a recital of that information, which is of little use, this type of bulky text is often used adversely to fill up space, and it can add to the 'illegibility' of the project proposal.

Key Conceptual Diagrams should explain the reasoning behind the design accompanied by a small amount of text if useful; they should be used as an introduction to the final drawings.

Keep the project introduction and conceptual explanation diagrams/drawings in the same area so they can be read together.

Logically they should follow on from the context information [normally we read left to right].

The information should not dominate any of the final technical drawings.

Avoid the use of longwinded paragraphs [especially cut and copied from the brief].

Use a title, subtext and body text rather than paragraphs [ABC text].

Font size should never exceed 16 points [11–16] in these areas as that is legible in print and on screen.

 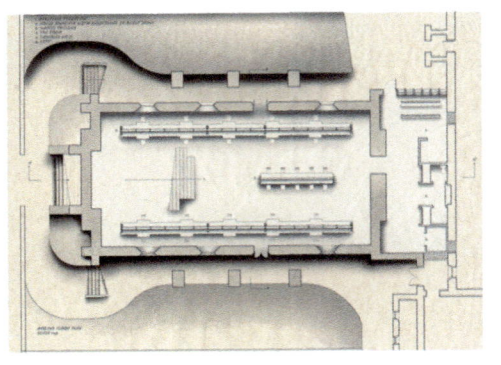

Figure 6.8 Diagrams used to accompany the orthographic drawings, expressing the key moves. Courtesy of Delyth Williams

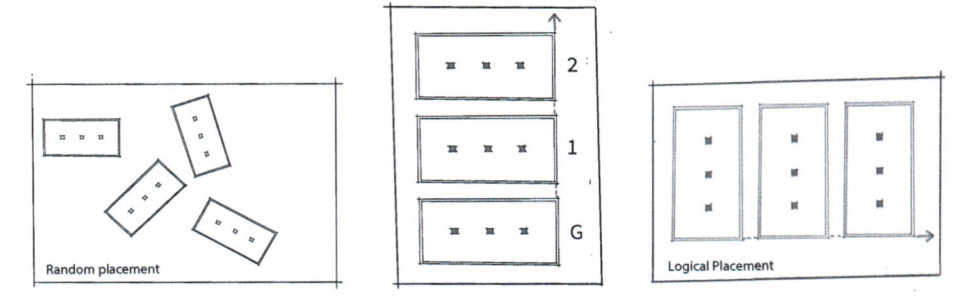

Figure 6.9 A diagram demonstrating the misplacement of multiple floor plans. Plans should be lined up vertically or horizontally – they should be placed from basement up

Design Drawings

Plans

Plans – A common mistake is to dot plans and sections around to add some 'graphic' intent to the presentation. For legibility this is not good practice as it makes the relationship between the drawing sets difficult to read.

Plans should be laid out in a sequential fashion so that they line up either vertically or horizontally; in this way you can read the structural and spatial information in parallel from floor to floor – ideally orientated towards north or a north arrow annotated next to plans.

They should be at the same scale laid out from ground [or basement if you have one] up, the same as a lift so G, 1, 2, 3, etc.

The ground floor plan should indicate context such as the pavement, garden, an adjacent building – subsequent floors do not need the ground context but any roof information per floor is useful to include.

A basement plan or subterranean floor should be surrounded with solid to indicate it is in the ground.

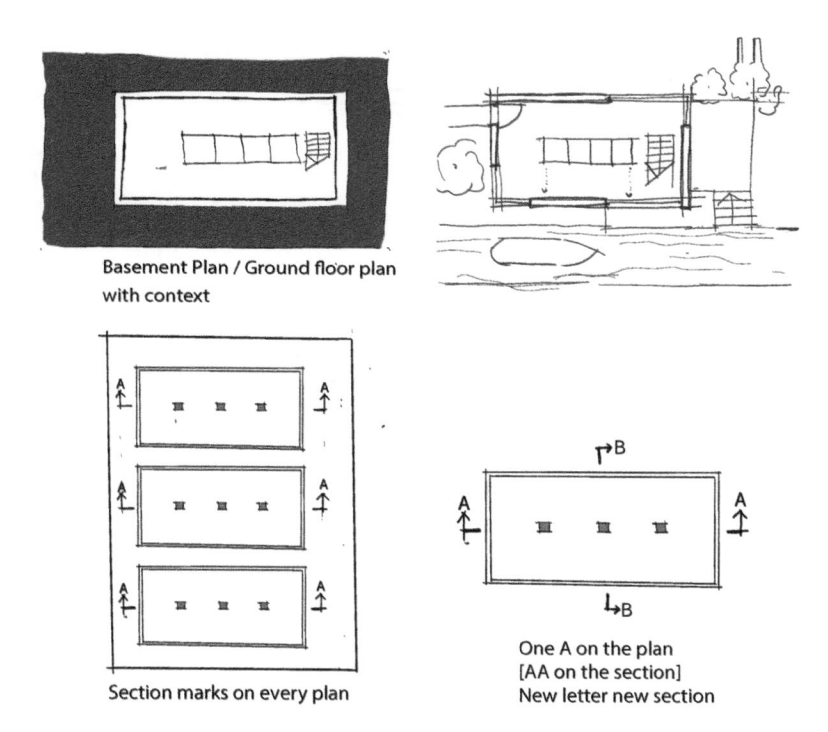

Basement Plan / Ground floor plan
with context

Section marks on every plan

One A on the plan
[AA on the section]
New letter new section

Figure 6.10 A basement plan if in the ground should indicate a mass around the plan. A ground floor plan should always define the exterior context if it has one; section marks should be in the same place on all floor plans – the arrow indicates the direction the section is looking. Use a new letter for a new section

Section Marks are important indicators of where the section has been taken; they are often left out or placed incorrectly on plans.

Create a new section mark for each section taken; e.g., section AA and BB.
The double letter AA or BB represent the two points where the section has been taken. Only label the singular on the plan and the double [AA] on the section drawing annotation.
Section marks should not go through the plan; they should be offset.

Line Weights play a very important role in describing the CUT so you can read the structure of the building and the new interventions that have taken place. Traditionally, line weights were set to ink pen widths .5, .35, .25, .18 so we still use that terminology. Today you're more likely to be on a computer so you can still set them in the traditional way; if drawing by hand you are likely to be using a technical pen set .1. 3 or .5, which is fine as long as you follow the basic line weight principles.

.5 or higher is used to indicate the cut through structure – sometimes a solid infill is used in black or grey; this can be fine if it does not detract from the detail of the drawing.
.35 [or .3] can be used to show the cut through fixed furniture and internal partitions – it is useful to be able to distinguish between the solid structure and the new build elements.
.25 [or .2] is used for other elements such as the stairs, doors, furniture that has not been cut through and basic window details.

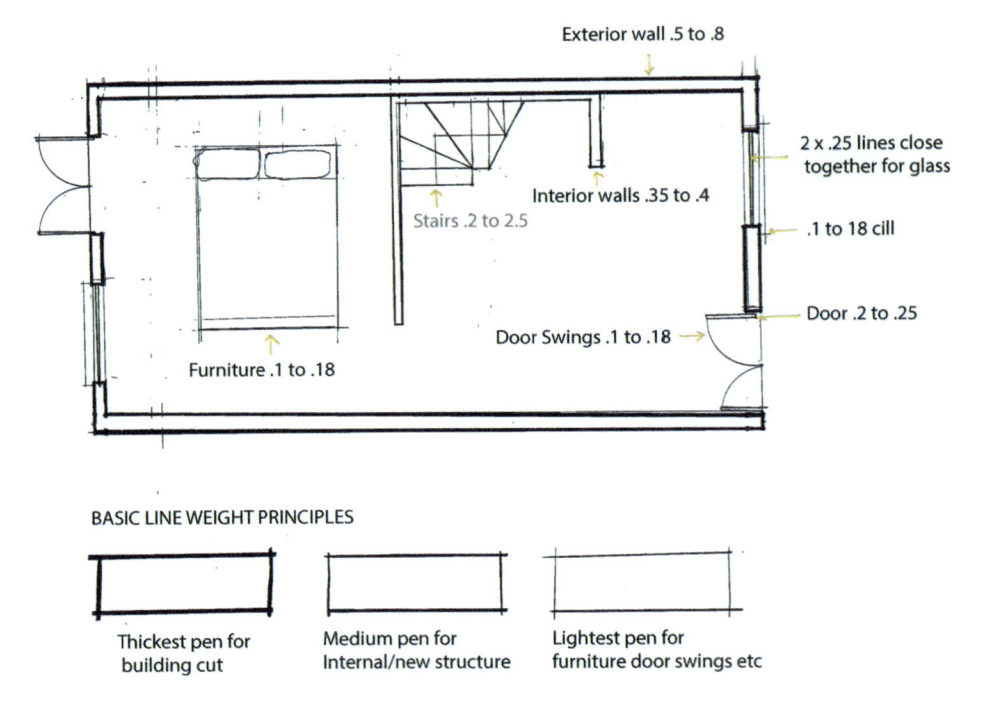

Exterior wall .5 to .8

2 x .25 lines close together for glass

Interior walls .35 to .4

Stairs .2 to 2.5

.1 to 18 cill

Door .2 to .25

Door Swings .1 to .18 →

Furniture .1 to .18

BASIC LINE WEIGHT PRINCIPLES

Thickest pen for building cut

Medium pen for Internal/new structure

Lightest pen for furniture door swings etc

Figure 6.11 A plan drawing indicating the line weights that should be used in a final drawing. Basic line weight principles

.18 [or .1] should be used for door swings, dotted lines [overhead and information through an object]. It is also used for insignificant elements such as floor patterns, plants, computers, etc.

Another line weight approach used is that the further away it is the lighter the line weight; so with relation to the cut being the thickest [closest] this may also work as a strategy.

> *Line weights are a guidance; you can always thicken up lines further to ensure you define the cut effectively.*
> *CAD: print regularly [even if digital] to check proportions and legibility as you develop your drawing sets. Print a 'small' section to print scale rather than the whole drawing.*

Stairs – A plan is generally taken at about 1m so it can show window openings and cuts though key structural and internal structural elements. Working on that principle a cut in the stairs should be shown at each level at about 1m [normally 5–6 steps]; the other principle is you only show what you can see below.

Starting at a ground floor or basement plan the stairs get cut at 1m and you only show the five to six steps [sometimes the above extents are dotted in to define the stair area].

Each subsequent floor will show the cut at 1m on that floor and everything you can see below, [sometimes with the previous floors cut for reference].

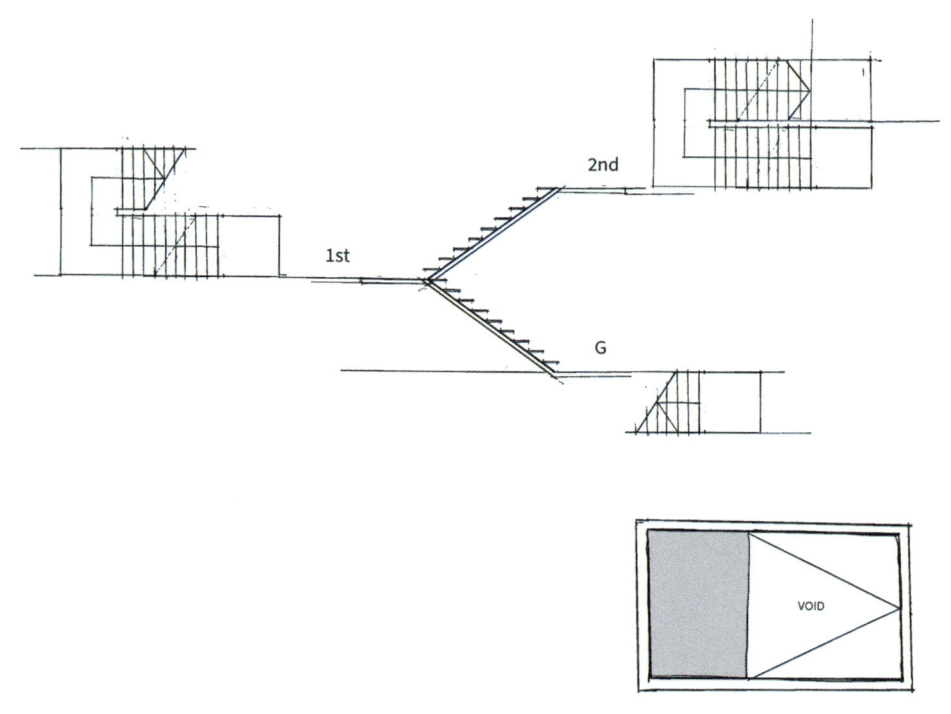

Figure 6.12 Diagram expressing how a dog leg stairs would look like in the floor plan of each drawing – note that on the ground floor you only show a few steps as that's what you can see when the plan is cut. Void – the different approaches to indicating a void in a plan – a fill/V through the space/or write void

Stairs are always shown going up [apart from the US].

It can be confusing to annotate up and down.

Voids – Void areas in a plan can be indicated with floor rendering to indicate solidity, V through the space [sometimes an X] or annotating void on the plan – normally just one approach is used rather than all.

Doors and door openings should be shown open, with the swing indicated with an arc.

Pocket, sliding, bifold, etc., are shown half open with dots to indicate direction of closure.

The main entrance to a building is indicated in a plan by a triangle.

Windows are not detailed in the same way as the structure when cut; the opening is defined in the structure, then the sill is drawn in a smaller pen weight (as you are not cutting through the sill). The glass is drawn using a thicker pen.

When drawing in the glass you normally use two to three lines close together [to indicate double or single glazing]; a .25 is normally sufficient to indicate a cut through glass; as the lines are so close together, they read thicker.

You do not show a standard window open in plan; you might if it is significant to the design proposal.

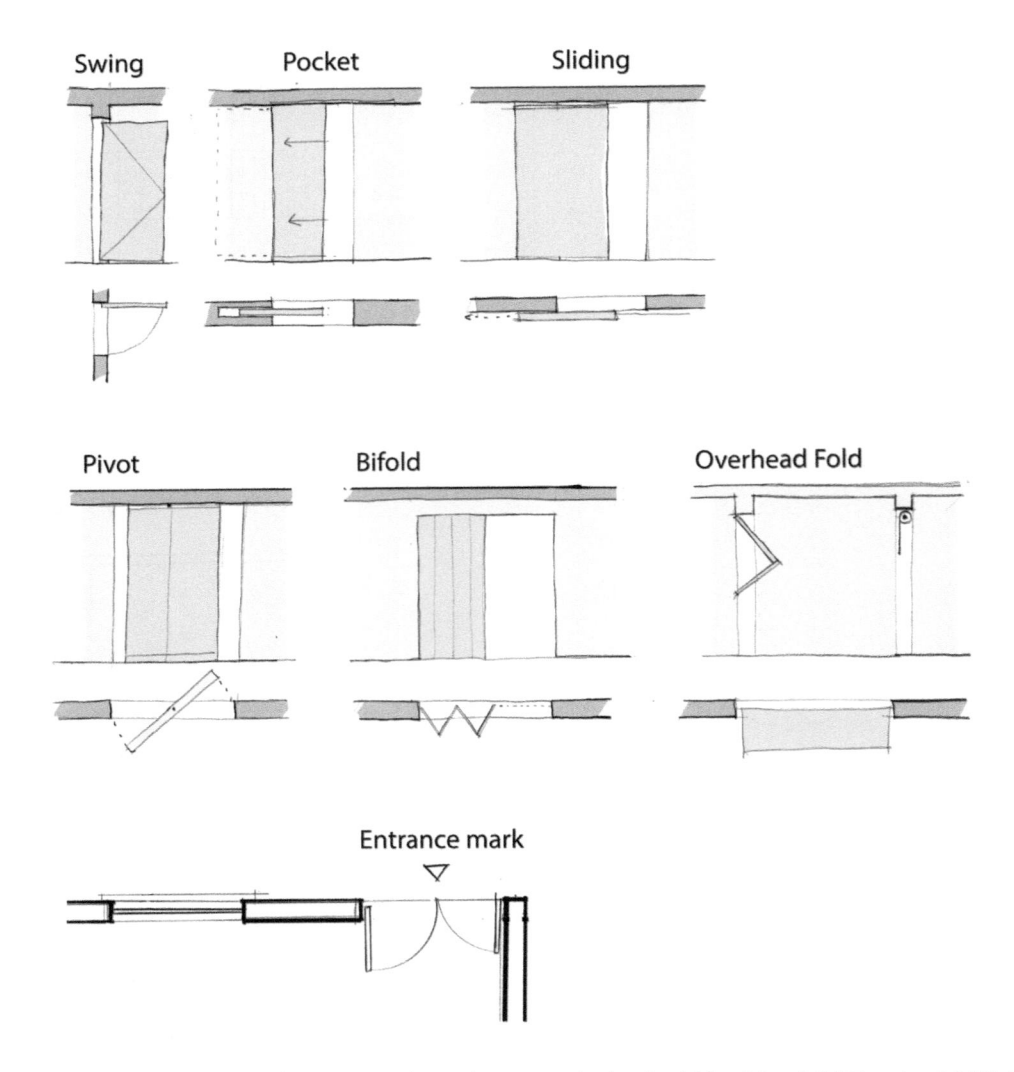

Figure 6.13 How to draw different door types in plan and section: swing/pocket/sliding/pivot/bifold/overhead fold/roller. A triangle indicates the entrance to a building

Sections

Sections are vertical cuts through the building and should in most cases include all the floors of the building; they should also include drawn references to any adjacent buildings. The simplest way to do this is to use a block or a few lines outside of the section, as we always read them as defining a new building/space.

Sections should be taken through the point of most information, through window openings, doors, voids, mezzanines, etc., to deliver as much spatial information as possible. It is a common fault to dodge these elements when drawing up a section as it will be easier [window dodgers]. That practice defeats the purpose of the section and can add to the illegibility of a drawing set.

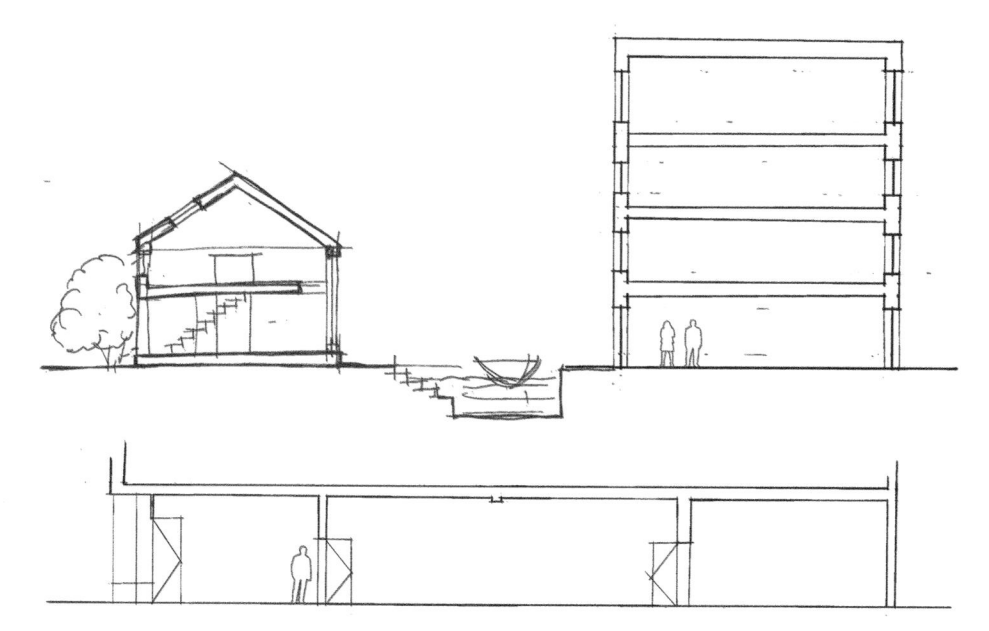

Figure 6.14 Sections through a double-storey and four-storey building – taken through the entire building. A section not including all the floors of the building – the vertical line caries on to indicate that there is another floor above

The section should show the contextual relationship – trees, rivers, anything that gives you an idea of the building's location.

All floors [where possible] should be included in the section to demonstrate exterior wall, floor, and roof thickness [even in an interior section]. If it is not possible then use the leading line technique.

Older structures are typically ornate so try to include that drawn information in the section.

The same line weight principles are applied to a section as they are to the plan. A section should relate to a plan to reinforce the understanding of the structure.

Use a scale person to indicate human scale in section [avoid infill silhouettes as they can be visually detracting].

> *You should maximise the information in the cut by taking the section through as many windows and door openings as possible [existing and new] to demonstrate the character of the building and to reinforce the spatial interventions made in the design.*

Stepped Section – a section can be stepped if that helps to show more – it should be a reserved action only happening once and still preserving the overall context of the drawing set.

> *Terms like long and short section are used when the building is rectangular and can be used to describe different spatial concepts.*

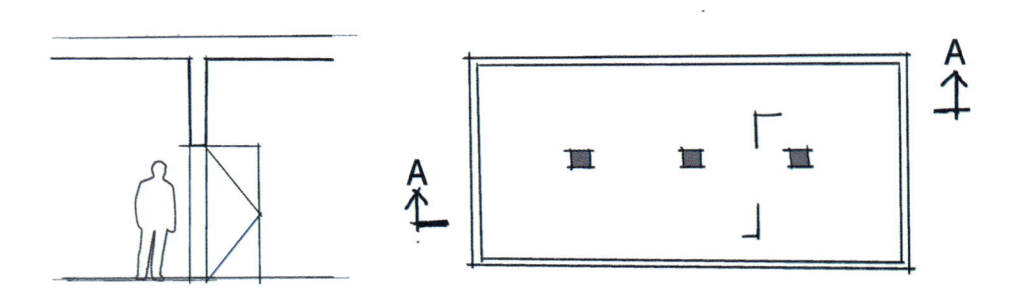

Figure 6.15 A triangle indicating door opening direction in section A. Stepped section moves within the plan from one point to another; it is indicated in the plan at the step point

You can show the direction of a door opening with a triangle [.18 pen].
A section is always a 2D drawing with NO perspective – unless it is a sectional perspective.
You see everything from the cut in the direction that you look – such as background windows, doors, furniture.

Elevations

Elevations are 2D exterior views of the façade; there are typically four façades on a building. They should be annotated by their orientation to a compass point, south elevation, west, east, etc.

Interior Elevations are not interior sections or exterior elevations; they are typically used to describe the interior elements of design such as wall finishes, kitchens and bedrooms – for example, a hotel room or specific seating area in a bar.

They should not be used as a replacement [because it is easier] to a section
It is good practice to include some additional information about the host building such as the thickness of the floor and ceilings – alternatively they can be profiled with an interior boundary line.
They are typically 2D drawings with no perspective.

Drawing Sheet Annotation

Key, **Legend**, and **Drawing Blocks** are important to describe accurately the spaces that have been created in a design. In well-developed drawings you will be able to tell what the spaces are as they would have gone to the next level of drawing, such as adding toilets [also known as blocks in CAD], beds into bedrooms or dining tables into dining areas. This helps describe the space but also to test out if the space works, to see if there is enough space to walk around the furniture, etc.

A Drawing Block/Template contains a note section, name of drawing, name of drafter, revision number, drawing number and date. It is a professional format that is an industry standard.

Rendered zones with a 'colour' key can be used to identify spaces but best used at smaller scales such 1:100 as it can eliminate the drawing detail.

Figure 6.16 An elevation that includes a wide context to contextualise the building, Sands End Arts and Community Centre, MAE Architects, 2020

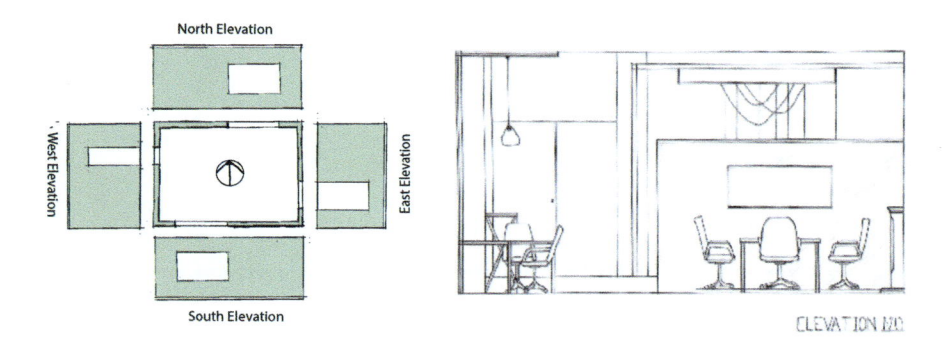

Figure 6.17 Elevations are arranged around a compass direction, south-south-west and east. A student interior elevation. Credit: Abigail Newton

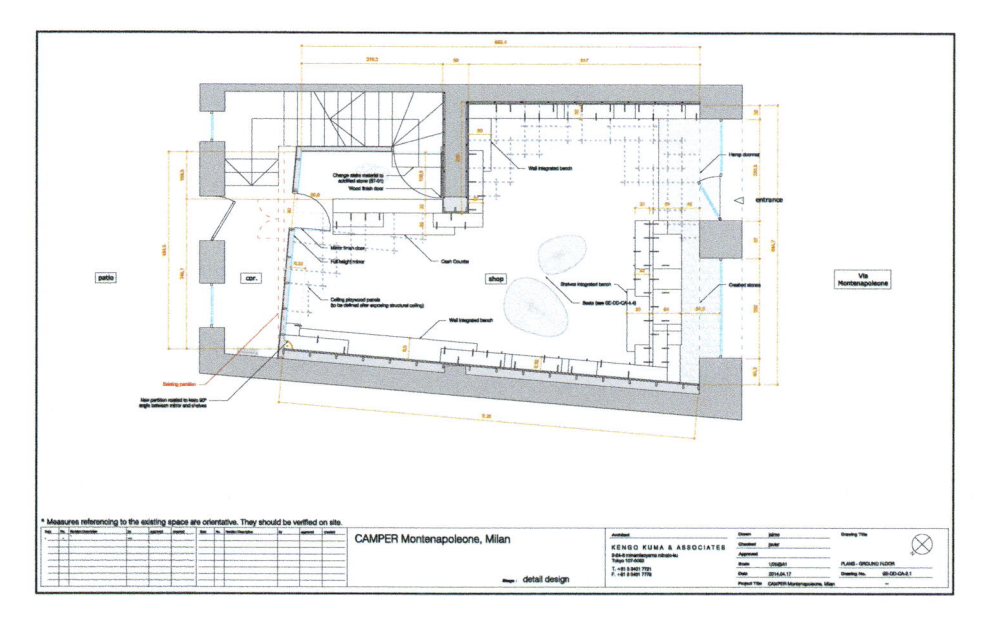

Figure 6.18 A commercial plan drawing with template title box. Credit: THE CAMPER SHOP – MILAN. KENGO KUMA ASSOCIATES, 2014. Design Team: Javier Villar Ruiz/Jaime Fernandez Calvache

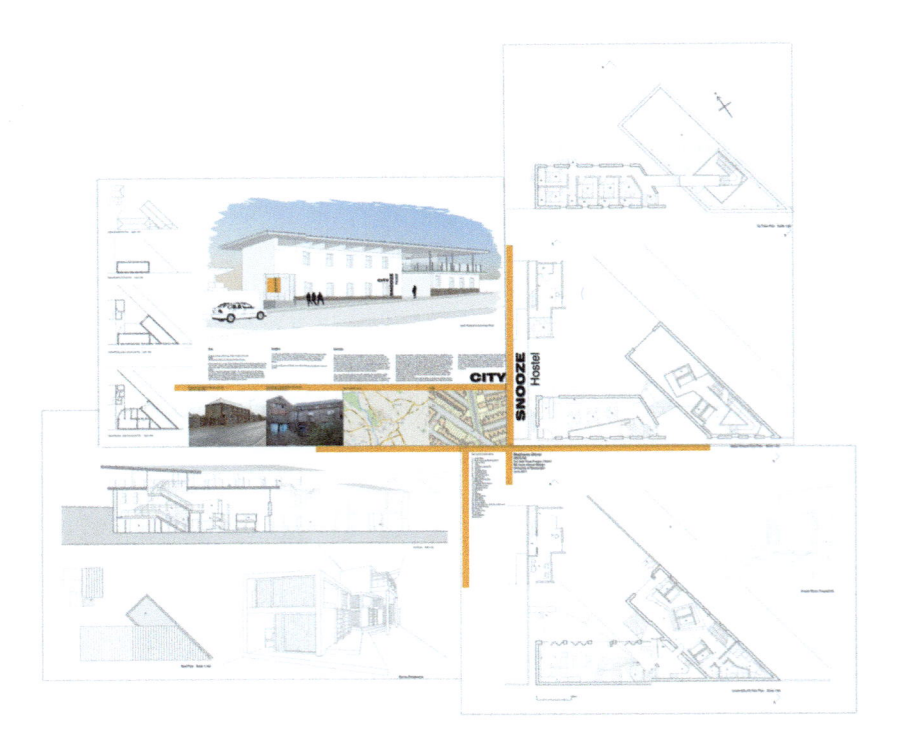

Figure 6.19 A student presentation that is annotated with a numbered legend/key to the spaces – presented in a graphic way but logical to the plan placement. Credit: Steph Glover

Basic Annotation – The scale of the drawing should be annotated to each drawing in the paper space [in the same position] or be specified in the drawing template box or a scale bar can be used. Only one method is required.

Annotation such as ground floor scale 1:100 font size should not dominate the drawings [16-point rule].

A key or legend is a layer of annotation and should not overwhelm the drawing it is describing [16-point rule]. You can use numbers and a key rather than text on the drawing if you are short on space.

> *Be careful of the style of furniture; some furniture blocks are very traditional and do not sit well in a contemporary space – most modern-day manufacturers supply 2D furniture blocks such as Vitra.*

3D REPRESENTATION – CONVENTIONS/PORTFOLIO

Most scheme proposals are accompanied by a model, visual or axonometric to reinforce what it would look like three-dimensionally. With the introduction of the computer and quick modelling programs such as SketchUp it has never been easier to generate a 3D representation.

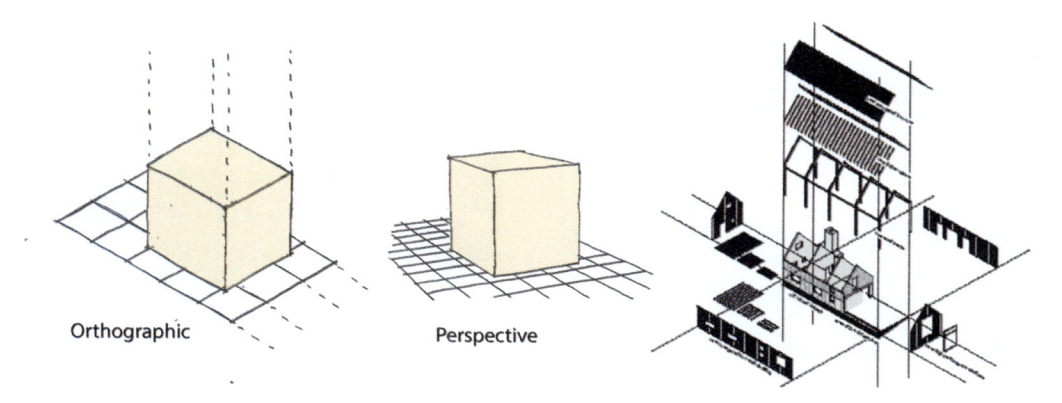

Orthographic

Perspective

Figure 6.20 3D orthographic view vs a perspective view. An exploded isometric that explains not only the scheme proposal but the way it works together as a set of building components. Credit: David Connor Design

An axonometric, perspective or model shot can help communicate a design scheme, but it will not replace the need for well-communicated plans and sections. Whether drafted and rendered by hand or on the computer they should also follow a set of conventions that will aid the legibility of the project communication.

Axonometric/Isometric – In computing it is extremely easy to toggle three-dimensionally around a drawing grabbing multiple views, sometimes without giving any additional design content. Be selective and pick one or two views that communicate the most relevant design content. If using a computer-generated model, you can post edit the image to work it up a higher level of detail.

If it is a complex view, consider exploding the axonometric rather than using multiple drawings to communicate how the space and structure work together.

Dot in walls that are in way of important design information.

Set the angle of the 3D model to 30/60 or 45/45 and if it is an axonometric/ISO set the view to orthographic NOT perspective – perspective can distort the spatial information.

Perspectives – If drawing by hand a perspective can be one, two or three points [you can also set this up within a CAD interface], all increasing in complexity of draughtsmanship. Like computing with a 3D model, CAD perspectives are easy to generate multiple times.

Be selective in your view selection as one good perspective is always preferable to ten poor ones. When first starting out keep it simple and use your artistic skills to post edit in Photoshop.

Set the perspective view to eye height [keep the viewers' feet on the ground and not levitating] for a natural view, as you would personally experience in the space.

Set an asymmetric view to make the view more dynamic and give more emphasis to a design feature.

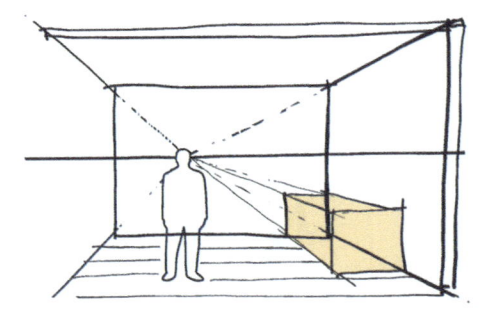 

Figure 6.21 A one-point perspective view [see Chapter 3] set to an asymmetrical view. A CAD-generated perspective that has had materials, shadows and context added in Photoshop

Figure 6.22 A model used to explain the shelving insertion/structure within the given space. Malin + Gotetz, Islington London. Jonathan Tuckey Design

A one-point view is as effective as a three-point view in communicating space – keep vertical and horizontal lines parallel in one point – use one perspective as a key drawing.

Post edits of materials and finishes in Photoshop can save wasted time when rendering a view in CAD [see Chapter 7].

3D Physical Models – Models are a valuable resource in communicating a design; they can be a holistic object – the plan, section and axonometric in one. When the pressure is on, a model can be a good avenue to present a design. They are limited by scale; it is rare to get a whole building modelled up at 1:20 so it is important not to get too wrapped up with modelling chairs and tables. As defined in Chapter 3 choose a modelling material that is easy to work with.

> *The bespoke designed interlocking shelves utilised a modular construction process, minimising waste and expenditure on site.*
>
> (Jonathan Tuckey Design)

Try and keep external model shots in axonometric view so they complement the drawings

Get inside the model [if you can] and take interior model shots at an equivalent eye line of the perspective views.

Think about the model construction in a series of elements – preferably that can pull apart to define the tectonics of the scheme.

Select a series of simple materials to use such as brown card and white paper – avoid trying to replicate too many specific materials as the model can soon look doll's housey.

2D PROTOTYPING – LASER CUTTER

The process of laser cutting has become increasingly important in the model making process. A play on words Lazer cutter, lazy cutter can cut various substrates/sheet materials such as paper, card, Perspex, leather, etc. You will not normally find laser cutters in the classrooms of universities that can cut metal, but engraving metal can be an option with most machines.

A laser cutter is a two-dimensional cutting machine that cuts patterns or drawings that have been prepared in 2D/*XY* space, though more complex machines will have an option for an additional rotational axis to allow engraving and cutting in the *Z* axis.

Like cutting a pattern for a dress or putting together an IKEA flat pack, the flat components are assembled to create a 3D object. Cutting 2D elements from a flat sheet and assembling them into a 3D object is a useful way to get to grips with 3D object creation [see Chapter 3].

If we look back at the discussion of vector and raster image [Chapter 7], the laser cutter will typically use a vector line to define a cut and a raster image to engrave an image. It is possible to engrave very successfully with a vector image but a laser cutter cannot effectively cut from a raster image as it has no path to follow.

Figure 6.23 Garland, design by Tord Boontje. Garland was designed in 2002. Garland detail. Photography by Angela Moore

If you have used a laser cutter or are going to use a laser cutter, then the software on each machine will be quite different but will share a common 2D flat *XY* format. It will have the capability of cutting or engraving. When the substrate is denser it will typically take longer, more power will be needed and the laser will move slowly. Each machine will have its own guidance on power and speed settings.

You can prepare a laser cutter drawing in most of the software listed in Chapter 7 but typically programs such as Illustrator, CorelDRAW or AutoCAD are used. The file format used by different machines can vary but typical formats used are IA, which is an Illustrator file, DXF, which can be generated by AutoCAD or Vectorworks, or in some cases a PDF file or SVG file can also be imported into laser cutter software.

> *When engraving an image, the format will typically be raster based, a BMP [file format] and in greyscale.*

Good Practice

Start a new file to avoid drawing fragments outside of the cutter extents.

Work out the scale of the element that are to be cut. One cut is better than two [it's quicker and uses less material]; arrange your layers in cut order to ensure the detail gets cut last.

Try and create a clean drawing for use in the laser cutter:

If you use an existing drawing [created in 3D] you may have multiple lines. The laser cutter will follow exactly what it is given in terms of information.

If there are fragments outside of your limits, then the laser will possibly go to that area to perform a cut. If your bed size is 400mm by 600mm but the fragment is at 12000mm the machine may try to go, there 'crunching' the laser cutter.

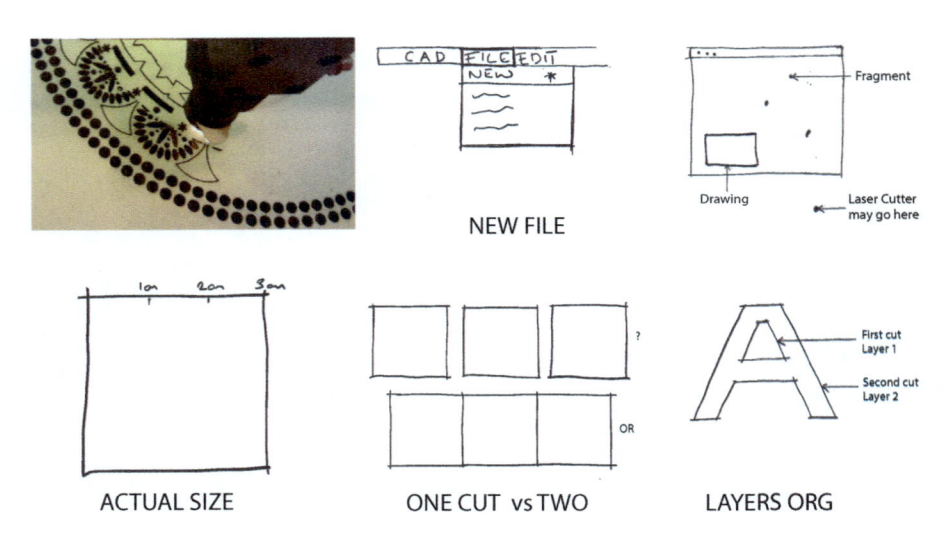

Figure 6.24 Tips for preparing a laser-cut file

Work to the appropriate scale or scale your drawing to the actual units' need for the cut and the size of the machine: for example, a wall of 3m × 3m at a scale of 1:100 would be 30mm × 30mm and that is what you want the cutter to cut, so draw it that size or resize the drawing to that scale.

Try to ensure that any shapes that are going to be cut are closed lines.

The laser cutter will follow paths, often in the series of construction. Many shapes are made up of individual lines and the cutter will be bouncing around doing one bit here and another there.

Why do two cuts when you can do one?

Plan out your sheet to use the least number of cuts. It is good practice as you get more out of your material and in many cases it speeds up the time it takes to cut the sheet.

Use colours/layers to organise the cuts' sequence effectively.

Useful if you are cutting text or enclosures as you want the internal cut first, then the external cut. Also, engrave first and then cut after.

3D PRINTING/CNC MILLING

3D PRINTING – With 3D printers now costing less than a budget mobile phone, they really are an accessible tool to a model maker and interior designer. A model for a 3D printer can be produced on most mainstream CAD software; AutoCAD, Rhino, 3DsMax, SketchUp and many more. Many printers towards the higher end will supply a basic three-drawing program with the machine.

A 3D printer works by 'additive' principles. It adds layers of plastic material [usually PLE] in fine layers, building up the form. Depending on the setting this can be solid [which is not an usual construction] or it is most likely to be a hollow or waffle type structure.

> *Models created in software packages such as AutoCAD or Rhino will normally need to be saved as a STL file – stereolithography.*

Most 3D printers have a dedicated software to prepare the file for printing. The software will size the model for the printer bed size, slice the model into flat horizontal layers [the finer the slice the finer the detail – the longer the print process] that can be printed within multiple passes. It will also set the density and length of time to create the object – the information is compiled into G-code, which is a common file format for most 3D printers. The G-code contains a set of instructions for the printer.

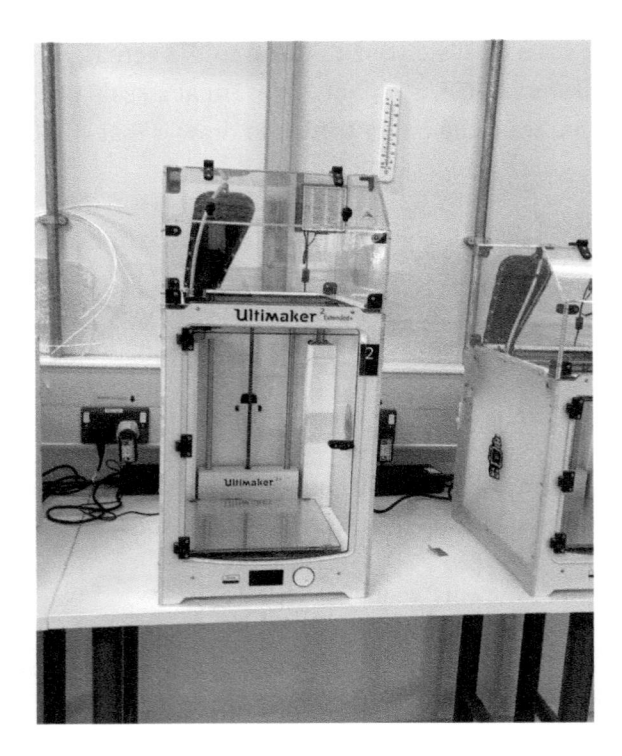

Figure 6.25 3D printer

You can often download for free the software of a specific brand of printer, such as Ultimaker, which will allow you to format and prepare files on your own computer before visiting a workshop provision.

Files are normally sent to the printer via a computer, or they can be copied to removable media – most 3D printers have a SD slot so you can load and operate the printer without the use of a dedicated computer.

Good Practice

3D prints everything? Not yet! Some limitations that are worth considering before going down the route of a 3D printed model are as follows:

Time – To print any model of volume takes a long time, and a basic small element may take 3 hours, whereas a 250mm × 250mm × 250mm may take over 24 hours to print depending on the level of detail and the quality settings of the slice.

If you consider making a model in CAD, setting up the machine and print time, could that time be better spent on a sketch model?

Unless you have exclusive access to a printer there are normally time restrictions at print time [so do not rely on last-minute 3D printing].

Taller parts will usually take longer to 3D print than shorter parts, even if their volume is the same

Printer Size – 3D printers normally have small printer beds, less than A4 in width, length and height, which can limit the size of your model.

Things Can Go Wrong – Even with the careful set-up of a machine, code can be corrupted, leading to string rather than solids. If unsure about a machine's collaboration look at printing 'components' when dealing with a large-scale object.

A Working Strategy

A 3D printer is exceptionally good at modelling fine detail, and it is within this area of model making that you are likely to get satisfactory results and plan out a realistic time scale to make a model.

You can use a printer to print out detailed fussy elements that are hard to model by hand – such as windows openings, stairs, basic interior furniture.

A laser cutter is very precise when cutting openings in walls, façade and floor plates – you can create big volumes very quickly using planes cut on a laser cutter and infill details with accurately 3D printed details.

> *When working on a large-scale model [1:50 and above] the print times can be far too long; a hybrid approach is needed – the laser cutter should be used to cut planes to form the volume and the 3D printer used to print the architectural details such as the doors and windows.*

CNC Milling – CNC routing is a subtractive process. It starts with a solid volume such as blue modelling foam or a high-density MDF material; the material is taken away from the volume. The tolerance of the material and the 'Bit' used can develop detail to less than a mm of accuracy.

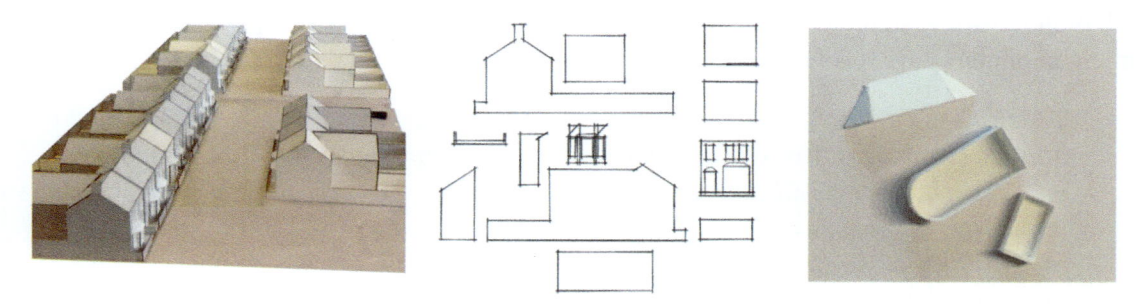

Figure 6.26 Large-scale model, template of laser-cut elements taken from a 3D CAD model; small details printed on a 3D printer

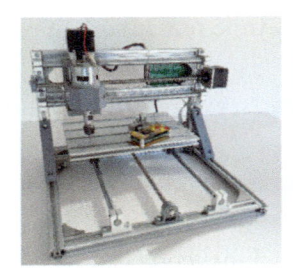  

Figure 6.27 Affordable CNC DIY kit using a Dremel type tool. CNC-routed blue foam model. Venice Architecture Biennale, 2016; wooden routed model, 2018

A CNC router can work in the same way as a laser cutter, cutting planar materials; the main difference is that a laser cutter is likely to do it with a single pass whereas a router will take multiple passes to subtract the material – it can be useful for materials that are heat sensitive.

You can work with thicker materials [Bit dependent] than you would with a laser cutter – the depth of the cut and detail are dictated by the tool size.

You can cut metal.

A router can set up contour landscapes for a model very effectively; it is also a quick way to set up context when using light foam material.

> *Easel is a free software that allows you to convert or develop a 3D model ready for routing [processing G-code] and in most cases is compatible with most DIY routers.*

MICROCOMPUTERS

Raspberry PI – The Raspberry Pi has revolutionised affordable computing [from £10] and simplified coding tasks so they can be approached by novices. The most important part of the interface is the GPIO that provides 40 pins that can be configured as inputs and outputs – for example, you can set pins as the on-off switch for a motor that drives a kinetic shaft or switch an LED on or off. Built in with what today can be regarded as fast processers and Wi-Fi capability, these budget microcomputers have revolutionised what is possible in terms of DIY robotics.

> *Arduino is another microcomputer aimed at quick programming and circuit prototyping; each board has its own advantages and disadvantages.*

Microcomputers have replaced the need for a laptop for driving software; their small form factor means that they can be easily integrated within components or hidden within small-scale architectural models.

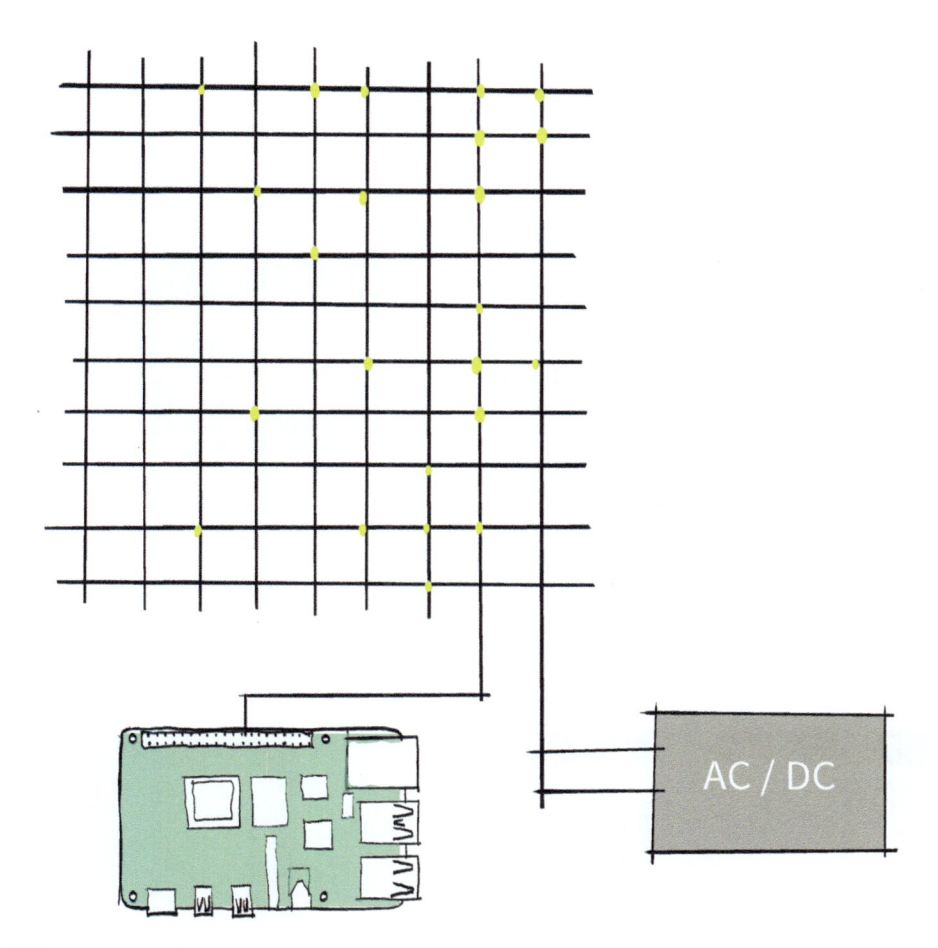

Figure 6.28 Microcomputer diagram

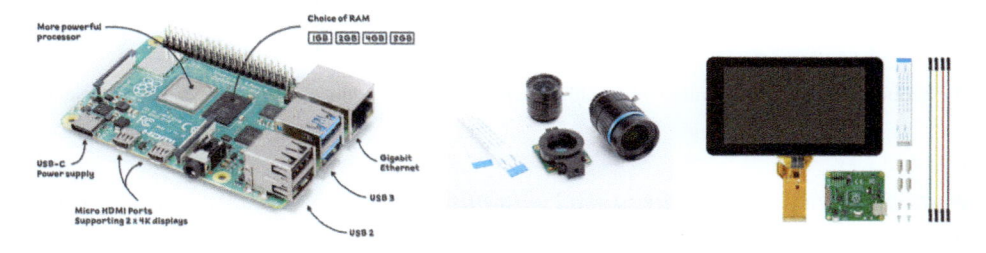

Figure 6.29 Raspberry Pi 4/camera attachments/touchscreen attachment. Image Credits: The Raspberry Pi Foundation

Uses of the Microcomputer

As a computer numeric controller (CNC) for a 3D printer, laser cutter or robotic arm.

Orchestrate complex light sequence [through addressable LEDs] and kinetic movements.

Sensory computation using cameras and sound recognition to make something move or respond.

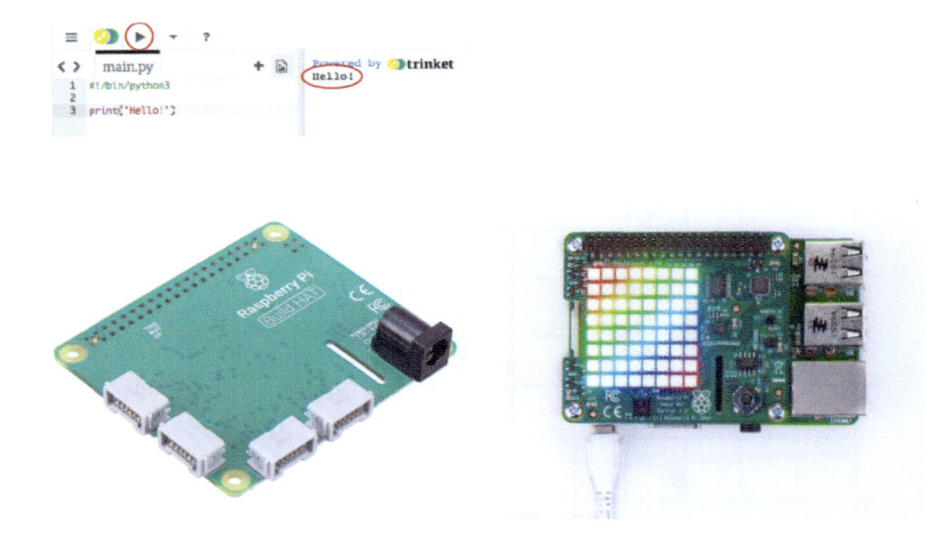

Figure 6.30 Basic Python scripting interface. The build HAT [left] allows you to control four elements [motors or sensors] individually. The Sense HAT [right] has an 8 × 8 RGB LED matrix and a five-button joystick and includes the following sensors: gyroscope, accelerometer, magnetometer, temperature, barometric pressure, humidity. Image Credits: The Raspberry Pi Foundation

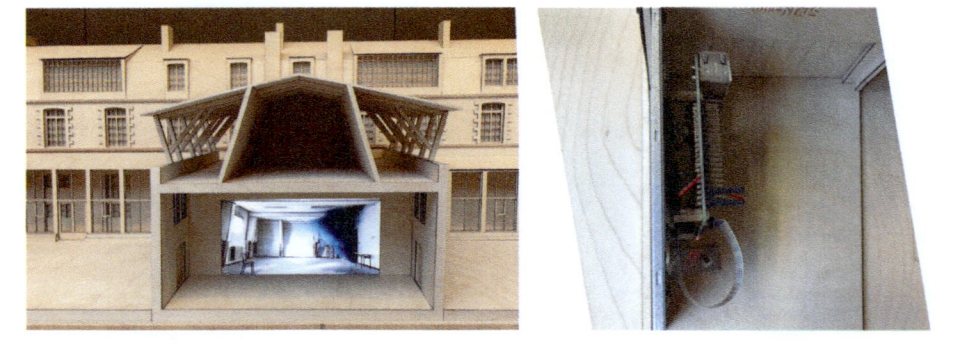

Figure 6.31 Raspberry Pi screens integrated into multiple models to visualise the interior space, the Venice biennale, 2017

If you are a novice the best way to start with microcomputing is to buy an SD card with the operating system already loaded – so you can boot it up and use it straight out of the box.

Python is a basic coding language that can be used to tell an element such as light or motor to do something – you can normally find scripts that are already written online, and copy paste it into a script editor/for example, trinket, which can be used online.

Most Python code is freely distributed so you can copy and paste it to use it.

You can find many scripts online for free to drive videos on a loop or play sound, easier to than trying to program the unit yourself.

HAT – A simple add onto the microcomputer is called a HAT; it plugs into the GPIO to provide an easy way to multiply functionality of a microcomputer – they often come with a Python library of scripts that can tweaked to the user's preference.

CHAPTER 7

CAD

- Introduction
- 2D CAD Drafting
- 3D CAD Drafting
- CAD Visualisation
- Digital Output/Annotation
- Digital Print – Resolution
- CAD Tools – Drawing and Modelling
- Tips and Hints/Common Problems

INTRODUCTION

Chapter 7 is a digital reference, listing the tools and diagrammatic workflow of mainstream software used in interior design. It's a selective list and misses out some titles due to the expanse of the subject area [it's a book in itself]. An overview is given of the basic tools, enough information to initiate a confidence to create any shape, object or drawing. Mapping along the 2D to 3D CAD route, clarification is given to how the CAD drawings can be effectively annotated, visualised and formatted for printing or output as a digital file. Further, the focus is on how to present professionally using a key set of tools such as Photoshop and Illustrator, with clarification on how they fit into the process of communicating a design proposal.

Figure 7.1 Student CAD/Photoshop visual. Image Credit: Oliva Laxton

DOI: 10.4324/9781003120650-8

Overview

In this chapter we elaborate on the working practices of digital production. The introduction of CAD to architectural practice has revolutionised the architectural design profession. CAD has provided an unprecedented level of accuracy that is essential to modern building practice and with its evolution into BIM [Building Information Management] it has become deeply embedded in the professional design and build process.

With that said, one of the first misconceptions is that everything needs to be completed on the computer, but nothing could be farther from the truth; the process of drawing, modelling and sketching by hand is integral to effective design development [as expressed in Chapters 1–6]. CAD and the use of multiple softwares do have their role to play in professional practice, but it is part of a bigger 'design' process.

The focus of this chapter is to illustrate that 'swapping between software' can be very beneficial [as practised in industry]. Final outputs can be very varied from an annotated plan and section to a 3D CAD visual. The important thing to always remember is when that output is digitised into a PDF or printed it's near on impossible to tell what it was produced on.

2D CAD DRAFTING

One of the first major differences between analogue and digital interfaces is the drawing field/ screen size. You are unlikely to get a computer screen at A0 drawing board scale so a navigation [zoom and pan] graphical interface (GI) system is used. Within the GI you can zoom in and out in an instant giving you the ability to see a drawing at 'whatever' scale, which later in the design process allows you to develop an unprecedented level of detail and accuracy.

2D Drawing Environment

Screen Size – Most CAD programs will allow you to use a predefined template to set up the correct units or you can set the 'working units' in the options menu. In ID UK mm is the default unit to define a working space [plus global examples]. Unlike the drawing board you will not set an initial scale [unless using Vectorworks]; you will draft at a scale of 1 unit = 1 mm at actual size [plus global examples].

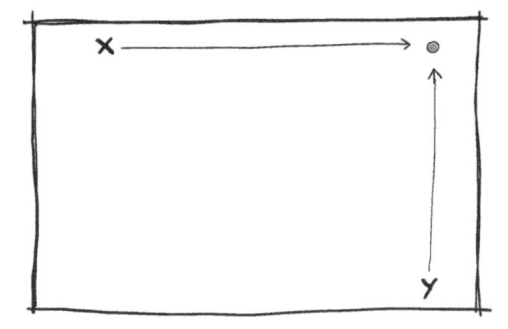

Figure 7.2 CAD screen diagram/XY points in CAD space

Navigation XYZ – The *XYZ* coordinate system is universal in CAD programs. It is a mathematical coordinate system for navigating and creating objects in virtual space. As a default in CAD, *X* will be the horizontal direction and *Y* the vertical; *X* and *Y* are the 2D coordinates that make up the 2D environment [*Z* equals 3D height]. A straightforward way to get to grips with the *XY* coordinates is to relate *X* and *Y* to the location grids found in most 2D maps such as an ordnance survey or sightseeing map.

> *It can be quite easy to lose your drawing in CAD while navigating around – use Zoom EXTENTS to fit all in the screen.*
>   *Middle mouse button allows you to zoom in and out – if you hold it down you can PAN around the drawing.*

Set Views – Many CAD programs open with a plan view as default such as Auto-CAD and Vectorworks; 3D programs such as SketchUp and 3ds Max open in 3D mode. Initially it might be useful to set the viewpoint to a plan 'top' view so you can focus on the plan view, but if you do this you will need to remember to use 2D tools rather than 3D tools to draw.

> *If you have not set up drawing limits [a way of fixing the screen size to building size] draw an initial line along the full width of the building, then use ZOOM extents to set the limits.*

Drawing Aids

There are various drawing aids that are present within all CAD software to help you draw accurately. The most important aid is the orthographic setting Ortho and POLAR [Angle] that ensure your lines are kept straight.

The Ortho mode is a user-set drawing aid similar to a set square that ensures every horizontal and vertical line is drawn straight; often this is also activated by pressing the **shift key** while drawing a line.

The POLAR mode allows you to draw a line at set angles similar to an adjustable set square.

SNAPS [endpoint, midpoint, etc.] allow you to snap to an endpoint of a line, so the lines meet up and there are no gaps in the geometry. Check they are ON.

> *Use the drawing aids to keep your line straight – set ORTHO or hold down the SHIFT key for straight vertical and horizontal lines.*

2D Drawing Tools

POINT – In a 2D CAD environment a point is located using the *XY* coordinate system. CAD comes into its own when dealing with the organisation of points in space. The ability to copy, multiply, move, scale and add further attributes such as parametric transformations means that the 'prime' element of the point can become a highly sophisticated conceptual design element.

> *The point is used as a point of reference in basic geometry, and is commonly referred to as endpoint, midpoint and centre point [in 3DS Max it is known as Vertex].*

LINE – If you have followed the principles of drawing up a basic plan on the drawing board, then it will be much easier for you to start drawing up a plan in CAD as you will be well acquainted with the construction process.

Construct a working grid with singular lines.

Draw in the structural walls, grids and columns.

Draw thickness to walls and add openings. The OFFSET TOOL will help you add parallel thicknesses quickly.

At each stage of development you will need to delete construction lines or TRIM LINES.

Then add major design elements walls, door swings, stairs and fixed furniture.

> *In programs such as Illustrator, a line is called a path [when it has no attributes]. Programs such as AutoCAD have nominal attributes to lines, the default being .25 thickness.*

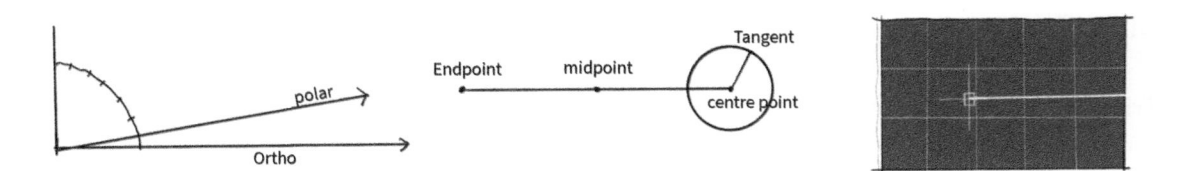

Figure 7.3 Different types of drawing aids – Ortho setting keeps a line straight. A line or object can be selected and modified by a specific point by snapping to it

Figure 7.4 Line drawing in CAD – on a rectilinear plan you will click a start point and use the mouse to show the direction [*X* or *Y*], then enter a distance into a command line or measurement box

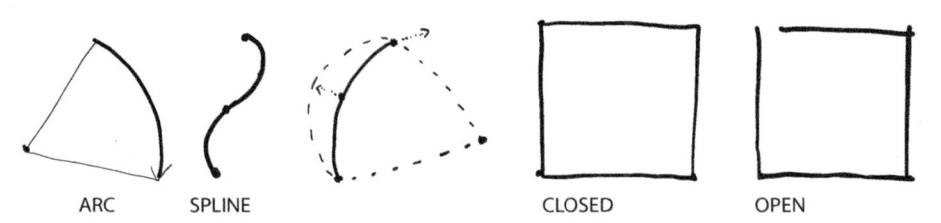

Figure 7.5 Arc and splines are created with three points – it's possible to adjust the arc after drawing it in. A closed and open shape

Line is always a continuous linear object unless additional properties have been applied to it such as a pattern; further line options are available in CAD programs such as a spline or freehand spline, which are made up of multiple connected lines.

Arc – The arc tool is a variation of the line tool and allows you to create an arch using various methods, normally by assigning three points on screen.

> *It is easier to draw in an arch and specify the points loosely NO SNAPS, then move/modify the arch to fit the geometry.*

Closing Lines [and **Arcs**] – When trying to draw a shape from a series points **double click** or type **C** to close a shape.

> *Using just the line tool and arc it is possible to draw very complex shapes so try to master basic 2D tools first before moving onto more complex tools. The close command will allow you to turn the line quickly into a shape.*

2D Modification

Once you have drawn a basic layout you can utilise a series of modifications to the lines or objects:

Offset: it is a tool available in some shape or form in all CAD programs and allows you to create a parallel line to a set distance [either on screen or by typing in a number].

Trim: the command allows you to trim crossing lines. Remember you cannot trim lines that don't cross!

Extend: this command allows you to extend a line either by entering a new distance or you can specify a line or object to extend to, useful to tidy up a drawing.

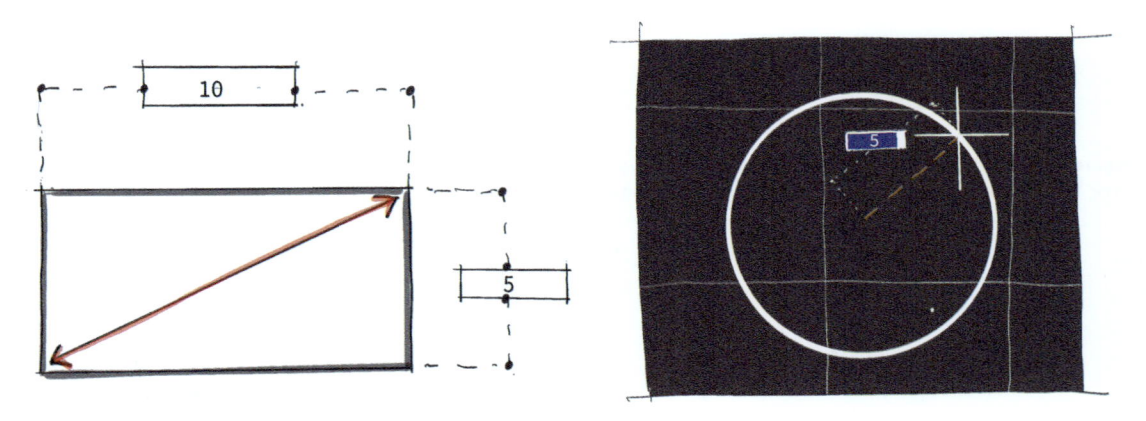

Figure 7.6 Two points being selected to create a rectilinear shape – often the measurements will be highlighted to allow direct keyboard entry, which is more accurate

2D Shapes

There are a series of basic shape tools in CAD starting with the rectangle, then normally followed by the circle tool. Other more complex shapes are available through the parameters of the object or predefined as a tool icon. Using the 'shape' tools will create a closed object: one object rather than a series of lines [apart from SketchUp]. A closed object/predefined shape can be useful:

When you move the object, it moves as one. You can also use the group command to do this.
It will be a **Surface Plane** that you can apply surface attributes to.
If extruded into 3D it will be a true SOLID.

Rectangle – A basic rectangle is drawn by specifying two points on the screen using the mouse or entering them into a measurements box or command line [e.g. @200,200].

Circle: A circle is drawn by defining a centre point and then specifying a radius. Often the circle will be made up of facets. The number of facets determines the smoothness of the circle. In most programs you will find further complex shapes based on the circle such as polygon stars and ellipsis.

> *You can use the TAB key to move onto the next measurement rather than mouse; it helps keep the shape accurate.*

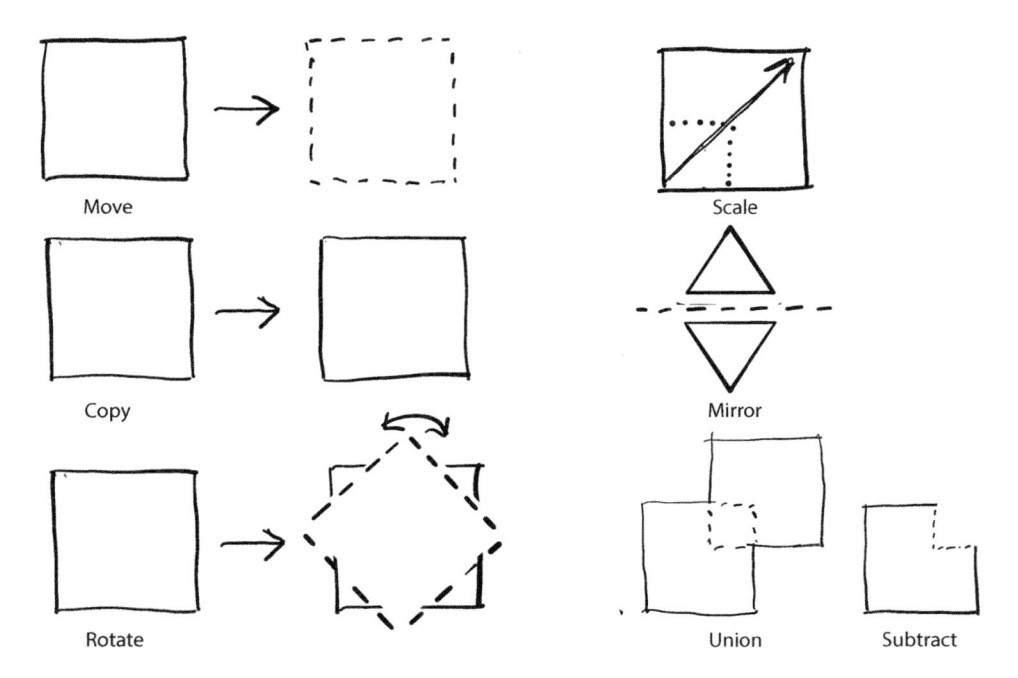

Figure 7.7 Different types of transformation diagrams – the iconography will be different in each program but the functionality the same

Transformations

Transformations are a series of moves or modifications that can be applied to a line, surface or object. Basic transformations are **Move, Copy, Rotate, Scale, Mirror – Offset, Trim, Extend** are also basic transformations that edit the size or shape of the object.

Other more complex transformation include **Union, Subtract, Array** [a multiple copy]. The transformations in CAD relate directly to those discussed in Chapters 2–4 but are digitally processed.

When performing a transformation, you can use a keyboard entry rather than toggling with the mouse [which can get complicated!]:

You can usually use the up and down keys to nudge an object a small set distance in a move or rotate tool.

2D transformations are set to the *XY* axis – 3D transformations use *XY* and the *Z* axis [see 3D CAD transformations].

3D CAD DRAFTING

3D CAD is an exciting prospect for any student or professional. It is a very powerful tool both in design terms and in visualisation potentials. In reality it's not that different from 2D but with the additional *Z* axis. In workflow terms it's useful to move between 2D and 3D environments to develop and modify models – they are both equally important and have a symbiotic relationship.

3D Drawing Environment

The environment of 3D CAD typically opens up in an *XYZ* 3D interface.

Model space is often set to a perspective view [so will have perspective distortion].

While you will be keen to spend as much time as possible in 3D development remember that specific 3D tasks can be easier handled in a 2D view, which is why all programs provide a multi-paned view where the plan and elevations can be viewed along with the 3D view.

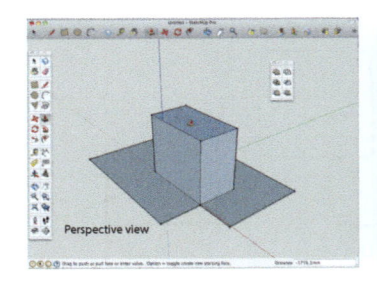 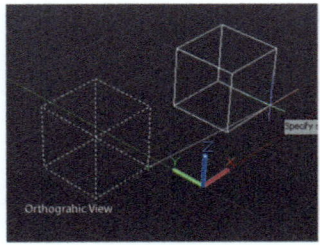 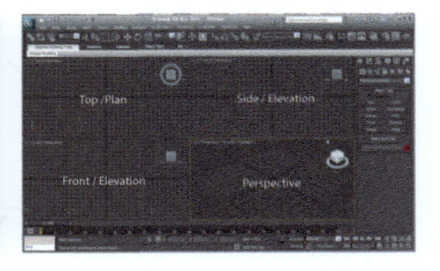

Figure 7.8 3 Different ways a 3D view can be represented in CAD. A Perspective view [by default] in Sketch Up AutoCAD orthographic/parallel view [with a *XYZ* reference]. 3DS Max – multi view four panes – 3D Perspective 2D – plan/front/side

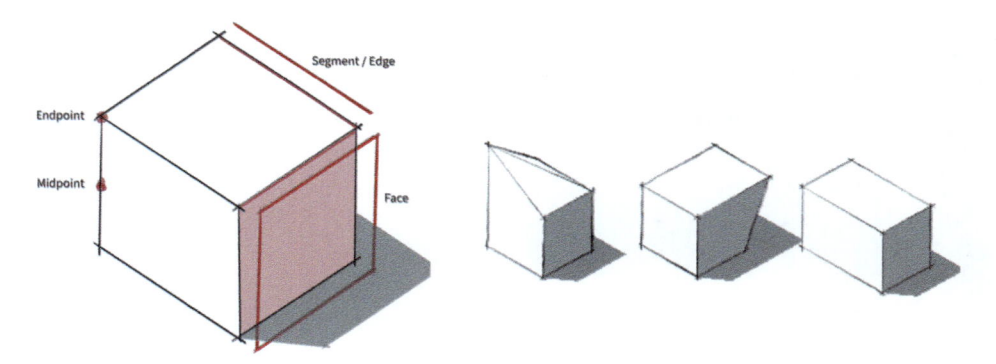

Figure 7.9 Basic topological levels of a cube: object, face, segment, endpoint, midpoint. A cube moved by point, edge and face

> *3D and 2D views can normally be found in the view's pallet. For technical tasks you may want to set the view to orthographic 'parallel,' as described in Chapter 6 [perspective/Orthographic].*

3D Drawing Aids

Ortho aids are as they are in the 2D section with the addition of the Z axis. Snaps are also similar with selection being available by topological point – endpoint, midpoint, segment, face, object. What is specific to 3D modelling is the possibilities of UCS (User Coordinate System) orientation.

UCS (User Coordinate System): The UCS defines the direction of the XY plane around the central point, also called the work plane or construction plane. You can rotate the UCS to pick up specific planes or to model extra elements in a desired direction. The default is XYZ, but you can alter that with the UCS to be ZYX or in any direction needed.

> *Programs such as SketchUp have a dynamic UCS that picks up automatically the face you would like to work on.*

Primary Forms

While drawing a 3D cube, cubes can be called by different terminology within different CAD programs but follow a similar definition, to create a cube you are likely to:

Use a 3D **Cube Tool** to directly create the 3D form using keyboard entry or by click XYZ dimensions in screen.
or **Extrude** a 2D shape – enter the Z height.
or **Presspull** a closed shape – which allows you to make the solid a positive or negative.

CAD Objects/Solid and Enclosures

Using 2D shapes as the starting point many different forms can be created – solids or enclosures – the forms can also be developed to a single point to create a cone or pyramid form.

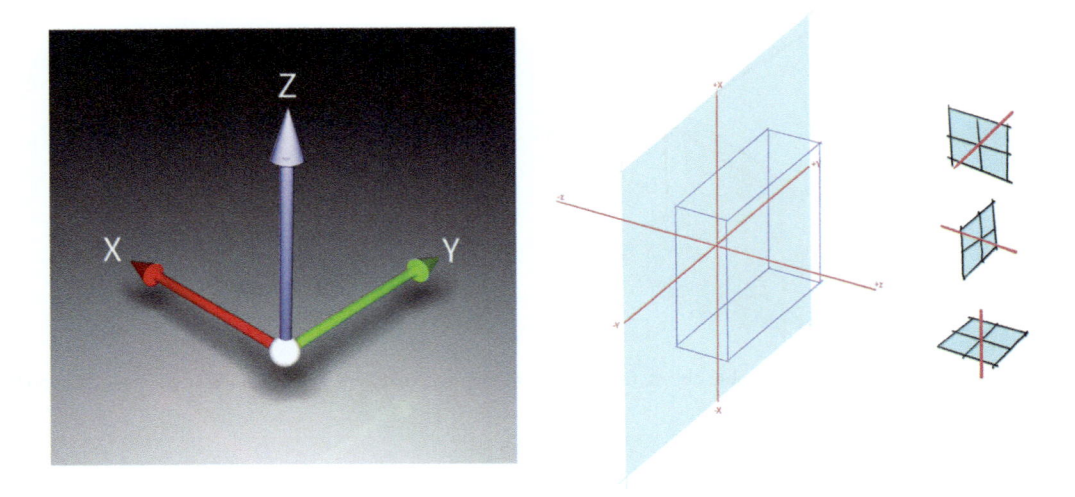

Figure 7.10 *XYZ*, the Cartesian coordinates of a point in space. UCS rotating the ground plane to extrude objects in a different direction to the traditional ground plane

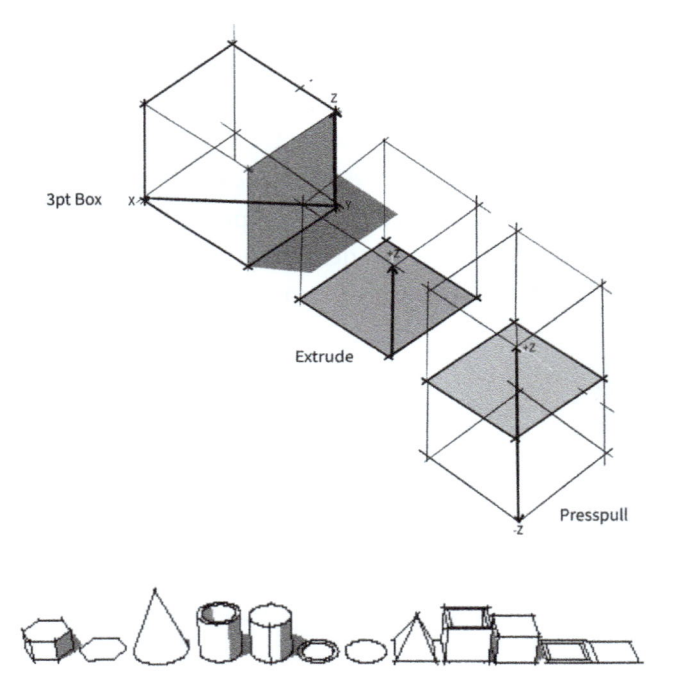

Figure 7.11 Basic cube object creation – direct creation on screen or by keyboard, extruding a surface, presspull. Various 3D solids that can be created from a shape

Complex Forms

A complex 3D shape can be developed from a simple shape through modification and transformation. Other complex forms are created using specific tools that mesh or skin a user defined path.

The most common tool used to create complex forms are the sweep and revolve commands, which are available in most 3D software – both work on the principle of a sectional shape as the

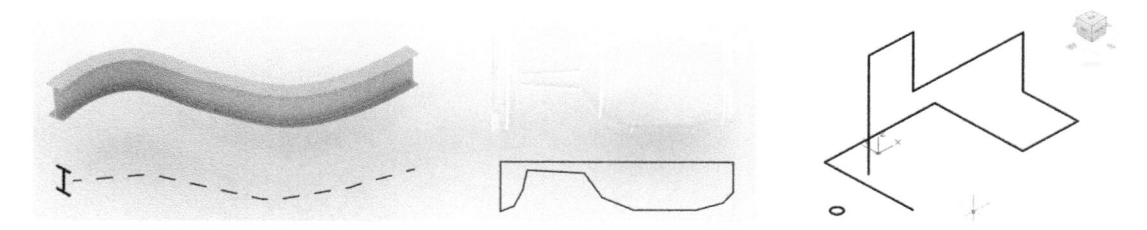

Figure 7.12 I section being swept along a path. Revolve section being rotated around a central axis. The *3Dpoly* line in AutoCAD allows you to draw a line in the *Z* axis

source of the 3D shape and a path or axis to follow. Adjustments can be made in real time to the object as they have controls that can be altered after creation, in principle [some may disagree] a simple type of parametric modelling.

Sweep is a command that sweeps a 2D section along a path – the shape in essence is a section of the 3D form that gets swept along a path.

Lathe/Revolve works like a turning lathe; the command will rotate a section around a central axis – a useful command for symmetrical forms.

3D Poly – programs such as AutoCAD have 3D line tools 3D Poly, which allows you to create a complex 3D framework, allowing you to draw continuous line utilising the *Z* axis.

> *A closed or open shape can be swept along a continuous line – a continuous line helps resolve the tricky junctions when the 3D object is generated.*

3D CAD Modifications

In CAD, a 3D solid can be modified from a 3D volume into an enclosure or series of 2D surfaces. In a comparable way that you break down a form in hand drawing a CAD object can be broken down into facets and manipulated/modified to develop a more complex form.

3D CAD Formal Transformations

All the formal transformations in the 2D section apply equally to the 3D environment. The only difference in using the 2D tools is that you are restricted to the *XY* ground plane. Nearly all software will have a 3D move section and some use it by default such as 3DS max.

Using 3D transformations gives the user good control over the three axes *XYZ* – you can pick an axis and then move in the chosen direction, which helps with accuracy. As in 2D you can often type in the relative distance that you want to move using the keypad.

> *Further transformations include mirror and 3D array.*

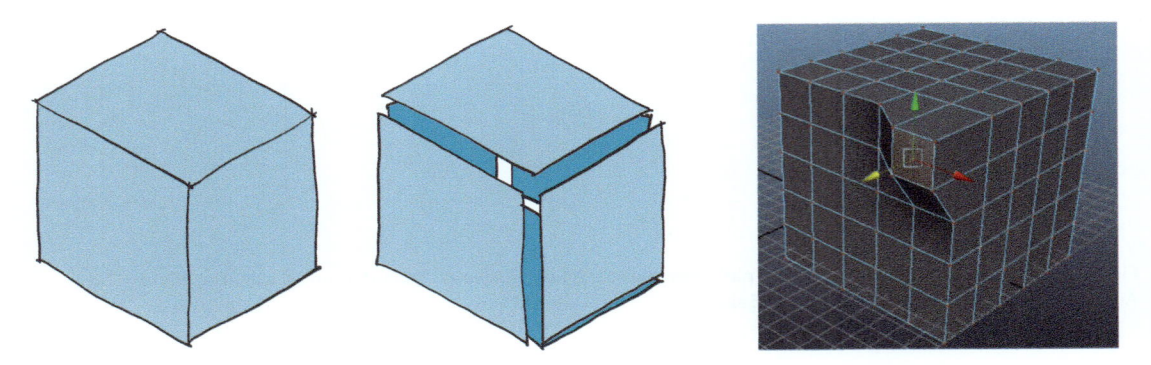

Figure 7.13 A solid form that has been modified [exploded] into planar elements. A solid form that has subdivisions applied – allowing you to modify the object using topological levels: point, edge, face

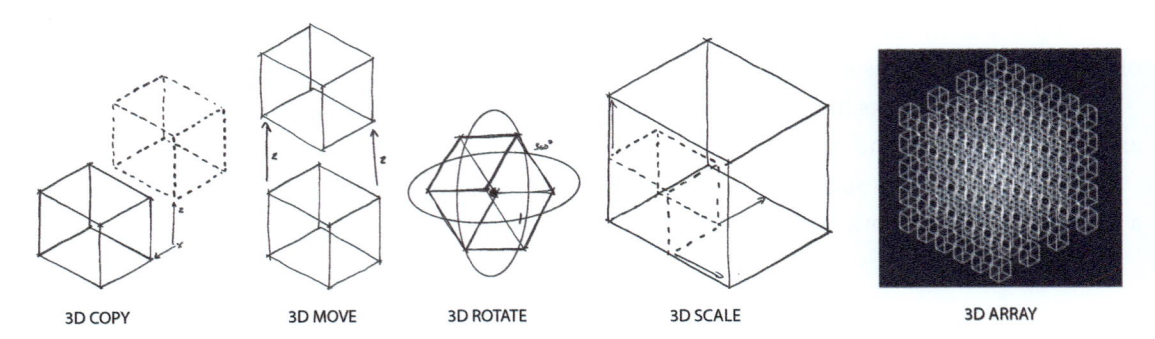

3D COPY   3D MOVE   3D ROTATE   3D SCALE   3D ARRAY

Figure 7.14 3Dmove, 3Dcopy, 3Drotate, 3Dscale, 3D array

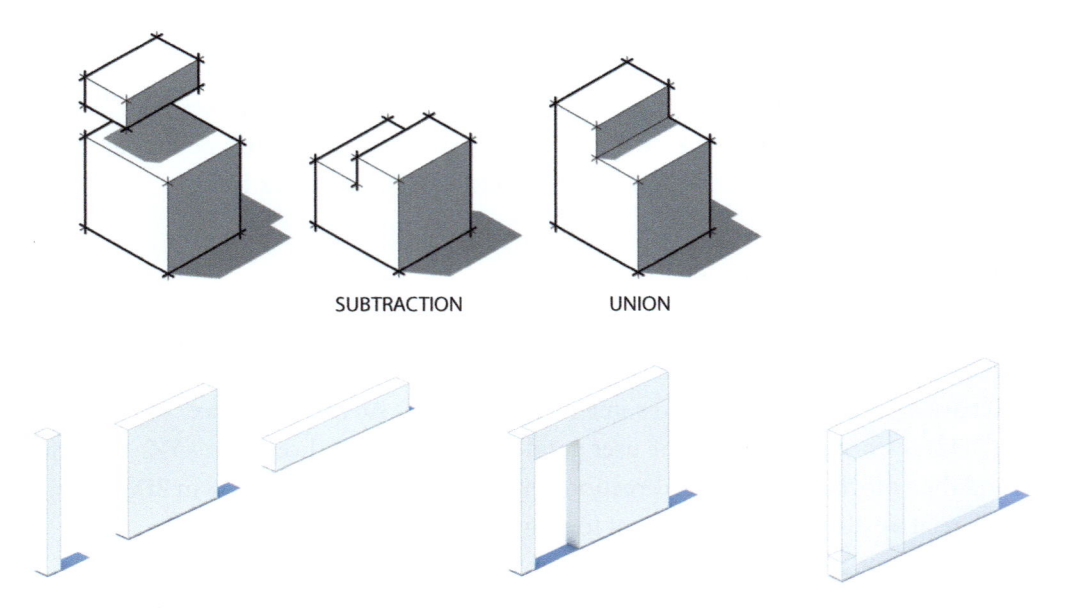

SUBTRACTION   UNION

Figure 7.15 A smaller cube being subtracted and added to a larger cube – Boolean moves unite an object removing the join. The Lego [using union] approach to construction – or the subtraction from the primary object method

3D Union and Subtractions

BOOLEAN MOVES – Union and subtract are important modifications of both the design process and the development of more complex forms in CAD. A union will make two or more objects into one solid. A subtraction will take away a set volume from an object.

You can use union and subtraction to create highly complex shapes/objects. You can take two approaches when using this set of modification tools:

Build up a shape by assembling the blocks, like building with Lego.
Or you can subtract one object from another to create an opening.

> *It's often a good idea to use a placement block to help you assemble complex arrangements – and to delete them when the model is complete.*

CAD VISUALISATION

Materials can be applied to a CAD 3D model and combined with a light source to produce very realistic interior simulations. The process of visualising material finishes in CAD is also an extremely useful tool for developing a palette of materials – to see how they work together. As technology moves forward the application of materials in a real-time VR environment allows the designer and client to experience at first-hand the spatial and material properties of the designed environment even before they are built.

The process of visualisation can be quite daunting and complex but following a series of logical steps it can be a relatively simple process. When starting out it is important not to overcomplicate or expect too much from CAD visualisation. Yes, you can put lights into a space but don't expect them to react as a specific light object. You can put materials onto a wall surface but don't expect them to tile seamlessly or go in at the correct scale; this and many other multiple 'trip ups can add unnecessary pain to visualisation–.'

In the end it's the product [the image] produced rather than what it was produced on that will be the success of the visualisation. That often involves multiple softwares and an understanding of when to move between them, which is what this section illustrates – the workflow of visualising with key advice to gain successful outcomes.

Modelling the Scene

Try and avoid complex objects with lots of facets/polygons. Normally the space you model up is made up of simple geometric forms; try and keep the simplicity of the model.

> *If using the model only for a visual/s don't model everything up; just model up the bit you are going to visualise.*

When you import complex objects [such as the toilet in the clay render scheme] they can slow down the rendering of the scene considerably.

> *Put complex imported objects on their own layer so you can easily take them out of the scene when developing the overall image – you can switch them back on for the final render.*

Setting Up a CAD Perspective

Following the same principles as the hand-drawn perspective try and set up the view at eye height. It's easy to take multiple shots of a model from every direction but the consistency of the natural view gives a true perception of what the space will be like to the user.

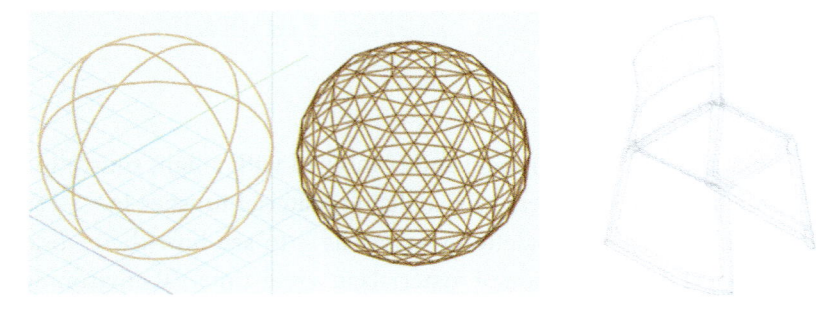

Figure 7.16 Low- and high-resolution sphere/Hi Res mesh chair object

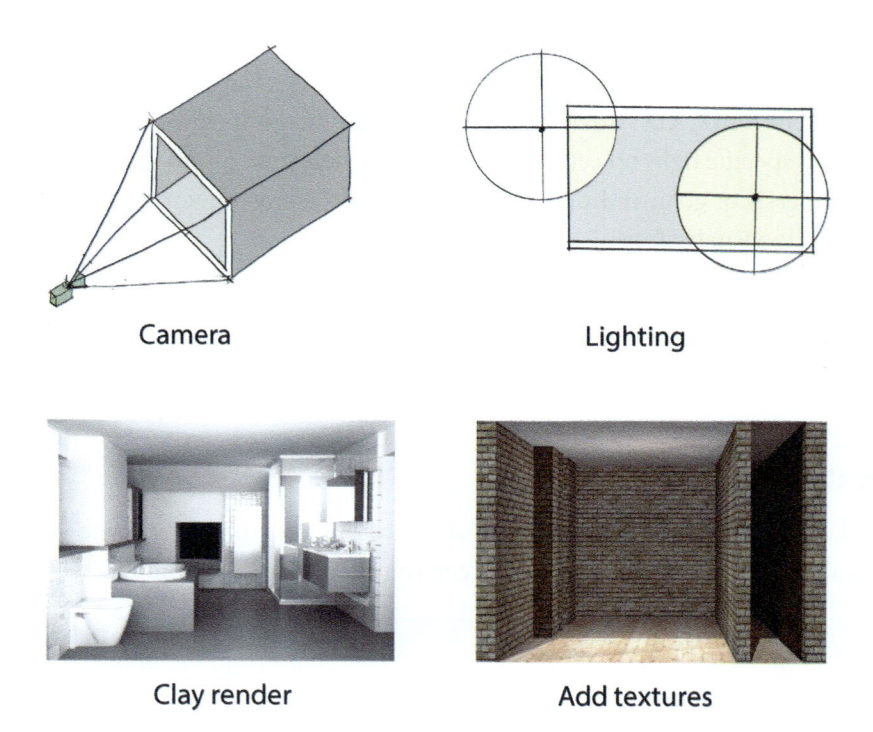

Camera

Lighting

Clay render

Add textures

Figure 7.17 Workflow for setting up a 3D model for rendering

You can remove walls to get a greater depth of perspective.

It can be good practice to work up materials while in a camera view.

Set/save one or two views that you can work up – if one is not responding in the same way as the other, save the CAD file into a file per view.

Adding Materials to the Model

It's good practice to render the composition in white first before adding materials [which can be processer intensive], often referred to as a CLAY RENDER.

Take your own pictures/textures to add realism to your work.

Tricky textures that don't work when first imported can be edited in Photoshop while still loaded into the CAD program [cropped or increased in scale] so you can get real-time updates.

A big texture file will slow down the rendering – you can use Photoshop to reduce the file size.

Too much reflectivity can adversely affect lights and wash out a scene.

Adding Lights to the Model/View

It may come across as an odd principle – Don't use light to be lights, use lights to add light and depth to a scene. Less is more; don't add too many lights, for example, lots of ceiling spots, and expect the computer to not slow down to a crawl.

Use one main light in the space and use Photoshop to post edit the image.

Add a natural daylight outside the scene to add depth; sometimes if you remove a wall, it can help add light to the scene.

Turn the light shadows **ON** to add depth to the scene.

Developing the Render View

It is rare that a rendered scene just works; it will need developing. Materials will need tweaking or in some cases replacing; lights will need increasing, decreasing or moving around the scheme to get to a desirable outcome.

When working up a render keep the resolution low – a screen size 600–400 pixels is fine to get an overview of the lighting and materials.

Most render packages have an option to pick a window to render rather than the whole image – useful to save time and focus on a particular area.

Up the resolution as high as is possible for the FINAL RENDER as that will be your final image – this may take many hours to process [even with a fast computer].

Save an image as a high-quality file such as a TIFF; if saved as a Jpeg it will automatically be compressed [you can't get back the compression].

Figure 7.18 A visual using CAD modelling, Photoshop and an original photograph of the site. Credit: Olivia Laxton

DIGITAL OUTPUT ANNOTATION

Professional CAD programs such as AutoCAD, ArchiCAD, Layout for SketchUp, Vectorworks, Revit and so on have page layout facilities. They are vector-based programs that allow you to change the scale of the drawing while retaining resolution. You can drag and drop raster-based images into the layout, annotate drawings effectively and define a professional drawing template.

Remember within all outputs is the 'art' of the drawing and the craft of the process. There is no quick fix for Photoshop, Illustrator or CAD. A drawing that has been 'worked up' is always evident in the same way a drawing that has had a quick graphic fix reads the same with or without the 'graphic treatment.'

Within most orthographic drawing's programs, you will reach a point where it may be more effective to move to another program for a final tidy up or for the application of line weights. It's all in the workflow and making sure that you switch at a key point rather than get tied up trying to master a program just before a deadline.

AutoCAD Annotation

Annotation in AutoCAD is notoriously layered with pitfalls [which is why it's the only software covered here] for the novice user; even with recent program developments from R14 to 2022 some scale issues remain along with common display and print problems. That said, it is a great tool for orthographic drawing.

Paper Space/Model Space – Basic drawing takes place in model space [black]; a view is imported from model space into paper space – the paper size is set in paper space. You can zoom in and out when the viewport is open [thick black line]. You can set the scale of the drawing when the viewport is open [not when shut].

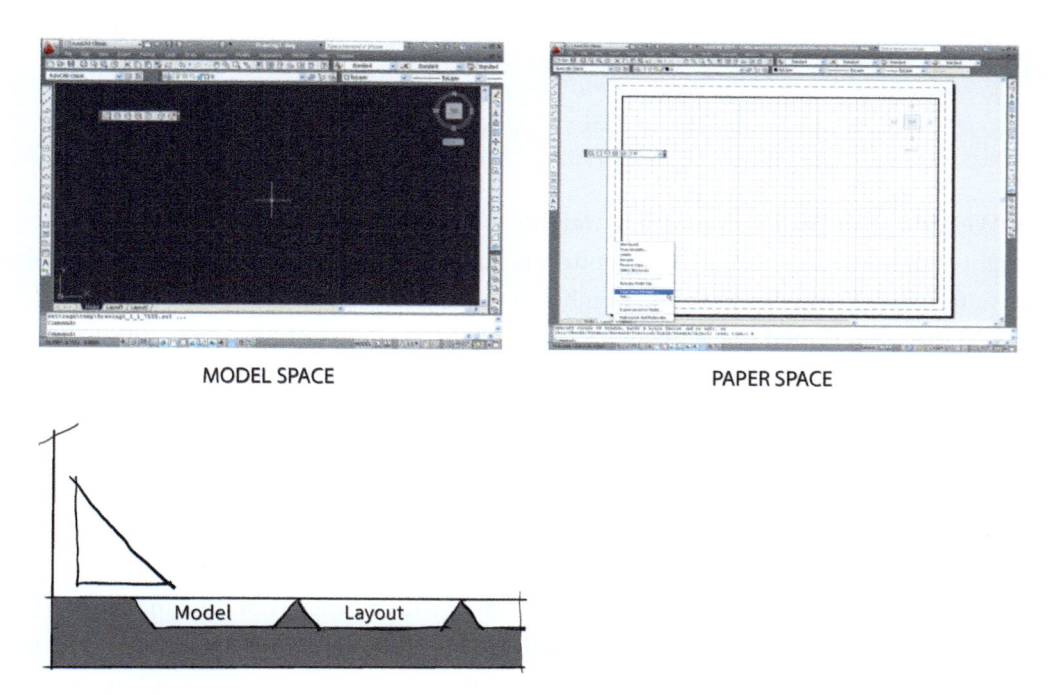

MODEL SPACE   PAPER SPACE

Figure 7.19 AutoCAD model space; black and paper space, white model and layout tabs in the bottom left-hand corner of AutoCAD

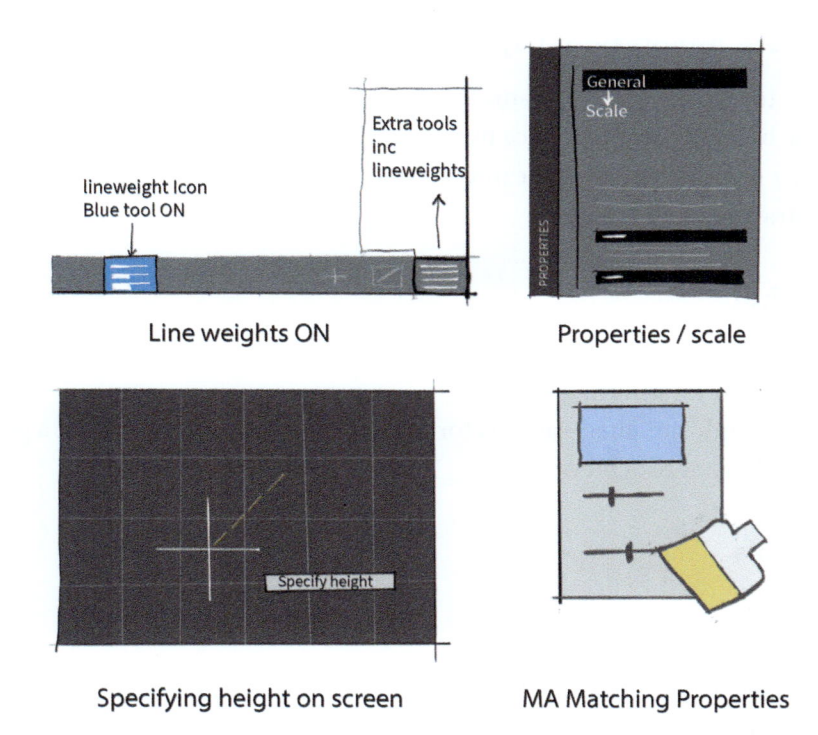

Figure 7.20 Line weight button, bottom right-hand corner or in the right-hand roll out. The properties palette contains all the parameters to the objects you have drawn – the object must be selected for the properties to come up in the tab. Specifying the size of text on screen can be useful to judge the size of the text next to the drawing. Match properties tool can be activated by typing MA – it's a great tool to tidy up a drawings line weights and annotation

Paper space is often referred to as layout space [activated by the tab in the bottom left – if you get lost then use the tabs to get to the right space].

Line Weights – AutoCAD assigns line weights to a line [the default is 2.5]; you won't see the line weight unless the line weight view button is activated. It's hidden away in the right-hand corner – alternatively you can type line weights in the command box [the easiest way!]

Dotted Line – No dotted line showing is normally associated with the scale of the line; most dotted lines are for big buildings rather than interior ones; you can change this in properties 'Line Type Scale.' A quick way to get there is to select the line/type in the command line PROP and change the scale in the properties tab.

Dimensions – The same is true of dimensions – you need to set the size of Arrows and text in properties to see the dimensions on screen – but they may be formatted for layout space.

Text – Text is the simplest type of text to get used to – Type TEXT in the command line/specify the height on screen. Text size again can be problematic; you can use properties and the **Text Size**.

Match Properties – Probably the most useful tool in AutoCAD annotation, it works in the same way as the format painter in word. Enabling you to copy the format of text, dimensions, line weights over to another object.

'Other' Software Annotation: Layout and Post Format

It might be better to use different programs for annotation; often you can get much better results. If you can get the basic line work in place using a program like AutoCAD or Vector works, there are plenty of other software options. The next section covers the basic tools that might be used in post formation drawings and images.

Adobe Photoshop

Pros – Good for layout graphics, Photoshop is great to iron out render issues and to add textures to a perspective – good for inserting images.

Cons – It is not good with lines – any vector work will be converted to pixels; a good outcome for line weights is difficult to achieve.

Photo shop Tools

Adobe Illustrator

Pros – Good at line weights, Import DWG or DXF files, assign line weights/dotted lines in the stroke panel, very good at text Infill colour fills onto plans, etc.

Save as a PDF that still retains the vector graphics so great for printing and screen view.

Cons – Some of the terminology and ways of editing can be very different from other interfaces [such as CAD and Photoshop].

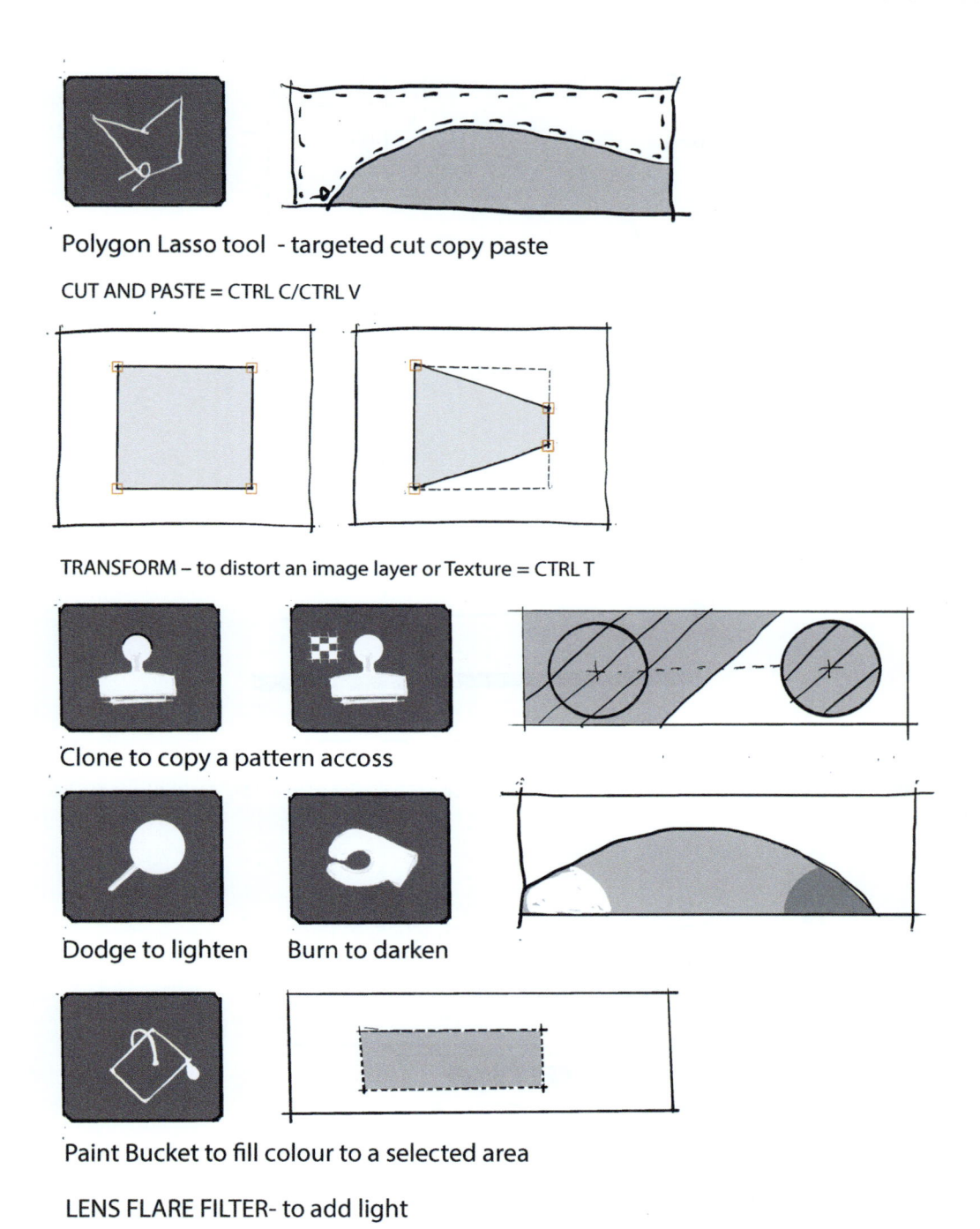

Polygon Lasso tool - targeted cut copy paste

CUT AND PASTE = CTRL C/CTRL V

TRANSFORM – to distort an image layer or Texture = CTRL T

Clone to copy a pattern accoss

Dodge to lighten   Burn to darken

Paint Bucket to fill colour to a selected area

LENS FLARE FILTER- to add light

Figure 7.21 Useful Photoshop tools for the interior designer

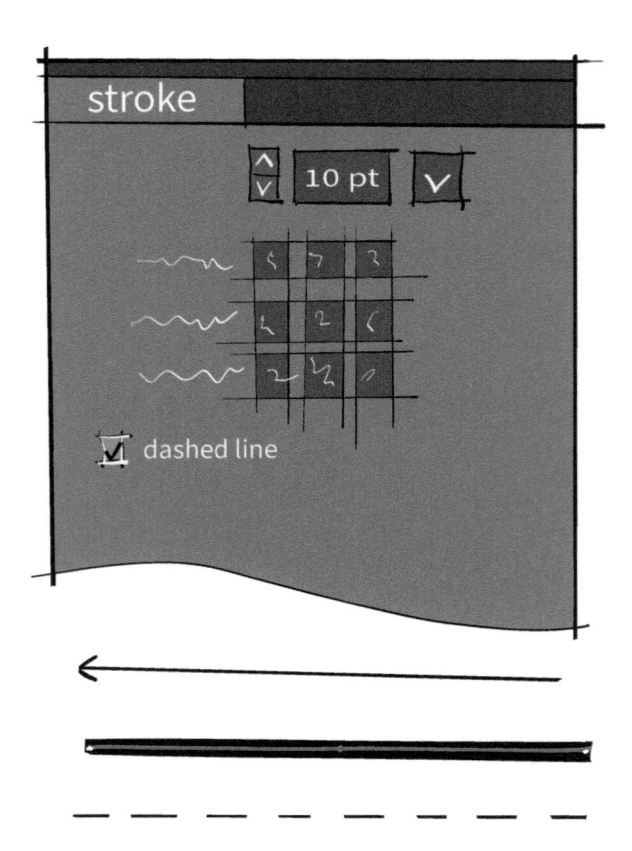

Figure 7.22 The stroke panel and the various types of line types that can be assigned to a DWG drawing imported into Adobe Illustrator

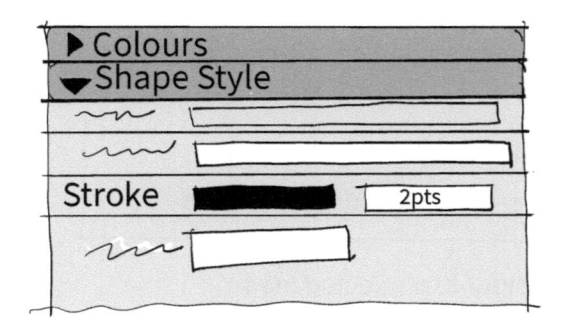

Figure 7.23 SketchUp stroke panel, under the *shape* style tab

SketchUp Layout

Pros – A small but good program for formatting; it is a more stripped back interface than Illustrator, very easy to use with the ability to page set at page size such as A3 and annotate in that view. Saves as a PDF or a DXF.

Cons – Limited tools as the output gets more complicated, e.g., multiple drawings.

Figure 7.24 A typical document page layout created using InDesign

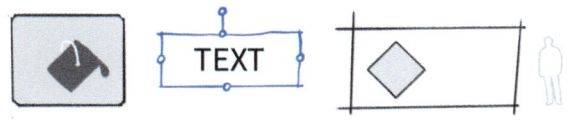

Add text,Images, fill colour , use shapes

Figure 7.25 Basic tools available in Fresco, bucket fill, text and shapes

Adobe InDesign

Pros – Very good for general page layout styles, the template sheet can get repeated for every page you make to take full graphic control of the layout. You can update Photoshop or Illustrator files even when they are in the document window. Rather than imbedding files into the page design, InDesign links to them so when you come to print you don't lose any of the quality from the original drawings.

Cons – You must set up the template. It's easy to lose linked files as you move between computers.

iPad/Adobe Fresco/Pro Create

Pros – The iPad is great at post drawing annotation – you can thicken up lines; it's good at filling in colour. Overall, it's very simple to use; files can be saved as a PNG or PDF and still retain the Vector information.

Cons – Some advanced functionality can be limited by screen size [works best on a larger tablet]. You need a pen – it's easy to lose the resolution of an original image.

Digital Print – Resolution

For presentation and print the sheet size of a presentation is likely to be set at A3 or A1; occasionally A2 might be required. You can approach the page set-up in a few ways, some of which might be preference but more likely to be a set format being requested. Whether print or digital the likely end format will be a PDF. A PDF has the capacity to be vector based or raster [pixel] based [see below]. While this may seem like an insignificant choice it can make a big difference to the quality of the output.

Unless producing your composite sheets by hand you are going to have to assemble them digitally and there is a set series of industry software to do that with [see software PROS and CONS]. Each one has its strengths and weakness, but it is generally accepted that vector-based graphics with line drawings offer the most flexibility in resolution.

Vector/Raster

Vector – Vector-based images are based on a path or specific points in a field [such as *XYZ*]. The advantage of a vector-based drawing is it can be scaled up or down without any loss of resolution and doesn't suffer from 'pixelation' when being manipulated.

Vector   Raster / Pixel

Figure 7.26 Vector line PDF AutoCAD plot; a low-resolution image expanded to reveal the pixels

When drawing and outputting orthographic drawings such as plans, sections, axonometric, etc. From vector-based programs the output will be a crisp line that is appropriate to the scale of the drawing.

Formats such as a jpeg or tiff are 'Raster' based so if you output a drawing for use later; then you risk 'pixelation' of the line work. A safer option when outputting any drawing work in CAD is to use the PDF format as that will in most cases preserve the vector attributes of a drawing [this can depend on your settings]. You can often see this when you open a PDF generated by a CAD program as the lines stay crisp even when you zoom in.

> *You can always convert a vector image to a raster, but you cannot convert a raster image to a vector.*

Raster images are based on a pixel. You may have seen individual pixels in a low-resolution image. In this image of the line icon, you can clearly see the pixilation. Its image size is 18×26 pixels, which equates to a total size of 468. It's a very small image but when used as a small image/ an icon, it works fine.

Photoshop is the most used software that is raster based and because of the fluidity of the pixel format it can prove extremely useful in editing drawings with photographic imagery, colour and context. **MS Paint**, **GIMP** freeware and **CorelDRAW** are some of the alternative raster-based software available.

If you are going to output to Photoshop then you need to ensure that you have enough resolution in your image to retain the clarity of the line. As a rule, that would require that your drawings be outputted to print size [A2/A1, etc.] and at a density of at least **300 DPI** dots per inch.

Figure 7.27 Sometimes you don't need CAD. A simple Photoshop [raster] visual with textures overlaid on an original photograph. Image Credit: James Gould

At A1 the ideal size is 300 dpi [9933 × 7016 pixels] and the file size will be about 199 mega-bytes, which is fine with most of today's computer hardware.

> *A common mistake made when converting drawings from vector to raster is to select Dot per CM. Don't do this as an A1 image at 300 dots per CM equates to a file size of about 1.26 gigabytes, enough to print an image the size of house!*

CAD TOOL – DRAWING AND MODELLING TOOLS

AutoCAD

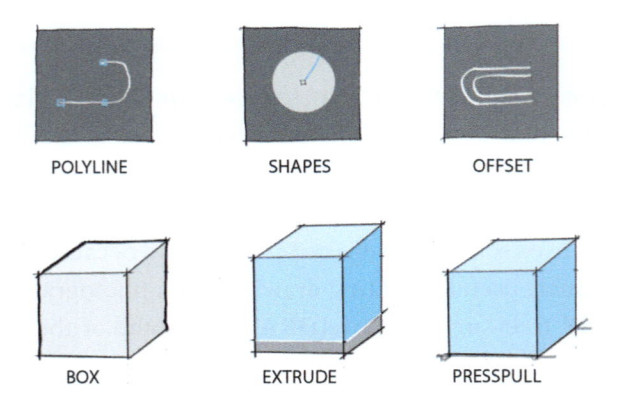

Figure 7.28 2D tools: polyline tool, shapes, offset – very useful for creating enclosures. 3D tools: Box, Extrude, Presspull

AutoCAD Tools

Line – AutoCAD has a few variations of the line tool offering construction, parallel, etc. For the most flexibility you should use the polyline tool option as you can apply attributes such as line thickness and arrow heads, etc.; it also translates well into a 3D solid.

Shapes – AutoCAD shape tools are closed shapes; you can use the pedit command to create an object made up of separate lines and the explode command to make single lines from a rectangular shape.

Offset can be made by entering a set distance or referencing on screen – remember to follow the command prompts for the next move.

> *There are three ways to create a box solid in AutoCAD so if one does not work you can always try another.*

Box is the direct generation of the object and requires the selection of an X and Y point [or enter the direct measurements and TAB through] then enter the Z measurement to give the box a height.

Extrude transforms a rectangle [or shape] into a 3D object – the shape should be closed to create a true 3D solid.

Presspull finds a field to extrude.

Illustrator

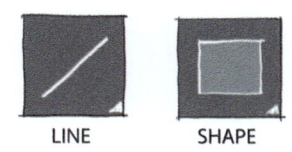

LINE   SHAPE

Figure 7.29 The line and rectangle tool in Illustrator

Line – In Illustrator the line tool is known as the 'line segment tool.' Attributes are set prior to drawing the line or can be applied after. Stroke [attributes] sets a thickness to the line and appearance allows the selection of colour, line type, etc.

Shapes – Drag on the artboard to draw a rectangle. As you drag, look for a diagonal magenta guide that shows a perfect square polygon tool and type the number of sides for your shape – for example, type 6 to create a hexagon.

SketchUp

Line – Click two points to define the length of the line. Define the direction with the mouse and enter the distance in the measurements box; type in directly the distance you want to go. You can apply basic attributes through the styles pallet.

Shapes – To draw a rectangle accurately: define a starting point, type a length value, a comma, a width value, and then press Enter. Circle tools enter the radius; more complex shapes can be constructed using the polygon or line tool.

Solids – Solid shapes in SketchUp need to be drawn in 2D then extruded using the presspull command – they can then be modified by point, edge or face.

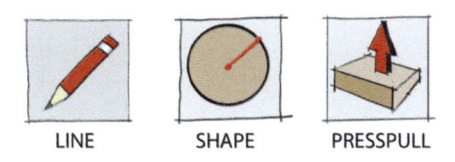

LINE   SHAPE   PRESSPULL

Figure 7.30 The Line, Shape and Presspull tools combine to create a 3D form

Vector Works

Line – The constrained mode constrains the line to be vertical, horizontal and 30 degrees or 45 degrees from vertical or horizontal in any direction.

Shapes – To create a square (1:1 rectangle), press and hold the Shift key while drawing [applicable to many vector programs].

Solids Basic 3D Shape Tools – The 3D poly allows you to create complex shapes when used with the push pull command.

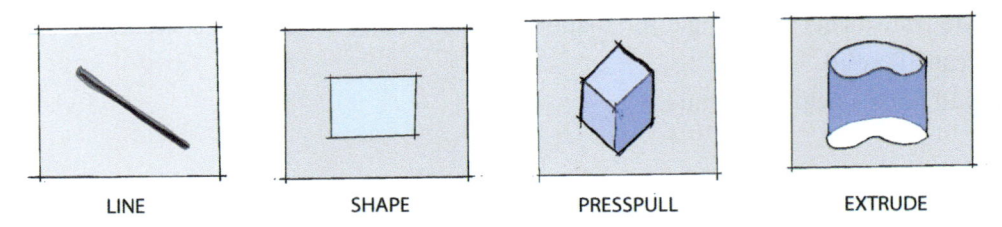

LINE   SHAPE   PRESSPULL   EXTRUDE

Figure 7.31 Line, shape, solids and presspull/extrude

Revit

> *Windows, doors are inserted into the wall and the subtraction is made automatically as are stairs. Objects are kept in families such as furniture, lights, doors, etc.*

There are two ways to approach Revit:

Mass Model: You can create a 3D mass model and then break it down into its components such as floor roof, windows, etc. That is the BIM [Building Information Management] process of developing a model in architecture.

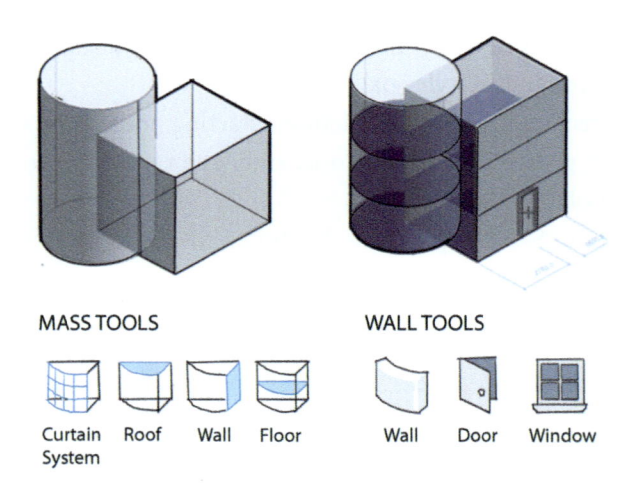

MASS TOOLS   WALL TOOLS

Curtain   Roof   Wall   Floor   Wall   Door   Window
System

Figure 7.32 A mass Revit model subdivided into floors and defined with walls. Revit basic massing tools/wall, door and windows tools that can be added to an imported plan

Revit is also used to model interior environments which requires a different approach. A ground floor plan is imported into the program; walls, ceiling, furniture, etc., added from the model. You can extract door schedules, take sections, plans and visualise.

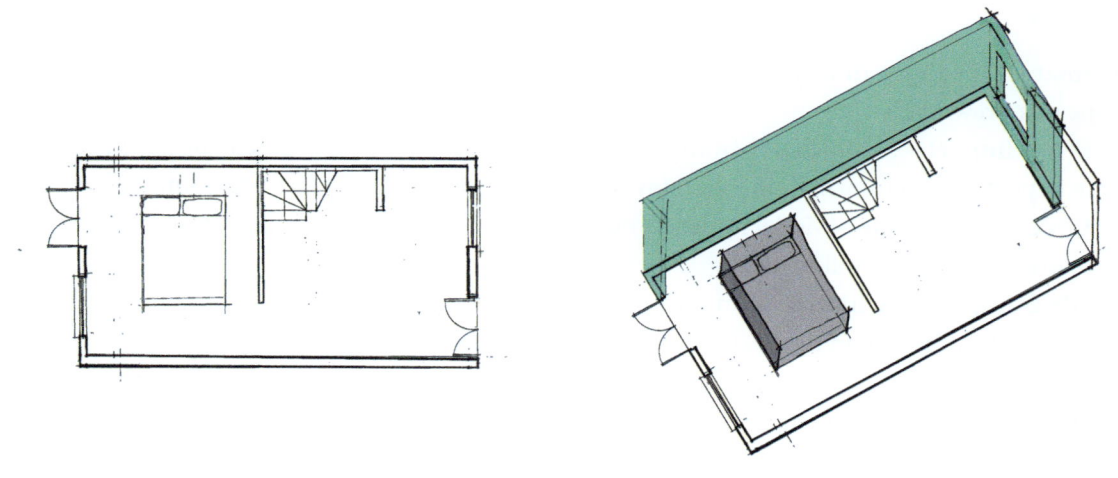

Figure 7.33 A plan imported into Revit which then has a wall, doors and windows added

TIPS AND HINTS/COMMON PROBLEMS

The following are some common problems and advice that may happen to you when using the CAD software. The list is not extensive or software specific as that may well take a book in itself. You may want to keep a small journal to write down any problems and solutions you have encountered while using your chosen software; you can refer to it when needed, even share the information with colleagues. In this internet age it is possible with some rigorous searching to find the solution to any problem encountered when using CAD software.

Working Ethos

Computing in CAD is by its very nature a problem-solving exercise and as with most problems we are presented with there may be many ways of reaching the same solution. If you don't succeed, then try another way. As a learning process it's like riding a bike; once you resolve a problem, you will always remember that solution. You build knowledge through experience and that can be rewarding, as there is a sense of achievement in building a skill base. As CAD computing is such a progressive medium it's refreshing to acknowledge that there is always someone who knows more around the corner; it's the very fact that you learn something new every day that makes the subject so interesting.

Install

Activation – After you register and install software you may need to activate the software. You may need to register a new account during the activation process.

30-Day trials: You can often install a 30-day trial; 30 days can often be enough time for you to complete the project you are working on.

Import

Format – Opening a drawing and if it is in the wrong measurement format change the **UNIT** Type of a drawing.

DWG Import – 3D IMPORT [into SketchUp particularly] can be problematic; often you will only import the 2D information – test any move between software before you commit.

DWG Import Scale – Model imports and disappears – scale the drawing before import; work in metres rather than millimetres.

DWG Import Orientation – Imports on its side or way off the origin – prior to import; rotate and place the drawing on the 0,0,0 origin in your drawing software.

3D Model Import – Model imports as a single object – use an Entity or check if a group option has been deselected in the imports dialogue to preserve the individual objects.

Import Scale – Often when you import a pre-built object, such as a chair, it may not be at the correct scale – use the scale option to resize.

Display/Environment

Zoom – Losing your drawing – **Zoom Extents** will fit all the drawn information in the working window.

Line Weights [no line weights] – Ensure the display line weights dialogue is ON.

Dotted Line [cannot see line weights] – Set the scale of the dotted line in the properties so you can see the dots.

XYZ Unable to draw on the default *XY* axis: – Reset the **XYZ** to **World**.

Slow Machine – Use wireframe rather than a realistic visual mode when working on a project.

Visibility – You create something and it's not showing – check if it's visible or the layer options are set to visible.

User Interface you lose any tools – Reset the user interface to default.

Create and Modify

AutoCAD Command – Unable to use a command: use the escape or return key to exit a tool.

AutoCAD Keyboard Entry – Remove your hand from the mouse when entering any dimensions in a data/command field.

AutoCAD Command Input – Read the command line/tool info at all times; it will inform you of the next move or of your tool options.

Wonky Lines – Ensure the Ortho mode [or Shift] has been selected.

Gaps in Linework – Check your snaps are activated and you are snapping to the end of the proceeding line.

Presspull won't presspull – Check for broken lines; ensure NO gaps.

Array: Create a simple array and then use the properties palette to format the array to your requirements.

Separate Elements Object will only move in bits – Use the group, compound, union option to make it a solid object.

Move – Only able to move up or down – Check whether Ortho or parallel is deactivated.

Isolate/Hide – Use the isolate hide option to work on an individual object.

Rendering

Flat Image – No shadows on.

Lights – Not working. Check and alter the intensity/decay settings in the light edit properties.

Overexposed – Check the light values and reduce.

Global Illumination – Use low light volumes and multiply with the global illumination multiplier to gently increase light levels in a scene.

Textures – Textures don't show up when assigned – make sure the show in viewport option is selected or the UVW/texture map has been applied to the object.

Poor Resolution – Ensure that the set resolution of the render is at a suitable size for print.

Slow Render Preview – Reduce the image size and the other render settings to draft or lower.

Not Enough RAM – To render an image, use the region option to render a bit at a time.

Antialiasing – Increase antialiasing values if the image becomes jagged or with fuzzy details.

Post Process

Rendering Faults: Use the clone tool to iron out any mistakes.

Photoshop Incorrect Layer: Ensure you have the correct layer activated that you wish to alter.

Dull Image: Use Photoshop image adjustments to add depth.

3 Bits: Combine the best bits of images to create a final image.

Resolution: There is no point increasing the resolution of an image in post process as it is set at point of creation, render/photo.

Index